The Crisis of Method in Contemporary Analytic Philosophy

The Crisis of Method in Contemporary Analytic Philosophy

Avner Baz

OXFORD
UNIVERSITY PRESS

OXFORD
UNIVERSITY PRESS

Great Clarendon Street, Oxford, OX2 6DP,
United Kingdom

Oxford University Press is a department of the University of Oxford.
It furthers the University's objective of excellence in research, scholarship,
and education by publishing worldwide. Oxford is a registered trade mark of
Oxford University Press in the UK and in certain other countries

First Edition published in 2017

Impression: 1

Published in the United States of America by Oxford University Press
198 Madison Avenue, New York, NY 10016, United States of America

British Library Cataloguing in Publication Data
Data available

Library of Congress Control Number: 2017941746

ISBN 978-0-19-880188-7

Printed and bound by
CPI Group (UK) Ltd, Croydon, CR0 4YY

For Tal

Contents

Acknowledgments

Even more so than *When Words Are Called For* (Harvard, 2012), this book was written with my students in mind, and helped by their hard questions. I would like to thank, in particular, the students in two seminars on philosophical method that I taught at Tufts: Maisoon Al-Suwaidan, Alicia Armijo, Sophie Derugen-Toomey, Megan Entwistle, Larry Kenny, Jonatan Larsson, Qiu Lin, Chris Litscher, Sam Lundquist, Aileen Luo, John McCrary, Michael Mitchell, Kiku Mizuno, Leo Moauro, Brad Pearson, Hannah Read, Gabe Santos-Neves, Clare Saunders, and Michael Veldman. I have sometimes felt guilty for encouraging my students to question received philosophical positions and procedures while offering them nothing determinate in their stead; but I do not know what else the teaching of philosophy might be.

I would like to thank Peter Momtchiloff, for his help and support along the way; Steven Gross, for an exemplary set of comments—at once generous and penetrating—on the whole manuscript; Juliet Floyd, for sound advice and criticism, and for her encouragement; Jonah Horwitz, long-time friend and much-trusted personal editor; Michael Mitchell, for carefully reading the final proofs and generating the index; two anonymous reviewers for Oxford University Press, for their detailed comments and suggestions; two anonymous reviewers for *Philosophical Psychology*, for two rounds of meticulous comments on a paper that became the basis for chapters Five and Six; and an anonymous reviewer for *Philosophy and Phenomenological Research*, for helpful comments on a paper that became the basis for chapter Two.

Earlier versions of portions of this book were presented to audiences at: Tufts University; The University of Porto; a conference on "The Form of our Life with Language," in Munich; the Annual Conference of the Boston Phenomenology Circle; The University of Chicago; Western Michigan University; Boston University; Université Paris 1, Panthéon-Sorbonne; Åbo Academy, Finland; Amherst College; Tel Aviv University; The Nordic Wittgenstein Workshop; University of Göttingen; California State University, Fullerton; and the University of Oxford. I would like to thank members of these audiences for their suggestions and criticisms.

Introduction

Armchair Philosophy, Experimental Philosophy, and the Minimal Assumption

[T]here are experimental methods and *conceptual confusion* . . . The existence of the experimental method makes us think we have the means of solving the problems which trouble us; though problem and method pass one another by.

Wittgenstein, *Philosophical Investigations*,
Part II, section xiv

There is, I believe, little question that experimental philosophy constitutes one of the most significant developments in analytic philosophy in the last couple of decades. What is less clear is what its philosophical significance is, or has been. Whereas its proponents tend to present it as a way of moving forward in philosophy,[1] I would argue that its singular contribution thus far has been that of pressing analytic philosophers to reflect on their favored method of inquiry, thereby helping to bring out fundamental problems with that method. More specifically, the present book argues that the new experimental movement and the responses to it by traditional, "armchair" philosophers have helped to make clear that what is known in contemporary analytic philosophy as "the method of cases"—that is, the widespread philosophical practice of theorizing on the basis of the "application" of terms to "cases"—rests on substantive

---

[1] Fischer and Collins have recently proposed that experimental philosophy heralds an "exciting" "new framework" that "provides both philosophical and metaphilosophical discussion with a fresh set of specific methods and distinctive approaches beyond 'just following our argumentative noses'" (Fischer and Collins 2015: 23).

and challengeable assumptions about language. But if so, then experimental philosophy, insofar as it too has, by and large, proceeded on the basis of such "applications"—albeit mostly ones performed by lay people, as opposed to trained philosophers—has rested on the same challengeable assumptions.[2]

"Applying" a term to a case is what both professional philosophers and participants in philosophical "experiments" are supposed to do when, having been presented with (or having presented) a description of the case, they are asked (or ask themselves) questions such as "Does the protagonist of this story *know* that such and such?" or "Is the protagonist's belief that such and such *justified*?" or "Is the protagonist of this story *responsible* for doing this or that?" or "Did the protagonist of the story do this or that *intentionally*?" or "Did the protagonist's failure to water the plants *cause* them to wilt?" or "Would the differently constituted liquid on that other planet be *water*?" ("Is it a *necessary* truth that water is H_2O?"). The general form of such questions is "Is this (or would this be) a case of x?" where "x" is the term that the question invites us to "apply" to the described case, either positively or negatively. I will call any question of this general form, when it is raised in the context of philosophical theorizing—armchair or experimental—"the theorist's question."

I put "application" in quotation marks in order to register the fact that the word, as commonly used in contemporary analytic philosophy, and particularly in the recent discussions concerning the method of cases, is a piece of philosophical jargon.[3] As a piece of jargon, it has helped to cover

---

[2] Experimental philosophy is not an altogether homogeneous movement. While many of its practitioners have presented it as a constructive extension of traditional practice, others have mostly focused on questioning that practice on the basis of experimental results. It might therefore be thought that experimentalists of the second, skeptical sort might not object to my general characterization of the movement's most important contribution to philosophy. As we shall see, however, even where experimentalists have focused on questioning the traditional practice, rather than on extending it experimentally, they have done so from within the perspective of the assumptions about language that have underwritten the practice and which are questioned in this book. As a result, their critique of the practice has been useful, but ultimately misplaced: it has failed to bring out, and in effect has helped to cover up, what is most deeply problematic about that practice.

[3] In general, I put words in quotation marks even when I'm not quoting a particular text whenever I take those words to be jargon. So there is a sense in which I am quoting in those moments, even though I'm not quoting anyone in particular. I also signal in this way that I myself may not be clear on what, if anything, those words mean, or could mean, in the particular philosophical context(s) in which they appear.

up the assumptions that this book aims to bring out and question. Outside philosophy, to apply a word, or anything else for that matter, is to put it to some *use*—do some *work* with it. By contrast, I will argue, the philosophical "application of a word (or concept)" is, precisely and by design, not a use. It might perhaps be thought of as a *simulated* use that is meant to serve theoretical purposes; but if, as I will argue, the ordinary and normal *conditions* for the felicitous use of the word (or concept) under investigation are lacking in the theoretical context— and, again, lacking by design—then there is good reason to worry that the theorizing is bound to distort what it aims to clarify.

In both modern Western philosophy and contemporary analytic philosophy, reliance on answers to versions of the theorist's question has arguably been even more pervasive than participants in the recent discussions concerning philosophical method have tended to recognize.[4] Just how pervasive that reliance has been will become evident once it is noted that it may also be found in works that do not appear to deploy the method of cases in its paradigmatic form. Every time a philosopher theorizes about some philosophically interesting subject X, and takes it that some cases just are, or are not, cases of X, irrespective of whatever might lead someone to *count* those cases as cases of X, and irrespective of the *point* or *function* of such counting and of the *conditions* under which the counting may felicitously, or intelligibly, be carried out, she is relying, in effect, on some particular answer to a version of the theorist's question.[5] Thus, even though I will mostly refer to the target of my critique as "the

---

[4] Fischer and Collins propose that the reliance on (what they call) "intuitions," or "judgments" about given "scenarios," has been the central "theme" of analytic philosophy in the last few decades (Fischer and Collins 2015: 3 and 10–11; see also Machery 2015: 189). Knobe, Buckwalter, Nichols, Robbins, Sarkissian, and Sommers similarly observe: "Contemporary work in philosophy is shot through with appeals to intuition. When a philosopher wants to understand the nature of knowledge or causation or free will, the usual approach is to begin by constructing a series of imaginary cases designed to elicit prereflective judgments about the nature of these phenomena. These prereflective judgments are then treated as important sources of evidence" (Knobe et al. 2012: 82). What Fischer and Collins, as well as Knobe et al., refer to by "intuitions," or "(prereflective) judgments," is what I less committedly refer to as "the answers we (find ourselves inclined to) give to the theorist's question." The reason for this less committed way of talking will become clear as I go along.

[5] I do *not* contend that this reliance would *always* be problematic; but I will argue that it is problematic and bound to lead us astray when it comes to philosophically troublesome words such as "know," "cause," "free," "mean," "understand," "see," and so on.

method of cases" (in either its traditional-armchair version or its new experimental version), it should be kept in mind that the actual target of the critique is broader, and arguably much broader, than this title suggests. Should it be objected that, even so, there is *still* much work in contemporary analytic philosophy that the argument of this book leaves untouched, I would answer that a clear demarcation of *that* work, and a clear understanding of how it escapes the argument, would be useful.[6]

This book continues lines of thought originally broached in my previous book, *When Words Are Called For*. But whereas that earlier book was primarily focused on defending what I there call "ordinary language philosophy" as an approach to the understanding and dissolution of philosophical difficulties, against the widespread notion that it has somehow been shown to be misguided and may safely be ignored by contemporary analytic philosophers, in the present book I go on the offense, so to speak. Also, and to the chagrin of some of my Wittgensteinian friends, I'm arguing a little more theoretically, or less purely therapeutically, than I did in *When Words Are Called For*.

This *slight* shift of orientation—there is still quite a lot of Wittgensteinian therapeutic intervention in this book, especially in the first two chapters—is due in part to my wish to engage fruitfully with mainstream analytic philosophers, many of whom have long dismissed the works of Wittgenstein and his devout followers on the ground that they offer no "positive" theoretical understanding of anything. But another reason for this shift is that I have come to think, under the inspiration of Maurice Merleau-Ponty, that it is possible to have an understanding of perceptual and behavioral phenomena—including our acquisition and use of natural language—that on the one hand is positive and in some clear sense beholden to empirical reality, but on the other hand is *neither* reductive-mechanistic *nor* necessarily empty or nonsensical. (I say more about this in the Appendix to this book.)

---

[6] Huw Price (2011, 2013) has similarly argued that much of the work in contemporary analytic philosophy is a response to difficulties that owe whatever sense and urgency they seem to have to a "representationalist" conception of language that may be questioned on (what Price considers to be) naturalist grounds. Price's focus, however, is not on the method of cases but rather on metaphysical "placement problems," as he calls them, and on philosophical responses to those problems. So between the target of Price's critique and the target of mine, and if we add to that much of the work done in semantic theorizing (which neither of us focuses on), it seems safe to say that *the bulk* of the work in contemporary analytic philosophy arguably rests on substantive and challengeable representationalist assumptions about language.

One main source of motivation for writing this book is the sense that experimental philosophy's laudable aspiration to connect our philosophizing more securely to empirical reality has actually partaken in encouraging a false picture of what's involved in our wording of our world—a picture on which, as speakers, we may stand outside the world, and simply apply our words to worldly "things" or "items" as labels. Except that, normally and ordinarily, even just labeling things is a worldly, intersubjectively significant activity whose specific sense, or intelligibility, depends on a suitable worldly context and on its having a point.

My underlying concern, in other words, is that the theorist's questions have encouraged us to forget what phenomenologists have called our "being-in-the-world," and in particular what is involved in positioning ourselves in the world and in relation to others by means of words. In order to bring what's involved in wording our world clearly into view, it would not do just to ask lay people the same sorts of questions that philosophers have tended to ask themselves for millennia, and then try to either explain or draw lessons from the statistical distribution of the answers they give. The questions themselves, together with the framework that has made them seem just the right questions for philosophers to ask, will need to be rethought.[7]

I will not, however, commit myself theoretically beyond what is needed for the purposes of the argument of this book. For example, though I believe, and will argue, that there is much truth in Huw Price's critique of "representationalism" in the philosophy of language (Price 2011 and 2013), I will remain silent about his "*global* expressivism." For my present purposes, it is enough to show that representationalism has led us astray when it comes to philosophically troublesome words such as "know," "cause," and "meaning." I can therefore set aside the question of whether it might be right, or not obviously or harmfully wrong, when it comes to words such as "table" and "lion."[8]

---

[7] A common theme of what has been called "ordinary language philosophy" is the idea that at the root of any number of traditional philosophical difficulties lies not this or that mistaken answer, or set of mistaken answers, to some perfectly legitimate and intelligible question, but rather, precisely, the question itself, and the assumption that, as raised in the philosophical context (either explicitly or tacitly), it makes clear sense and has a correct answer (see Wittgenstein 1958: 169; Austin 1964: 4; and Ryle 2000: 22).

[8] After all, Price too argues for what he calls Wittgenstein's "functional pluralism"—the recognition that some words, or "vocabularies," may function very differently from others.

My basic plan is to argue that theorizing on the basis of answers to the theorist's questions rests on substantive, and challengeable, assumptions about language, and then to question those assumptions, both philosophically and empirically. As we will see, virtually all of the participants in the recent debates concerning the method of cases—both critics and defenders, both "armchair" and "experimental"—have tended to rely on the assumptions I will question. They have thereby participated in covering up what, by my lights, is most deeply problematic about the method.

It might seem implausible that all of the participants in the recent debates concerning the method of cases, and all of those philosophers who have theorized on the basis of answers to the theorist's questions, share a commitment to a set of substantive—that is, nontrivial, and challengeable—assumptions about language. Surely, it might be thought, participants in those debates think of language in a variety of ways and disagree with each other about any number of fundamental issues regarding language. No doubt they do. And yet I claim that they have all committed themselves, sometimes explicitly but for the most part implicitly, to certain substantive and questionable assumptions about language. More precisely, I claim that there is at least *one* assumption they all share— I will call it "the minimal assumption." The minimal assumption is that the theorist's questions, as presented in the theorist's context, are, in principle, in order—in the simple sense that they are clear enough and may be answered correctly or incorrectly—and that, as competent speakers, we ought to understand those questions and be able to answer them correctly, just on the basis of the descriptions of the cases and our mastery of the words in which the questions are couched.

The widespread commitment to the minimal assumption is evidenced by the fact that much of the recent discussion has focused on the question of the *reliability*, or "warrant," of the answers we (find ourselves inclined to) give to the theorist's questions.[9] The question of reliability presupposes that the answers we give to the theorist's questions are, in principle, correct or incorrect, true or false.[10] So it presupposes that the

---

[9] See Fischer and Collins 2015: 21–2.

[10] Even if only relative to the content of someone's or some community's concept of X (see Goldman 2007: 15). The assumption that the theorist's questions are, in principle, clear enough to be answered correctly or incorrectly has been made even by the strongest critics of the method of cases, not to mention its defenders. In pressing his "calibration" objection to the method, Cummins, for example, never doubts that our answers to the

questions themselves are in order, in the above sense. As I develop my critique of the method of cases, I will take its practitioners—traditionalist and experimentalist alike—to be committed at least to this. Those who are not thus committed fall outside the intended target range of my critique. But it is hard to see how they could nonetheless be proponents of the method *as commonly practiced*.

I have just italicized "as commonly practiced" for two reasons. First, as I note below and discuss more fully in Chapter Four, contemporary semantic "contextualism" represents an important—albeit ultimately insufficient—move away from the minimal assumption. It is actually striking that though semantic contextualism has in recent years become a—if not *the*—dominant position in the philosophy of language, experimental philosophy has by and large proceeded without letting the contextualist insights affect the design of its experiments.[11] Second, as I note in the Conclusion, it is possible to revise the method of cases *beyond* the introduction of the contextualist's "semantic ascent," in such a way that it would no longer rely on the problematic assumptions about language that are questioned in this book. The philosophically motivated question would then invite us to *project ourselves imaginatively into situations of speech*—situations in which the philosophically troublesome words would actually be *used*—rather than inviting us, as it now does (even

theorist's questions may or may not be "accurate" (Cummins 1998: 124). And Jonathan Weinberg, who among the experimentalists has been one of the most skeptical of the method of cases in its armchair version, has asserted, in a co-written paper, that the theorist's questions invite us to "track philosophical truths" (Weinberg et al. 2010: 332 and 338; see also Weinberg 2015: 172). The philosophical truths may be relative, or context-sensitive (Weinberg et al. 2010: 332); but they are nonetheless truths, which means that the theorist's question is taken to have a correct answer (even if only relatively and context-sensitively). Weinberg's skepticism concerns our ability, and specifically that of philosophers, to track those "truths" reliably; it does not concern the existence of such truths or the sense of the questions they are supposed to answer. See also Weinberg 2007, which is premised on the assumption that intuitive answers to the theorist's questions are true or false, correct or incorrect. For other lines of skepticism about the method of cases that presuppose the minimal assumption see Nado 2015; and Machery 2011 and 2015. On the other side of the field, those who have responded to the skepticism on behalf of armchair philosophizing have all presupposed—as armchair philosophers themselves have all presupposed—that answers to the theorist's questions are, in principle, either true or false, correct or incorrect, and may therefore be assessed in terms of their reliability (see, for example, Williamson 2007, Jackson 2011, Ichikawa 2012, Nagel 2012, Cappelen 2012, and Sgaravatti 2015).

[11] There *have* been a few experiments, which I'll discuss in Chapter Four, designed to test contextualism itself.

after the contextualist amendment), to "apply" our words to cases from a metaphysically detached position, where nothing hangs on what we say but some philosophical theory. So it would invite us to practice some form or another of ordinary language philosophy. But for that we would need to also transform our expectations of philosophy, and how we think about philosophical difficulty, and progress.

My more detailed plan is as follows. In Chapter One I examine, on the one hand, John Hawthorne's introduction of the "lottery paradox" in *Knowledge and Lotteries* (2004), and on the other hand, texts in which experimental philosophers describe their practice and offer a rationale for it. Hawthorne's text illustrates well the deep confusion about the method of cases on the part of its armchair practitioners; the experimental philosophy texts show that the new movement has done little to alleviate the confusion. The aim of the chapter is to demonstrate this, and at the same time to raise some of the main issues that will occupy us in subsequent chapters.

In Chapter Two, I examine Timothy Williamson's and Herman Cappelen's attempts to defend the method of cases in its traditional, "armchair" form. The aim of that chapter is to continue the work of Chapter One of exposing the *internal* difficulties that have presented themselves for those wishing to defend the method, and to begin to work toward establishing my basic contention that the method of cases rests on substantive and (therefore) challengeable presuppositions about language.

In Chapter Three, I articulate more fully the representational-referential and atomistic-compositional[12] conception of language that underlies Williamson's and Cappelen's arguments in defense of the method of cases, and I show that essentially the same conception underlies Frank Jackson's argument in defense of the method; and this despite the fact

---

[12] By "atomistic-compositional" I mean to refer to any conception of language on which the overall sense of an utterance is made up of the independent and determinate senses of the individual words that make it up, and on which, as producers and perceivers of linguistic sense, we first find out or determine the sense of each of the words that make up an utterance—the contribution each of them makes to the overall sense of the utterance—and then put those senses together to arrive at the overall sense of the utterance. The atomistic-compositional view tends to go together, as we will see in Chapter Three, with a representational-referential view, in which case the sense of each individual uttered word is understood in terms of its "representational (or semantic) content," where *that* is understood—at least for most words—in terms of the word's "reference." Contextualists, as we'll see in Chapter Four, reject the atomistic-compositional part but hold on to other key features of the traditional, representationalist conception.

that Jackson seems to disagree quite fundamentally with Williamson and Cappelen on what the method is supposed to accomplish. It should be noted, however, that my critique of the method of cases (as commonly practiced) does *not* depend on attributing to its practitioners or defenders *that particular* conception of language; nor will that critique be undermined by the possibility of more or less significantly different conceptions of language that might be taken to support the minimal assumption. For my critique of the method ultimately consists of questioning the minimal assumption itself, both philosophically and empirically.

Chapter Four is a transitional chapter and is devoted to contemporary semantic "contextualism." In arguing that the contribution a word makes to the overall sense of an utterance depends in part on the context of the utterance, contemporary contextualism already challenges the minimal assumption that takes the theorist's words (and case) to suffice for ensuring the clear (enough) sense of his question. At the same time, in holding on to the representationalist tenet of the traditional conception of language—continuing to think about language as an instrument first and foremost for communicating useful information, and about linguistic sense primarily in terms of truth-conditions and truth-value—this form of contextualism encourages a misleading picture of what is involved in positioning ourselves intelligibly in the world by means of words, and does not go far enough in bringing out what is wrong with the minimal assumption. And this, I propose, despite the fact that contemporary semantic contextualism, *thought through*, actually points us away from the representationalist conception, or picture, of language.

Chapters Five and Six are where I get a little more theoretical. Chapter Five presents a conception of language on which the minimal assumption—and therefore the method of cases as commonly practiced—is fundamentally misguided. This alternative conception draws on ideas of Wittgenstein's and of Merleau-Ponty's, and may very roughly be characterized as combining key elements of contextualism and pragmatism while at the same time emphasizing the synchronic and diachronic plasticity of language. It should in itself be interesting that despite significant differences in their respective philosophical backgrounds, orientations, and methods, these two philosophers think of language in strikingly similar ways. (In the Appendix to this book I say something about where, and why, they part ways, and about why, where they do part ways, I choose (for now) to continue with Merleau-Ponty.)

In Chapter Six, I argue that empirical studies of first language acquisition lend support to the conception of language presented in Chapter Five, as against the conception that underwrites the method of cases in either its armchair or experimental version. That empirical studies have lent no support to the representational-referential and atomistic-compositional conception ought not to surprise us, since, as Wittgenstein's remarks on rule following make clear, we do not really know what it would be for a natural language to be such that what its words bring with them from one utterance or speech act to another—call it "their meanings"—would by itself ensure the sense of the utterance, or determine how it should be understood (as the theorist in effect assumes). So I could have stuck to Wittgensteinian therapy. My aim in considering the empirical findings is twofold: first, to undercut a contextualist but still representationalist understanding of the upshot of Wittgenstein's remarks—an understanding that takes utterance-sense to always be cashable in terms of truth-conditions (however context-dependent), and takes the sense of a word (on an occasion) to be a matter of its contribution to utterance-sense *thus* understood; and second, to bring out and underscore the striking fact that, whereas many in contemporary analytic philosophy regard and present themselves as open and attentive to empirical science, they have tended to rely—not only in their semantic theorizing and reflections on language but in employing their favored method for gathering data for theorizing just about anything else—on a conception of language that has been supported by no empirical evidence.

If the argument of this book is successful, it will show that there are good reasons for suspecting that the minimal assumption is false, and therefore good reasons for suspecting that the method of cases as commonly practiced is fundamentally misguided. More broadly, the argument (if successful) will show that despite considerable recent efforts to denounce, or undo, the so-called "linguistic turn" in philosophy, questions about language still lie at the very heart of the question of philosophical method.[13]

---

[13] In recent years, analytic philosophers such as Kornblith 2002 and 2015, Soames 2003, Williamson 2007, Sosa 2007a, Stanley 2008, and Cappelen 2012, have made considerable efforts to convince us that the so-called "linguistic turn" in philosophy was a mis-turn, because, as they claim, it is not true that philosophical problems are all, at bottom, linguistic problems. What philosophers are mostly interested in, they have insisted, are *things and their natures*, not words and their meanings. By the light of the argument of this book, the

Though the argument of this book is meant to stand on its own, there is one respect in which it presupposes the argument of *When Words Are Called For*. In that earlier book, I looked closely at certain areas of philosophical difficulties—mostly difficulties concerning knowledge (skepticism, for one), or else "knowledge" (the seemingly unresolvable debate between "contextualists" and "invariantists" about "know," for example)—and tried to show that those difficulties are due entirely to certain assumptions that philosophers have made about language: essentially the same assumptions that this book will question at a more theoretical level. In the present book, my discussion in Chapter One of the opening pages of Hawthorne's *Knowledge and Lotteries*, and my discussion in Chapter Four of John Austin's anti-representationalist way with "knowledge," should give the reader some sense of what I mean when I talk about philosophical difficulties that are due entirely to certain assumptions about language; but beyond that, I must rely on the reader to know what sorts of difficulties I am talking about. Anyone who has not been sufficiently impressed with the difficulties—anyone, that is, who truly believes that theorizing on the basis of answers to the theorist's questions has been delivering on its promises and yielding satisfying results—would be less inclined to follow me in questioning those assumptions. But then, that there *are* difficulties with the method is something that experimental philosophy *has* made harder to deny.

Finally, I need to say something about my use of notes. Many of the notes, especially in Chapter One, are substantive, and quite a few of them are rather long. The main reason for this is that it was sometimes hard to strike a good balance between developing a critique of the method of cases *at a foundational level* (the "forest") and responding to some of the more *specific moves* that have been made by practitioners of the method—whether "armchair" or "experimental"—or by participants in the recent debates about method (the "trees"). My solution was to relegate much of the latter material to footnotes.

---

irony here is that this very idea—that it should be possible not merely to distinguish, but to separate in practice, philosophically interesting phenomena from our concepts of those phenomena, as those concepts manifest themselves in our use of words—itself rests on a particular, and questionable, conception of language. And if so, then questions about philosophical practice are inseparable from questions about language, just as so-called "linguistic philosophers" such as Wittgenstein and Austin have maintained.

1

Methodological Confusion in Armchair and Experimental Philosophy

One obstacle that must be overcome *before* one attempts to question the method of cases—or for that matter any other long-standing practice—at a foundational level, is the sense on the part of its practitioners that they *already know* what the method is, what it is supposed to accomplish, and how it is supposed to accomplish it. And no doubt we do, on *some* level, know and understand the method of cases. Fairly early on in our formal philosophical education we encounter versions of the theorist's question and are prompted to answer them. We may feel—I do not believe I am the only one who *has* felt—that the questions are not quite or fully natural, that they, and so our answers to them, are somehow forced, and that in giving our answers to them we do not stand on the same kind of footing that we stand on when we employ the same words ("know," "cause," "intentionally" . . .) in the course of everyday discourse.[1]

---

[1] When Joshua Knobe, rather than asking subjects in his thought experiments whether they thought the chairman harmed [helped] the environment *intentionally*, and giving them just two responses to choose from, as he had done originally (see Knobe 2004), asked them instead whether they agreed or disagreed with the sentence "The chairman of the board harmed [helped] the environment intentionally," and gave them a Likert Scale that allowed them to choose from seven responses ranging from "definitely disagree," through "unsure," to "definitely agree," what he got was a "*moderate* agreement with the claim that the chairman harmed intentionally and *moderate* disagreement with the claim that he helped intentionally" (Knobe 2010: 318, my emphasis). The same kind of unsureness has been found in other philosophical experiments that used the Likert scale (see Cullen 2010 and Hansen and Chemla 2013). Of course, the empirical fact that people tend to be unsure about how to answer the theorist's questions can be explained in any number of ways. By itself, that fact does not show that there is something wrong with the philosophical method of cases. What may already safely be said at this point, however, is that apart from an

(This lack of familiar footing may actually add to the aura of profundity, or perhaps transcendence, that attracts some people to philosophy.) But, at the same time, the questions do *seem* clear and intelligible—in many cases, we could easily enough imagine the same form of words used to raise a perfectly intelligible question in the natural course of everyday life; and raised as they are in the philosophical context, especially by a figure of some authority, they encourage the very conception, or picture, of language on which there *is* nothing wrong with them.[2] And we *do* typically find ourselves moved to give some answer or another to the theorist's question (though, as I will later stress, it is important that people who otherwise agree in their everyday employment of the relevant words, quite regularly find themselves "disagreeing" with each other in their answers to the theorist's questions). We then learn to theorize on the basis of what are taken to be the correct answers to those questions, and how to challenge extant theories by way of the clever construction of counterexamples—that is, cases that tend to elicit answers to the theorist's question that seem to conflict with the theory under examination. Soon enough, some of us get the hang of the practice and even become proficient at it; and it seems safe to assume that those who become proficient at it, and who are moved to give or accept the "correct" answers to the theorist's questions, are more likely to pursue a career in professional analytic philosophy and be successful at it. That the theorist's questions are, in principle, in order (in the sense of "in order" specified in the Introduction), that we should be able to understand them and answer them correctly, and that theorizing on the basis of "correct" answers to the theorist's questions is a way, perhaps even *the* way, of coming to better understand philosophically interesting subjects— all of that tends to be taken for granted from the very beginning; and we

---

understanding of what the theorist's questions ask or invite us to do, and what our answers to them are supposed to reveal, and how, these sorts of experimental manipulations and their effects are bound to leave us in the dark about the significance of the data gathered by way of the method of cases, not to mention the peculiar phenomenology of attending to and answering the theorist's questions.

[2] In this way, I will later propose, what philosophers have called "theory contamination" (see Goldman and Pust 1998) begins earlier, and goes deeper, than they have suspected: it manifests itself not just in the answers we give to the theorist's questions, but already in our accepting them as having clear enough sense and a correct answer.

can easily and naturally come to *think* that we know exactly what we are doing, and why, when we pursue the method of cases.

For this reason, it would be worth showing, before I begin to develop my actual critique of the method of cases, that there are, just underneath the surface, considerable lack of clarity and considerable disagreements about the nature of the theorist's question and what our answers to it are supposed to reveal. The objective of this chapter is to show this, and at the same time raise some of the main issues that will occupy us in subsequent chapters.

1.1 Methodological Confusion in Contemporary Analytic Philosophy, Part I: "Armchair" Philosophy

I start with some basic questions. Suppose we utter (or, on the experimentalist's questionnaire, check the box saying) "knows" in response to the theorist's question "Does the protagonist of this story know that such and such?" Are we thereby saying, *asserting*, *that* the protagonist knows, and thereby expressing our *belief* that she knows?[3] If so, how might our believing this manifest itself in our conduct—as beliefs may normally be expected to manifest themselves—*beyond* our uttering of our answer? After all, beliefs may plausibly be thought to be identifiable by, or to even consist in, the set of commitments they carry for their holder; so what (more) are we supposed to be committed to in being committed to (the truth of) our answer?[4]

---

[3] For this understanding of the force of our answers to the theorist's questions, see Lewis 1983, Williamson 2007, and Ludwig 2007.

[4] Cova, Dupoux, and Jacob report an experiment in which they tested whether the answers people give in Knobe's "Chairman" experiment (Knobe 2004) correlate with their predictions of the chairman's future behavior. They found no correlation (Cova et al. 2010: 335). This of course is just one experiment, but its results should not surprise us: they bring out a crucial feature of the method of cases as commonly practiced—namely, that nothing (but some theory) hangs on the answers we (find ourselves inclined to) give to the theorist's questions. I see no reason to expect that "disagreement" in answers to the theorist's question about a Gettier case, for example, would systematically correlate with disagreement about what the protagonist would be likely to do next, or about what she *should* do next. Nor is there reason to suppose that such "disagreement" would systematically correlate with different patterns of (actual) responses to someone who (actually) stood in a Gettier-type relation to some proposition.

Or are we perhaps only saying that we are *inclined* to believe the protagonist knows,[5] which would normally commit us to far less than an expression of an outright belief would? I note that "being inclined to believe" relies for its sense on the sense of "believing"; so if it is not clear in what sense an answer to the theorist's question might be thought to express *a belief*, it is also not clear in what sense it might be thought to express *an inclination to believe*. Setting that worry aside, what might be the significance of what (we find) we are inclined to believe? How, exactly, is our inclination to believe she knows supposed to teach us anything about knowledge, or about our concept of knowledge?

Or perhaps we are saying something even less committing, such as what we find ourselves *inclined to say* in response to the question? (I shall ultimately propose that this third description of what we are doing when we answer the theorist's question is closest to the truth, or anyway is the least misleading.) Surely, the truth-conditions, and presumably also the philosophical significance, of an utterance of this last sort would be very different from those of an utterance of the first or second sort.

And what are our answers to the theorist's questions supposed to reveal? Do the questions invite us to reflect upon or discover the metaphysical nature, or essence, of such things as knowledge, causation, intentional action, freedom, and so on? Or do they rather invite us to reflect upon and become clearer about *our concepts* of knowledge, causation, intentional action, freedom, and so on? Does it even make sense to try to separate the traditional "objects" of philosophical reflection from our concepts of them?[6] If the philosophically elusive "objects" are taken to be separable from our concepts of them, as many philosophers seem to suppose, what sort of objects are they supposed to be? In what is their existence, or their identity over time, supposed to consist? And how do we know that our answers to the theorist's questions successfully and reliably track those "objects" (supposing they exist and are trackable by way of answers to the theorist's questions)? Why even presume that it ought to be possible for us to track those "objects," let alone track them

---

[5] See Sosa 2007a.

[6] Some armchair philosophers insist that it does, and that, for the most part, philosophers are primarily interested in "objects" such as knowledge, causation, freedom, and so on, as contrasted with our concepts of them. See Introduction, note 13, for references.

reliably?[7] These questions become all the more pressing when we find ourselves disagreeing with each other in the answers we (find ourselves inclined to) give to the theorist's questions. On the other hand, if our answers are supposed to reveal our concepts, can those answers be right or wrong? What would it mean for us to be wrong about our concepts? What *are* concepts, anyway, such that answers to the theorist's questions may plausibly be thought to reveal them?[8]

The above questions are not meant to be rhetorical. They are meant to be *pointed*; and the argument of this book is going to bear on all of them. Insofar as there are answers to be found in the literature to these and related questions, they are typically just asserted, not argued for, and they all tend to presuppose (one version or another of) the conception of language that will be questioned in this book. And all too often, these fundamental questions are ignored altogether, and the method of cases is practiced despite evident lack of clarity about what it is meant to reveal, and how.

---

[7] In Chapter Three, I will argue that the only plausible answer to this question is one that relies on the conception of language that will be questioned in Chapters Five and Six. For the idea that human beings are more or less reliable, but in any case the best available "detectors," of philosophically interesting "properties," see Weinberg 2015.

[8] There is considerable lack of clarity in the literature about this question (as acknowledged, for example, by Weinberg et al. 2010: 336)—a lack of clarity that plagues not only the debate between experimental and armchair philosophers, but theorizing about language and cognition more generally. The general tendency is to take the question "What are concepts?" as essentially empirical, and to assume that one could *first* identify concepts as objects of empirical study, *and then* answer the question by studying *those* objects. Only few theorists have taken it that the question "What are concepts?" *is itself a conceptual question*, to be answered by way of consideration of our ordinary and normal *use(s)* of "concept," and then have drawn the conclusion that given the difficulty of explicating far simpler concepts, there is no good reason for optimism when it comes to explicating our concept of *concept* (See Armstrong et al. 1999: 257). For most theorists, however, "concept" is a theoretical term, without any obvious or straightforward connection to the same word in its everyday use. Few theorists acknowledge this fact and, of those, some go on to draw the conclusion that in order to understand the theorist's "concept"—see what concept *it* "expresses"—it will not do to look for the worldly item or set of items to which it refers, apart from seeing *how the word functions in the theorist's thinking* and fits within his or her overall "view" (see Jackendoff, 1999: 305; see also Millikan 1999: 525). But even then the tendency is not to follow this line of thinking through to the conclusion that, as this might also be true of the concepts "expressed" by other words, the representationalist conception of concepts might be deeply misguided. For the most part, theorizing about concepts—both within philosophy and within the sciences—is controlled by the representational-referential and atomistic-compositional conception of language that will be questioned in Chapters Five and Six.

For an initial illustration, consider John Hawthorne's introduction of the "lottery paradox," to the dissolution of which he then devotes an entire book (Hawthorne 2004). The following discussion is not meant to be anything like a comprehensive criticism of the argument of Hawthorne's book (though the discussion does suggest that Hawthorne's book is responding to an ill-conceived philosophical difficulty). I focus on the opening paragraphs of Hawthorne's text because I find them useful for the purpose of raising certain basic issues concerning the method of cases.

Hawthorne begins by presenting his topic as "an epistemological puzzle [that] has received increasing attention in recent years" (Hawthorne 2004: 1). He then says that "in essence, the puzzle consists of a tension between various ordinary claims to know and our apparent incapacity to know whether someone will lose a lottery" (Hawthorne 2004: 1). So the tension, as Hawthorne here presents it, is between, on the one hand, *something ("ordinary") we sometimes do with our words* and, on the other hand, an *apparent fact* about what sort of knowledge may or may not be had by creatures such as ourselves. In the next couple of paragraphs, however, the tension that generates the philosophical puzzle is presented quite differently (all of the emphases are mine):

Suppose someone of modest means *announces that he knows* he will not have enough money to go on an African safari this year. We are *inclined to treat such a judgment as true*, notwithstanding various farfetched possibilities in which that person suddenly acquires a great deal of money. We are at some level aware that people of modest means buy lottery tickets from time to time, and very occasionally win. And we are aware that there have been occasions when a person of modest means suddenly inherits a great deal of money from a relative from whom he had no reason to expect a large inheritance. But despite all this, many normal people of modest means *will be willing, under normal circumstances, to judge* that they know that they will not have enough money to go on an African safari in the near future. And under normal circumstances, their conversational partners *will be willing to accept that judgment as correct*.

However, were that person to *announce that he knew* that he would not win a major prize in a lottery this year, *we would be far less inclined to accept his judgment as true*. *We do not suppose that people know in advance of a lottery drawing whether they will win or lose*. But what is going on here? The proposition that the person will not have enough money to go on an African safari this year entails that he will not win a major prize in a lottery. *If the person knows the former, then isn't he at least in a position to know the latter by performing a simple deduction?*

Are we to say that he doesn't know the relevant fact about his future vacations? Or are we to say that, after all, one can know that one will lose a lottery in advance of drawing and without special insider information?   (Hawthorne 2004: 1–2)

Since Hawthorne presents and motivates the puzzle, at least in part, by appealing to "ordinary" discourse, let me start by noting the oddness of the speech act Hawthorne invites us to imagine of *announcing* that one knows one will not have enough money to go on an African safari in the near future, where "knowing (that *p*)" is presumably supposed to mean here what it has traditionally meant in philosophy, and what Hawthorne needs it to mean given his purposes—i.e., something like "believing the true proposition *p* and possessing evidence (or proof) good enough for ruling out all (relevant) doubts as to *p*." I can easily enough imagine various sorts of situations in which the *form of words*, "I know I will not have enough money to go on an African safari this year," could felicitously be used, or intelligibly meant; I can even imagine those words uttered in the course of making some announcement or another; but it is very hard—I do not say impossible—to imagine a context in which the words would be used to make the *announcement* that one *knows* (in the relevant sense) one will not have enough money to go on an African safari this year. Knowledge, as traditionally thought of in philosophy, and especially in matters such as whether one will have enough money to go on an African safari in the near future, is something to *claim*, not *announce*.

Now, why should that matter? After all, I have just acknowledged that the words "I know I will not have enough money to go on an African safari this year" may be put to perfectly intelligible use under ordinary circumstances. Why, given Hawthorne's purposes, should it matter that no such use of those words would amount to an *announcement* that one *knows* something (in the relevant sense of "knows")? We can imagine the words used to express, for example, the speaker's *acknowledgment* or *acceptance* of the (presumed) fact that he will not have enough money to go on an African safari that year, perhaps after having fantasized for some time, in the face of other people's skepticism, about going on such a trip. Along the same line, the words may be used for expressing or introducing the premise, so to speak, of a piece of practical reasoning ("I (now) know I will not have enough money to go on an African safari this year, which has been my dream for some time; so I think I'll just stay home this summer and try to make the best of it"). Such speech acts are perfectly ordinary and intelligible, and they would seem to be all that Hawthorne needs in order to generate his puzzle. And would we not, under normal circumstances, be inclined to accept the speaker's words as *true*?

By way of anticipation of the main argument of this book, let me say that insofar as the (imaginary) speaker has succeeded in putting the words, "I know . . . etc." to some intelligible use or another, that *use* of the words—their contribution to the conversation—stands in no tension at all, not even *apparent* tension, with the undeniable fact that the world can be unpredictable and that our future may always outstrip even our wildest fantasies, not to mention our reasonable expectations. What you might call our metaphysical finitude and epistemic fallibility stand in no tension with the ordinary and normal functioning of our words, but rather are part of the background against which the words we utter acquire their particular significance, or sense. The tension, and indeed the whole philosophical puzzle that has gripped philosophers and with which Hawthorne is trying to grip his readers, only appear when the theorist comes onto the scene and supposes, and encourages us to suppose, that every utterance of a sentence of an indicative form, or anyway every utterance of a sentence of the form "N knows that such and such," irrespective of how the words are used, or meant, is assessable in terms of truth and falsity even from a metaphysically detached position—that is, the position we hold as readers of the theorist's imaginary "case"—in which nothing hangs on our assessment but the fate of some philosophical theory. In a way, the aim of this book as a whole is to throw this widespread supposition into question.

The audience of an intelligible speech act such as the ones imagined above may accept it as *reasonable* or *unobjectionable*—they may take it as perfectly reasonable or unobjectionable, that is, for the speaker to proceed on the assumption that he will not have enough money to go on an African safari that year, for example. Accepting the speech act, or the attitude it expresses, as reasonable or unobjectionable is not the same as taking some (knowledge-ascribing) proposition expressed by the speaker to be true. The question whether it is *true* that the speaker *knows* he will not have enough money to go on an African safari, *as the theorist understands that question*, would never arise naturally outside philosophy, and precisely because, outside philosophy, nothing would hang on how one chooses to answer *that* question.[9] *That* question is, in essence, the theorist's question; and Hawthorne, I wish to propose, is forcing it onto the imagined scenario, *thereby generating the (apparent) tension that he will subsequently look for ways to dispel.* The philosophical puzzle is generated not by ordinary and normal discourse itself, but rather by a theoretical construction that is forced onto it from the outside, so to speak.[10]

It is true that we could easily enough imagine another person challenging the original utterance by uttering the words, "You don't *know* this." I note first that the possibility of such a challenge—and more precisely the possibility that such an utterance would be (found) natural and intelligible under suitable circumstances—does not serve Hawthorne's purpose of gripping us with a philosophical puzzle by way of appeal to ordinary knowledge claims that we would be "inclined to accept as true"; for, if we had to assess the imagined exchange in Hawthorne's terms, we would

---

[9] This, as I note below, is brought out by the fact that philosophers such as Feldman and Williamson, who "disagree" with Hawthorne in their answers to the theorist's question about our knowledge of the future, would (presumably) have no problem interacting with Hawthorne in the sorts of situations he discusses, where that includes communicating with him smoothly and effectively by means of "know" and its cognates in conversations concerning the future. I emphasized "as the theorist understands that question" because, as I will note in Chapter Four, we do, of course, commonly ask whether someone knows that such and such, in the sense of "(already) has the information (has learned, has heard, has noted, has found out, has figured out. . .) that such and such"; but it matters that we use "know" in *this* sense in contexts in which such and such itself is taken for granted. "To Know," in *this* sense, or use, does *not* mean "to stand in some special position of authority arrived at by the elimination of all ("relevant") doubts, or by having a proof that such and such." So it does not mean what philosophers have traditionally taken "know" to mean. Nor does it stand in tension with our metaphysical finitude and epistemic fallibility. In Chapter Four, I will also discuss the use of "know(s)" in which it does mean something like "be in a position to rule out doubt, or prove." Following Austin, I will argue that that use too does not stand in tension with our metaphysical finitude and epistemic fallibility.

[10] Toward the end of his book Hawthorne turns to address the question of how it can be that our ordinary and normal employment of "know" and its cognates proceeds smoothly and effectively and without any trace of the "tension" that generates his "puzzle." "The smooth functioning of ordinary epistemic discourse in a person's life, despite apparent diachronic inconsistencies, is indeed a striking fact," he writes, "[b]ut it is not one that by itself solves our puzzles, nor one that unmasks them as mere pseudo-puzzles" (Hawthorne 2004: 187). Hawthorne suggests that what enables us to overlook the inconsistencies in our own practice in "ordinary life" is the fact that we do not "take in the gamut of knowledge ascriptions in one sweep" (in the way that he has done in his book) (Hawthorne 2004: 187). I am about to propose, and then to argue in greater detail later in subsequent chapters, that Hawthorne's puzzle is a pseudo-puzzle that is generated when the philosopher forces a certain conception of language onto the facts of ordinary discourse.

have to say that the challenger is, precisely, *not* accepting the original "knowledge claim" as *true*.

Moving beyond this prima facie difficulty for Hawthorne's story, let us consider a little more closely and carefully what we would actually need to imagine if we were to truly imagine the "You don't *know* this" challenge being made naturally and intelligibly. There are two basic ways of imagining the challenger meaning her words: we could either imagine her making some non-merely-theoretical point, using her words to express, and take, some non-merely-theoretical stand, or we could imagine her being merely philosophical, so to speak. Borrowing a distinction from Thompson Clarke (1972), we could imagine the speaker speaking "plainly" or we could imagine her speaking "philosophically" (or trying to).[11] Consider first cases of the former sort. One such case would be that in which the challenger's words are meant to *encourage* the first person, or rebuke him for having despaired of going on an African safari that year. In such a case, the disagreement between the first speaker and his challenger would best be described as a disagreement, not between two theoretical judgments about what the speaker does or does not (or can or cannot) know, but between two *attitudes*—roughly, those of hopefulness and despair.

A different case would be that in which the challenger has in mind some *particular* scenario in which the first person may come by a large sum of money. Here the imagined disagreement could be about the likelihood of that happy scenario, or about whether that likelihood is such that the scenario ought to be taken into account by the first person when he makes his plans. Disagreements of either the first or the second sort would *not* be merely theoretical disagreements about the "application" of "know" to a case; and none of them is philosophically *puzzling* in the way that Hawthorne's "puzzle" is supposed to be.[12]

On the other hand, if we imagine the challenger's words as meant purely theoretically—as meant merely to correct her friend's "false judgment" or "misapplication" of "know"—then the imagined case does *not*

---

[11] Clarke argues, in Clarke 1972, that the attempt to speak "philosophically" is liable to be self-defeating, and to result in the production of nonsense.

[12] These last two paragraphs anticipate my response, in section 6.3 of Chapter Six, to the "Frege-Geach" contention that from the fact that utterances may stand in logical relations to each other it follows that they must each have "representational" or "semantic" content that is independent and separable from how the uttered words are used, or meant.

show how *ordinary and normal discourse* contributes to the generation of Hawthorne's puzzle. (And anyway, as already noted, the challenger's "judgment" would be the opposite of what is needed for generating the puzzle). The conclusion, once again, is that the ordinary and normal functioning of "know," in the sorts of situations Hawthorne is inviting us to imagine, does nothing, by itself, to generate Hawthorne's "tension" or "puzzle." The seeming tension and puzzle only arise when a certain theoretical construction is forced on that functioning.

I started by pointing out the oddity of the speech act Hawthorne invites us to imagine not out of sheer pedantry but rather because it seems to me that his carelessness here is no *mere* carelessness: it is symptomatic of an ambivalence—by no means unique to Hawthorne—toward the question of how philosophically troublesome words actually function in ordinary and normal discourse, and what the conditions are for their functioning as they do. While contemporary analytic philosophers often find it useful, or tempting, to invoke "examples" of ordinary discourse in order to present and motivate philosophical concerns and theoretical responses to those concerns,[13] at the same time they tend to think of themselves as investigating a reality that lies beyond, or below, that discourse, and which is ultimately separable from it, at least theoretically. Many of them, Hawthorne included, take themselves to be investigating the metaphysical relation or state of *knowledge*, for example. Others, as we shall see, take themselves to be investigating our *concept of knowledge*, but think of that concept in terms of the "application" of "know" to cases, where the "application" is supposed not to require, or depend upon, putting the word to some *significant use* or another, in a context suitable for that use. On either way of looking at things, the philosopher's subject matter is taken by him to be theoretically separable, at least in principle, from how, and under what conditions, the philosophically troublesome word—"know," in this case—functions in ordinary and normal discourse. This, I think, is why contemporary analytic philosophers tend to allow themselves to be quite careless in their portrayal of that discourse.[14]

---

[13] Hawthorne continues to appeal to what he calls "ordinary practice" in subsequent pages (see, for example, Hawthorne 2004: 18 and 71).

[14] Throughout *When Words Are Called For* I give examples of this carelessness. Again and again we see contemporary analytic philosophers putting words in the mouths of the

By Hawthorne's lights, all he needs from the protagonist of his example is simply to *produce the sentence* "I know I will not have enough money to go on an African safari this year." In producing the sentence—assuming that he means his words "seriously and literally" (as if one could create at will the *conditions* of meaning one's words one way or another)—the protagonist, on Hawthorne's picture, "applies" "know" to himself and the proposition that he will not have enough money to go on an African safari that year; and that "application" is then supposed to be assessable in terms of truth and falsity irrespective of whether the protagonist has actually succeeded in performing an intelligible speech act in producing the sentence.[15] In the wake of Paul Grice's theory of "saying," "meaning," and "implicature" (Grice 1989), and of John Searle's alleged exposure of the so-called "assertion fallacy" (Searle 1999: 141–6) that is supposed to consist of confusing what it would make sense for someone actually to *say* or even just *think* under some set of circumstances and what would be *true* (to say, or think), many in contemporary analytic philosophy have come to presuppose, as Hawthorne does, that words may be vehicles of true or false contents ("propositions," Fregean "thoughts") irrespective of how, if at all, they are being *used*, or *meant*.

Not only does it not really matter for Hawthorne what, if anything, the protagonist of his example does with his words or how he means them, but—and for precisely the reason that *that* does not matter to him—it is clear that his protagonist might as well *say* nothing, as far as Hawthorne is concerned. As he puts it later in his book, "a sentence may serve as the vehicle of belief at a time, even if it is not asserted" (Hawthorne 2004: 83, fn. 87). And so, as Hawthorne sees things, all he really needs his

protagonists of their "examples" that are extremely hard to make sense of, given the circumstances described in those "examples." Or else—insofar as the words *could* be heard in such a way that they make, or have, sense—the example turns out not to support its author's express purposes.

[15] Witness in this connection Keith DeRose's anecdote about how his teacher, Rogers Albritton, responded to DeRose's early attempts to compose the sorts of examples to which contextualists have appealed in arguing for their position, and how he, DeRose, initially felt about Albritton's response:

> [Albritton] . . . objected, as near as I can remember, "Nobody would really talk that way!" I replied that it didn't matter whether people would talk that way. All I needed was that such a claim [a claim of the form "N knows (or does not know) that p"] would be true, and that certainly was my intuition about the truth-value of the claim. (DeRose 2005: 172)

protagonist to do is *judge* that he knows (or does not know) this or that. And this act of judgment is, for Hawthorne, a *purely* theoretical act—an act that consists of nothing more than "applying" a term (or concept) to a case, or, as it has sometimes been put in the tradition of Western philosophy, "subsuming a particular under a universal." And this means that, at the end of the day, the question Hawthorne's protagonist is supposed to be answering in his "judgment" is precisely what I have called "the theorist's question." It is a question that it should presumably be possible for us to raise, understand, and answer correctly or incorrectly, from *anywhere*, or more precisely from *nowhere*.

When, after inviting us to imagine the speech act of announcing that one knows one will not have enough money to go on an African safari that year, Hawthorne goes on to say that "we are inclined to treat such a judgment as true," it may not initially be clear who his "we" is supposed to refer to. Is it supposed to refer to Hawthorne and his readers as potential *actual participants* in such a speech situation, whose (imagined) response to the speaker may itself be humanly or interpersonally (as opposed to merely theoretically) *significant* in one way or another? Or is it supposed to refer to Hawthorne and his readers as philosophers reflecting on situations of that type from a metaphysically detached position, in which, by design, nothing hangs on their response—nothing, that is, but some philosophical theory? I will later suggest that the difference between the invitation to project oneself imaginatively into a humanly significant situation in which one's words may do interpersonally significant work of one kind or another and the invitation to reflect on a case from a metaphysically detached position may be all the difference in the world: the latter is precisely what defines the theorist's question and makes it philosophically and empirically problematic, in a way that the former type of invitation is not.[16] It

---

[16] Of course, for *some* purposes, detached reflection on a case may be appropriate. What I question in this book is the assumption that it is appropriate when our aim is to become clearer about what our philosophically troublesome words (may) mean in ordinary discourse, and so about the concepts those words embody and the world we articulate and express by their means. In talking about philosophically troublesome words (or concepts), I do not mean to suggest that it should be possible to come up with a definitive list of those words, or that we could know in advance which word is liable to give us philosophical trouble. It seems to me undeniable, however, that some words are more likely than others to get us into trouble when we "do philosophy"; and later on I will offer reasons for expecting this to be the case.

is clear, however, that from Hawthorne's perspective—which is the perspective of proponents of the method of cases in general—that difference makes no difference at all. From that perspective, declarative sentences in the mouths (or minds) of people are, in principle, always assessable in terms of truth and falsity, regardless of how, if at all, they are used, or meant, and regardless of the context in which the assessment itself takes place.

Coming back to the tension that is supposed to generate Hawthorne's puzzle, it should now be clear that, contrary to initial appearance, it is not really a tension between certain *speech acts* that we sometimes perform and some apparent fact about our capacity or incapacity to know certain things. Rather, it now appears that the tension is supposed to be between what such speech acts are supposed to express—certain "judgments," or "applications" of terms to cases—and some apparent fact (about what we may and may not know). Equivalently, it is supposed to be a tension between *our assessment of those "judgments" or "applications" in terms of truth and falsity* and some apparent fact. "Applying" a term to a case and assessing such an "application" in terms of truth and falsity are, for Hawthorne, essentially equivalent acts.

This does not end the complications, however. For note that it is not actually the truth-value of "judgments"—which may or may not be expressed in certain speech acts—that is presented by Hawthorne as being in tension with the apparent fact. It is rather our "*inclination*," "under normal conditions," to *treat such "judgments" as true*, or our "*willingness*" to either make those "judgments" or "*accept*" them *as true*.[17] And it also appears that on the other side of the tension that generates Hawthorne's puzzle there is not an apparent fact about knowledge but, once again, an "inclination" to accept certain *other* "judgments" as true—for example, the judgment that the imaginary speaker does not know that he will not win the lottery (assuming he has bought a lottery ticket, has no inside information, etc.). "[T]here is a strong inclination," Hawthorne writes later on, "to claim that the relevant lottery propositions are not known" (Hawthorne 2004: 8).

In Chapter Two, I will discuss in considerable detail Timothy Williamson and Herman Cappelen's complaint that analytic philosophers have tended

---

[17] This kind of language continues later: "I am inclined to think that I know where my car is parked right now" (Hawthorne 2004: 4).

to "psychologize their evidence" and have thereby misconceived their subject matter and how it should be investigated. Hawthorne's topic, Williamson and Cappelen would say, is, or anyway ought to have been, *knowledge*, and what people do and do not, or can and cannot, *know*, not what people are *inclined to say or think*. The topic here is, or ought to be, some "feature of the world," they would say, not some feature of "our psychology." Hawthorne, it should be noted, ultimately shares Williamson's and Cappelen's understanding of philosophy in general and of the method of cases in particular. This is evidenced by the fact that his attempted dissolution of the "lottery puzzle" ultimately consists of an argument for what he calls "subject sensitive invariantism," which is supposed to be a particular theory of *knowledge*, and not, or anyway not primarily, a theory of what *we count*—in different ways, in different contexts, and for different intents and purposes—as someone's knowing (or not knowing) this or that. And it is also evidenced, more immediately, by the fact that Hawthorne concludes his presentation of the puzzle, not with the question of how we should account for the inclinations he describes, but with the question of what we should say, *as philosophers theorizing about knowledge*, about what we may and may not know. Just like Williamson and Cappelen, Hawthorne takes himself to be investigating *knowledge* thought of as "a thing in itself" (to echo Kant)—that is, as a relation that either holds or does not hold between any pair of potential knower and fact (or true proposition), irrespective of what competent speakers count, in different ways, in different contexts, and for different intents and purposes, as someone's knowing (or not knowing) this or that.[18]

In Chapter Three I will argue that the "objects" of philosophical inquiry—*knowledge*, *causation*, *meaning*, *freedom*, and so on—as

---

[18] Contrast Huw Price, who argues, on the basis of Wittgenstein's "rule following" considerations, that "the applicability of a concept F to a new potential instance X is always, in the last resort, dependent on the disposition of the members of a speech community to regard X as F" (Price 2011: 91). This suggests further difficulties with the method of cases as commonly practiced. For one thing, if the disposition of members of a speech community to regard X as F is context-dependent, then, on Price's way of looking at things, with which I broadly agree, the applicability of F to X is also context-dependent, which means that X is neither F nor not-F *simpliciter*, which further means that the (theorist's) question "Is this a case of F?" if raised about X apart from any particular context, would lack a determinate sense and a correct answer. But this, as I will propose in Chapter Four, may only be the beginning of what is wrong with the method of cases as commonly practiced. Hawthorne, it should be noted, argues in *Knowledge and Lotteries* against contextualism about "know" and cognates.

Williamson and Cappelen conceive of them, are, at best, theoretical posits, since the idea that it should be possible for us to separate theoretically these traditional "objects" of philosophical inquiry from our concepts of those "objects," and to investigate the former *directly*— that is, not by way of investigating the latter—relies on substantive and questionable assumptions about language.[19] But for now let me just say that while the understanding of the work of philosophy that leads to the charge of "psychologizing evidence" is proffered, at least in Williamson and Cappelen, in an attempt to ward off a certain kind of skepticism about the method of cases, it actually invites skepticism of an arguably more powerful and less tractable sort. For if "know" (for example) is supposed to refer to some "item" or "feature of the world" that does not depend, for either its identity or presence, on what *we count*, under various types of circumstances and for various intents and purposes, as someone's knowing this or that, then why presume it should be possible for philosophers to track that "item" or "feature" in their answers to the theorist's question, let alone track it reliably, and to capture it with their theories? This is essentially Robert Cummins' "calibration" objection to the method of cases (Cummins 1998). In Chapter Two, we will see that it is very hard to respond to that objection in a truly satisfactory way, and that, in particular, Williamson's and Cappelen's responses to it will not do.

One thing that makes Cummins' "calibration" objection hard to ignore or dismiss is the empirical fact that even within the relatively homogeneous group of analytic philosophers, disagreements have emerged about how to answer this or that of the theorist's questions. (I note that "disagreement" is a tricky word here, for, if I am right, we do not know [yet] *what sort* of disagreement, if any, is manifested when different people give different answers to the theorist's questions.) One does not need to search very far for examples of such disagreements. Take Hawthorne's "puzzle," for instance. In its most compelling version, it requires that we judge (or be inclined to judge) that we know things about our future such as whether we will have enough money to go on an African safari this year, or spend our summer vacation on Cape Cod. Unfortunately for Hawthorne, Williamson "judges" not only that we do

---

[19] This is similar to what Price means when he says, in Price 2011 and 2013, that "object naturalism" rests on substantive assumptions that may be questioned from the perspective of "subject naturalism."

not know, but also that we know we do not know, such things (Williamson 2000: 255); and he is not alone in so "judging."[20] Such seemingly fundamental disagreements between people who are presumably capable of communicating smoothly and effectively with each other outside philosophy, and by means of the very same words that the theorist's questions are inviting us to "apply" to cases, provide at least prima facie reason for suspecting that answers to the theorist's questions might, in the end, reveal nothing more than how philosophers and nonphilosophers are inclined, for more or less traceable reasons, to answer those questions. Part of what I hope to accomplish in this book is to provide further reasons for this suspicion.

1.2 Methodological Confusion in Contemporary Analytic Philosophy, Part II: Experimental Philosophy

What the method of cases may reasonably be expected to accomplish, and how, is at best unclear. There are fundamental questions about the method that need to be answered, and difficulties with common answers to those questions that have not been dealt with satisfactorily. Experimental philosophy has helped to bring some of those questions and difficulties into sharper relief; but I do not see that it has brought us any closer to having truly satisfying answers to those questions. I will try to show in this section that, for the most part, experimental philosophy has extended the traditional practice experimentally without clarifying either its nature or its rationale. What Wittgenstein says in the last remark of the *Investigations* about the academic discipline of psychology would accordingly seem true of present-day experimental philosophy as well: there are experimental methods that encourage us to think we are making progress, and conceptual confusion that renders the progress mostly illusory. And it is hard to see how further experiments in which subjects are presented with one or another of the theorist's questions could help alleviate the confusion.

---

[20] Hawthorne chides Williamson for this (mis)judgment (Hawthorne 2004: 3, fn. 7); but Williamson is not alone in making it. The same judgment is expressed by Richard Feldman in his review of Hawthorne's book (Feldman 2007).

According to Knobe and Nichols, experimental philosophy proceeds by "looking carefully at people's intuitions about cases" (Knobe and Nichols 2008 (hereafter K&N): 4). They gloss "people's intuitions about cases" in terms of the "application" of concepts to cases (K&N: 5) and clearly mean to refer to the answers given by people to versions of the theorist's question. More recently, Knobe, Buckwalter, Nichols, Robbins, Sarkissian, and Sommers have described the motivation and rationale of experimental philosophy in the following way:

Contemporary work in philosophy is shot through with appeals to intuition. When a philosopher wants to understand the nature of knowledge or causation or free will, the usual approach is to begin by constructing a series of imaginary cases designed to elicit prereflective judgments about the nature of these phenomena. These prereflective judgments are then treated as important sources of evidence... [However, there has been] a persistent worry that the key claims made about intuition are not being subjected to empirical testing and that the approach as a whole is insufficiently attentive to psychological theories about how people's minds actually work... Experimental philosophy arose in part as a reaction to these worries. Experimental philosophers pursue the traditional questions of philosophy (free-will, mind-body problem, moral relativism), but they examine people's intuitions about these questions using the tools of contemporary psychology. Claims about intuition are tested in controlled experiments, and results are subjected to the usual statistical analyses. Most importantly, the patterns observed in people's intuitions are explained in terms of psychological processes, which are then explored using all of the usual methods: mediation analysis, developmental research, reaction time studies, patient studies, and so on.   (Knobe et al. 2012: 82)

In what follows, I will look closely at these ideas. My main aim will be to show that experimental philosophy has for the most part accepted without questioning the most fundamental, and problematic, assumptions that have guided and informed the method of cases in its traditional, armchair form. In particular, I will show that experimental philosophers have committed themselves, one and all, to the minimal assumption.

In using "intuitions" to refer to the answers people give, or find themselves inclined to give, to the theorist's questions, experimental philosophers have followed in the footsteps of many of their "armchair" colleagues. Fischer and Collins, who propose that the reliance on intuitions about cases may be seen as the central "theme" of analytic philosophy in the last fifty years or so (Fischer and Collins 2015: 10–11), observe that experimental philosophy similarly "builds on the assumption that, for better or worse, intuitions are crucially involved in philosophical work" (Fischer and Collins 2015: 3).

The tendency to refer to answers to the theorist's questions as "intuitions," or to describe them as expressive of "intuitions," has encouraged—but, as we will see in Chapter Two, is in no way essential to—two important lines of skepticism, alluded to in the above passage from Knobe et al., about the method of cases in its traditional, "armchair" version. The first line, originally broached by Stephen Stich (Stich 1988), follows from the thought that different people may have different intuitions, and, if so, it is not clear why philosophers should attach any special significance to what may merely be *their* intuitions. This line of objection to the method of cases has encouraged some of the first instances of experimental philosophy, in which lay people of various backgrounds were invited to answer different versions of the theorist's questions and, just as Stich had suspected, turned out to not always agree in their answers with either their peers or the professional consensus (where it exists).[21] The second line of skepticism about the philosophical method of cases originates from Cummins' "calibration" objection (in Cummins 1998), which I have already mentioned, according to which there is no way to *calibrate* philosophical intuitions—no way of verifying or ascertaining that they are indeed tracking, let alone tracking reliably, whatever it is they are supposed to track.[22] Much of the work of

---

[21] One such early attempt to establish cognitive diversity experimentally is Weinberg et al. 2001 (see also Machery et al. 2004). Nagel reports more recent experiments that did not replicate Weinberg et al.'s results in terms of a systematic pattern of *cultural* diversity, but in which, nonetheless, only "roughly two-thirds of participants" denied knowledge in a Gettier case (Nagel 2012: 515). So roughly one third of the participants did not share the Gettier intuition. Cullen reports an experiment in which 42 percent of the participants answered that the subject in a Gettier situation "knows" the proposition in question (Cullen 2010: 288). I will come back to the fact, and to the significance of the fact, of what Nichols and Ulatowski have called "*intra*-cultural" disagreements (Nichols and Ulatowski 2007), including disagreements among professional analytic philosophers.

[22] This, on Cummins' view, is true as long as we do not have an intuitions-independent and scientifically well-grounded theory of the subject matter under investigation. Once we do have such a theory, however, we have no use for the intuitions, Cummins contends. The upshot, according to Cummins, is that intuitions can only be calibrated when we have no real use for them (Cummins 1998: 118; see also Horowitz 2015: 246). In taking it that an empirical theory of X might not only bear on, but provide us with correct answers to the theorist's questions, Cummins is making some of the very same assumptions that are questioned in this book.

experimental philosophers has focused on pressing this worry, by producing evidence that people's intuitions about cases are subject to various sorts of "distorting" effects that render them "unreliable."[23]

It is worth asking what has motivated the widespread talk of philosophical "intuitions" in the first place. After all, the theorist's questions are typically couched in simple and perfectly familiar words; and they are often asked about cases that, while typically hypothetical, may well have been actual. This has led Timothy Williamson to protest, on behalf of traditional armchair philosophizing, that there is no fundamental difference between the theorist's questions and questions that are routinely raised and answered in the course of everyday life, and therefore no justification for calling our answers to the theorist's questions "intuitive" or referring to them as "intuitions." What the theorist's questions invite us to do, Williamson has contended, is simply to *judge* whether or not some case is a case of x, and philosophical judgments are "continuous" with everyday judgments and rely on the same "capacity" (Williamson 2007 (hereafter PP): 3, 136, and 192ff; see also Williamson 2004: 152). No one would be inclined to say that she relies on intuition when, in the everyday, she says or thinks that someone knows this or that, for example, or has done this or that intentionally, or is responsible for this or that; so why should we talk about intuitions, Williamson in effect asks, when in the course of doing philosophy (or answering the questionnaires of experimental philosophers) we do what is essentially the same thing? The same sentiment is also expressed by Cappelen, who refers to answers to the theorist's question as (expressions of) "judgments about cases" (Cappelen 2012 (hereafter PWI): 189), and asserts that the theorist's question of whether some given case is a case of x is essentially an empirical question that "clearly belongs" with questions such as what illness someone is suffering from, or how far away from some place you would be if you started at some other place

---

[23] See, for example, Swain et al. 2008, and, more recently, Tobia et al. 2012. Weinberg et al. 2010, in arguing against armchair philosophers' claim to "expertise," have essentially resurrected Cummins' original "calibration" objection to the method of cases. One of the most striking features of experimental philosophy, I will later note, is that while much of its work concerns the "reliability" of the answers people give to the theorist's questions— thereby manifesting commitment to the minimal assumption—it has shown little concern, if any, about *what it might mean* for those answers to be right or wrong, correct or incorrect.

and walked a certain distance in one direction and then a certain distance in another direction (PWI: 127–8).

I will call the claim that what the theorist's questions invite us to do is not different in any significant way (pertinent to the understanding and assessment of the method of cases) from something that we routinely do in the course of everyday experience and which underlies our ordinary and normal employment of our words, *"the claim of continuity."* In Chapter Two, we will see that Williamson's and Cappelen's defense of the method of cases boils down to the claim of continuity. Ultimately, I will argue that the claim is, at best, poorly supported and probably false, and that the philosophical talk of "intuition" is apt—for reasons spelled out in section 5.2 of Chapter Five, I do not say "correct"—precisely in that it registers the *dis*continuity between the answers we give to everyday empirical questions and the answers we give to the theorist's questions.

The claim, or anyway the assumption, of continuity, has been made in one way or another by many others in the recent debates concerning the method of cases.[24] It is central, for example, to Jennifer Nagel's defense of the method of cases in epistemology, and more specifically to Nagel's attempt to establish the reliability of the answers we give to the theorist's questions in this area. "While critics of philosophical methods have focused on deliberate assessments of hypothetical scenarios, we have reason to believe," Nagel writes, "that the abilities brought to bear on those cases would be equally operative in our very frequent and spontaneous assessments of real-life situations" (Nagel 2012: 501). More specifically, Nagel proposes that our ability to answer correctly the theorist's questions in epistemology is just our ability to "read" correctly the minds of others—to tell, for example, that someone else believes or knows this or that.[25]

---

[24] As far as I know, the only "armchair" philosopher who has not made the claim of (or else simply assumed) continuity is Ernest Sosa, who has proposed that our answers to the theorist's questions come from a *special* faculty of a priori intuition (see Sosa 1998 and 2007a). Sosa's proposal *invites* the sorts of skepticisms to which Williamson's, Cappelen's, and Nagel's claims of continuity are meant to respond.

[25] I think we can begin to see that something has gone wrong in Nagel's story when we consider that whatever we do when we attend to and attempt to answer the theorist's question about one of Gettier's (1963) original cases, for example, we are quite clearly *not* reading the mind of Smith (let alone the minds of people in epistemic situations such as his). Having been presented with Gettier's description of the cases, and whatever answer we will end up giving to the theorist's question of whether Smith knows the propositions in

Whereas Nagel, just like Williamson and Cappelen, has made the claim of continuity in an attempt to defend the method of cases, and more specifically to establish the reliability of our answers to the theorist's questions, Jennifer Nado has made the claim in an attempt to *cast doubt* on the method. Just like Williamson, Cappelen, and Nagel, Nado contends that our answers to the theorist's questions are *no less reliable* than the answers we give to questions that arise naturally in the course of everyday experience (see Nado 2015: 210). She argues, however, that while that level of reliability is more or less fine for the purposes of everyday practical life, it is insufficient for the more "demanding" purpose of philosophical theorizing (see Nado 2015: 212).

Most experimental philosophers have endorsed the claim of continuity, either explicitly or implicitly, and have relied on it in explaining and motivating their practice.[26] Knobe and Nichols, for example, though they mostly refer to the answers people (are inclined to) give to the theorist's questions as "intuitions," seem equally happy to speak of those answers, in perfect line with Williamson's and Cappelen's view of things, as expressive of "judgments" (K&N: 5 and 13), "opinions" (K&N: 6), "views" (K&N: 6), or "beliefs" (K&N: 7). And Knobe has claimed elsewhere that

question, we already know everything there will ever be to read, if you will, of *Smith's mind*. "Our intuitive mindreading," Nagel writes, "generates predictions about what others will do and say, and these predictions ... are subject to feedback and correction over time" (Nagel 2012: 497). But for the word "intuitive"—which is meant, I suppose, to encourage the idea of continuity, but would not normally be used to describe everyday instances of mindreading, *unless* we thought the reader was going on a hunch or a feeling, *rather than* the normal behavioral criteria for this or that state of mind—what Nagel says here is just right, and important; but it does not actually serve her goal of establishing the reliability in general of answers to the theorist's questions (in epistemology) by way of the claim of continuity. As I have already noted, there is no reason to suppose that those who answer "knows" in response to the theorist's question about one of Gettier's cases, for example, will make predictions about Smith's behavior, or about the behavior of others in similar situations, that are systematically different from the predictions made by those who answer "does not know." Nor, therefore, is it clear what sort of feedback and correction over time there might be for those who answer one way or the other.

[26] The only experimentalist I know of who has argued for a significant, and damning, *dis*continuity between answering questions about cases that naturally arise in the course of everyday experience and answering the theorist's questions is Weinberg (cf. Weinberg 2007). As I will note in Chapter Two, however, (even) Weinberg has failed to appreciate the extent of the discontinuity and its precise nature. The argument of this book is meant to show that the discontinuity is primarily a matter, not of *the sorts of cases* theorists have tended to focus on, as Weinberg has suggested, but of *the peculiar context* in which we attend to those cases and try to answer the theorist's questions.

the subjects in his experiments concerning "intentional action" "were guided . . . by the tacit understanding they normally use when deciding whether or not certain actions are intentional" (Knobe 2003: 318). In a more recent paper, Knobe says that "[w]e quite often wonder whether, for example, a person has a particular intention" (Knobe 2010: 357); and it is clear that he takes what we do when we thus wonder to be not essentially different from what we do when we attend to and try to answer a question in one of his questionnaires about "intentional action."

It seems obvious to Knobe, and to most other participants in the recent debates concerning the method of cases, that what we do when we attend to and give our answers to the theorist's questions concerning (for example) intentional action is not different in any significant way from what we do when, outside philosophy, we wonder, for example, whether a hurtful remark was made with the intention of hurting, or whether a dropped tea tray that somehow ended up dissipating an emotional storm that was about to break out was dropped intentionally (see Austin 1979: 176). One of the main tasks of this book is to break through this apparent obviousness.[27]

---

[27] We can begin to see, and appreciate, the *dis*continuity between answering the theorist's questions and answering similarly worded questions that arise naturally in the course of everyday experience once we note that when we ask outside the theoretical context whether a tea tray was dropped intentionally, for example, we are asking an essentially *empirical* question about the person who dropped the tray and what led or caused her to drop it; and there are ways of finding out, or trying to, whether she dropped the tray intentionally, and ways of showing, or trying to, that she did, or did not. (Often, a slight change of her expression—right before, or during, or after the dropping of the tray—will do.) Moreover, the question's sense would depend in part on the context in which it arose— a context in which the words expressing it could be found to express some particular interest in the dropping of the tray. The criteria for dropping the tray "intentionally" in order to dissipate a brewing emotional storm are very different from those of dropping it "intentionally" in a fit of rage or as an act of protest, for example, and what "intentionally" contrasts with or rules out would be different in each of those cases. Furthermore, in finding, or otherwise coming to hold that the tray was dropped intentionally, we become committed to indefinitely many other things: we may reasonably be expected to *respond* differently to the dropping of the tray, for example, or to the person who dropped it, depending on whether we have found that it was dropped intentionally. By contrast, when we are presented with Knobe's scenarios and invited to say whether the chairman harmed, or helped, the environment intentionally, we are not asked an empirical question that expresses some particular interest *in the case at hand*, in a context that makes *that* interest intelligible; and there is *nothing* we might do *to find out*, empirically, whether she did, or did not. The "case" has been given to us by Knobe and is, empirically, as clear as it will ever be: there is nothing to find out about *it*. There is also *nothing* we commit ourselves to in saying ("judging," "intuiting") that the chairman harmed, or helped, the environment

The claim (or assumption) of continuity and the minimal assumption are not strictly speaking equivalent,[28] but they tend to go hand in hand and lend support to each other: if you take it, as per the minimal assumption, that the (clear enough) sense of a grammatically well-structured string of words is ensured, in principle and at least in most cases, by the meanings of the words, regardless of the context in which they are used, then you would also be likely to suppose that, taken in itself, answering the theorist's questions is not essentially or significantly different from answering similarly worded questions that arise naturally in the course of everyday experience; and, on the other hand, if you take it that answering the theorist's questions is not essentially or significantly different from answering similarly worded questions that arise naturally in the course of everyday experience, that by itself would be likely to seem to you as sufficient reason for supposing that the theorist's questions make (clear enough) sense and that, as competent speakers, we ought to be able to understand them and answer them (mostly) correctly.

Both the claim of continuity and the minimal assumption are underwritten by (some version or another of) the conception of language that will be presented in Chapter Three and questioned in subsequent chapters. According to that conception, underlying everyday speech and thinking is something we might call "pure judgment"—the sheer "application" of terms, or concepts, to cases, where the application is supposed not to require any particular context for its sense (in just the way that the theorist's questions, and our answers to them, are supposed not to require any particular context for *their* sense). As we have just seen, Williamson tellingly describes this presumed element or dimension as that of "classifying empirically encountered cases" with respect to some term or concept.[29] Language, on this conception, is first and foremost an instrument for recording and communicating such classifications,

---

intentionally, as opposed to saying he did not—or anyway nothing but the truth of our answer; and we do not yet know what it might mean for it to be, or not to be, "true." There is, for example, no reason to expect those who say they "agree" with the sentence "The chairman of the board harmed [helped] the environment intentionally" to respond systematically differently to the chairman, or to an actual person who has done *just* what she did, from those who say they "disagree" with the sentence.

[28] Hence the possibility of denying the continuity while holding on to the minimal assumption, as, in different ways, Sosa and Weinberg have done.

[29] See also Jackson, who speaks of conceptual analysis as "concerned to elucidate what governs our classificatory practice" (Jackson 1998: 36–7).

where *what* classification is recorded or communicated by means of some expression is supposed not to depend on the expression being put to some particular, intersubjectively significant use or another, in a context suitable for *that* use.[30] The theorist's questions are taken to invite us *just* to classify given items, or cases; so they are taken to invite us to do, in a theoretically controlled setting, something that we are supposed to be doing regularly in the course of everyday experience and discourse. What is supposed to enable us to understand and answer Knobe's question regarding the chairman of the board, for example, is taken to be no different from what enables us to find, and say, in the course of everyday experience, that a tea tray was dropped intentionally, or not.

This way of thinking about what the theorist's questions invite us to do suggests plausible responses to Cummins' and Stich's lines of skepticism about the method of cases. If there is no significant difference between the theorist's questions and questions that we routinely have to answer in the course of everyday discourse, then it would seem, pace Cummins, that there is at least one thing that our answers to the question may reveal, and reveal reliably: namely, whatever it is—call it "our concepts"—that guides us in answering the everyday questions, and in assessing answers given to those questions as correct or incorrect.[31] And the answer to Stich's question of why we should attach any special significance to what may merely be *our* concepts would then be that they are *ours*; and becoming clearer about them is therefore a way of becoming clearer about the world they enable us to manage, and to express. Thus, *if* the claim of continuity is correct—*if* the theorist's questions are not different in any significant way from questions that we have to address and answer in the course of everyday experience—then theorizing on the basis of answers to the theorist's questions may plausibly be seen as (at least) a legitimate contribution to philosophy's ancient pursuit of self-knowledge.

---

[30] I set aside the much-debated question of whether the classifications are themselves somehow language-dependent. For a survey of the debate, see Gleitman and Papafragou 2005.

[31] Ludwig, for example, has proposed that the method of cases is meant to help us "get clear about the complex structure of concepts with which we confront the world" (Ludwig 2007: 151). For a similar understanding of the aim of the method of cases, see Bealer 1998, Jackson 1998, and Goldman 2007. Sgaravatti, who also gives a strong expression to the assumption of continuity (see Sgaravatti 2015: 132–3), argues that what gets revealed in our answers to the theorist's questions are not, or not primarily, our concepts, but rather "conceptions" that guide us in our applications of concepts (see Sgaravatti 2015: 139ff).

Neither Williamson nor Cappelen would be happy with the above characterization of the aim of the method of cases, which, by their lights, partakes of the tendency on the part of philosophers to "psychologize" their evidence. On Williamson's and Cappelen's way of seeing things, our answers to the theorist's questions are supposed to reveal "features of the world," and not, or not primarily, features of our concepts, let alone features of the psychology of concept application. The following chapters will challenge this way of seeing things.

Knobe and Nichols anticipate the charge of "psychologization of evidence." "How on earth could information about the statistical distribution of intuitions ever give us reason to accept or reject a particular philosophical view?" they imagine someone asking (K&N: 6). Here they might have been expected to respond to the anticipated charge by proposing that the aim of experimental philosophers is to become clearer about our philosophically interesting concepts, and by further proposing that those concepts best reveal themselves in our "applications" of words to theoretically significant cases. And they might have gone further and questioned the assumption that *knowledge, causation, meaning,* and so on, could be investigated philosophically fruitfully in some way other than that of investigating our concepts of knowledge, causation, meaning, and so on.[32]

---

[32] Kornblith is one of those who have proposed that philosophy should study "features of the world" as opposed to our concepts of them. Unlike many other "armchair" philosophers, however, Kornblith has therefore found little philosophical value in the method of cases (see Kornblith 2015). According to Kornblith, one such "feature of the world" (Kornblith 2002: 159 and 165), or "worldly object" (Kornblith 2015: 152) that may be studied *directly*—rather than by way of studying our concept of it—is knowledge, or the state of knowing this or that (cf. Kornblith 2002: 159 and 165; see also Nanay 2015: 228 for a similar idea). Knowledge, Kornblith claims, is "a natural kind" (cf. Kornblith 2002: 29); and we, and our concept of knowledge, may be mistaken about *it*, he says, in much the same way that we, and our concept of tiger, could be mistaken about tigers (Kornblith 2015: 152). In trying to characterize the natural kind that is knowledge, however, Kornblith opts for the externalist view that knowledge is "a reliably produced true belief" (cf. Kornblith 2002: 58 and 62); and, setting aside familiar "internalist" objections to this understanding of knowledge, I cannot see how anything attainable by way of empirical science could help Kornblith avoid the traditional *conceptual* entanglements concerning (what is meant by, or counts as) "(having a) belief" and "truth." Nor is it clear how the notion of "true belief"—relying as it does on *non-natural* (conventional) as opposed to *natural* (factive) meaning—could be of much use to the natural scientist, or even so much as given sense purely from the perspective of the natural sciences.

Interestingly, however, though Knobe and Nichols at some point suggest that *part* of what experimental philosophy studies is "people's concepts" (K&N: 12), they do not pursue this understanding of the method of cases, either in its own right or as a way of responding to the charge of "psychologization of evidence."[33] Nor do Knobe and Nichols say anything else by way of clarifying what they mean by "concepts" and by "the application of concepts." Instead, they respond to the charge of "psychologization of evidence" by arguing, in effect, that the subject matter of experimental philosophy *just is people's psychology*, or "how the mind works" (K&N: 13). "No one is suggesting that philosophers should stop thinking about what really causes what," they write—in what is clearly meant as a conciliatory gesture toward their "armchair" colleagues who take the method of cases as serving the investigation of worldly "features" such as *causation*, as well as toward naturalist philosophers such as Kornblith who believe that philosophically interesting phenomena like knowledge or causation could be studied by philosophers in much the same way that rocks and tigers and brain processes are studied by natural scientists—"the suggestion is just that, whatever else we do, we should *also* be looking at people's intuitions about causation as a way of coming to a deeper understanding of how the mind works" (K&N: 12; see also Knobe 2007: 120). In seeking to reveal hidden psychological mechanisms and processes, and to "inquire into basic questions about human nature" (K&N: 13), Knobe and Nichols see themselves and other experimental philosophers as continuing the work of philosophers such as Nietzsche, Marx, and Feuerbach (K&N: 7; see also Knobe et al. 2012: 95–6).

There are at least a couple of immediate problems with this characterization of the aim of experimental philosophy, however. For one thing, though Knobe and Nichols are happy to talk, as other experimental philosophers have also done, about intuitive answers to the theorist's questions as "warranted or unwarranted" (K&N: 8), or "right or wrong" (K&N: 10)—thereby showing their commitment to the minimal assumption (I know of no experimental philosopher who is not committed to that assumption)—they tell us nothing about what those answers might

---

[33] Elsewhere, Knobe has gone as far as to claim that "[analyzing] the semantics of our concepts . . . is not the aim that most experimental philosophers were trying to achieve" (Knobe 2007: 119).

be right or wrong *about*, or about *what it might mean* for an answer to the theorist's question to be right, or wrong. Surely, Knobe and Nichols do not take those answers to be right or wrong about *how the mind works*, or about *our nature*. Indeed, one of the most striking anomalies of experimental philosophy in general, and of what Fischer and Collins call "the warrant project" in particular (Fischer and Collins 2015: 21–2), is that while it has centrally concerned itself with the "*reliability*" of the answers people give to the theorist's questions, and has sought to identify and establish experimentally various kinds of "*distorting*" factors that affect those answers, it has left altogether unclear what those answers might be true or false *about*, or *what it might mean* for them to be true, or false.[34]

Of course, if, following Williamson, Cappelen, Nagel, Nado, and many others, we *assume* continuity, and take answers to the theorist's questions to be not essentially different from answers given in the course of everyday experience to straightforward empirical questions, then we are likely to suppose that what it means for the former to be true or false is as clear as what it means for the latter to be true or false; and since we are surely entitled to speak of the latter as true or false, it would seem that we are equally entitled to speak of the former as true or false. This, however, presupposes the (truth of the) claim of continuity, as well as the minimal assumption; and those will be questioned in subsequent chapters.

Setting that important issue aside for the time being, and coming back to Knobe and Nichols' proposal that experimental philosophy is primarily concerned with the elucidation of "how the mind works," I note that another problem with this characterization is that it is terribly vague. After all, studying people's responses to *anything* could potentially teach us *something* about how the mind works (or about human nature). Why suppose that people's answers to versions of the theorist's questions are somehow especially or uniquely revelatory of how the mind works? What exactly are we supposed to learn about how our minds work

---

[34] As I've already mentioned, even Weinberg does not doubt that "there are truths to be had" (Weinberg 2015: 172) concerning such philosophically interesting subjects as "justice, goodness, agency, beauty, explanation, mereology, meaning, [and] rationality" (Weinberg 2015: 171), and that answers to the theorist's questions could express those truths. Following Cummins, Weinberg only doubts the possibility of ensuring, or ascertaining, that the answers we give *are* expressing those truths. Just like other experimental philosophers, however, Weinberg says nothing about the nature of those presumed truths, or about what it might mean for an answer to the theorist's question to express, or fail to express, one of those truths.

from studying those answers, or their statistical distribution? Accepting the traditional picture, according to which the theorist's questions simply invite us to "apply our concepts to cases," Knobe and Nichols write that the aim of experimental philosophy "is usually to provide an account of the factors that influence applications of a concept, and in particular, the *internal psychological processes* that underlie such applications" (K&N: 5). Elsewhere, Knobe has similarly summarized the findings of many of his own and other people's experiments by saying that those studies "indicate that people's moral judgments can impact their application of a surprising range of different concepts . . . [including] the concepts of intentional action, causation, freedom, knowledge, doing and allowing, desire, and many other concepts besides" (Knobe 2010: 353).

In thus inheriting without reflection the traditional notion of the "application of concepts to cases," however, Knobe and Nichols, and other experimental philosophers, have done nothing to clarify the notion or to vindicate its philosophical use. In particular, they have in effect granted the traditional philosopher, without reflection or argument, his assumption that what the theorist's questions invite us to do is not essentially different from what we do when we answer questions about cases, or apply our concepts, outside philosophy. In other words, they have accepted without reflection or argument the claim of continuity—a claim that, as we have seen, Knobe has explicitly made.

Now, *if* indeed the application of concepts to cases, *as traditionally understood*, *were* somehow fundamental to human experience and to human speech; and *if* our answers to the theorist's questions *were* expressive of such applications; and *if* the applications of concepts made in the theoretical context were not different in any significant way from the applications of concepts that are made outside that context, in the course of everyday experience and discourse; *then* the sorts of experiments conducted by Knobe and others *would have* revealed, in a rather straightforward way, fundamental facts about human experience and discourse, and experimental philosophy would have had a solid rationale and would have been well motivated. But these are very big ifs that have not themselves been established by experimental philosophy or by anyone else. I am going to question all of them.

If, as I will argue, there is good reason to think that what the theorist's questions invite us to do is fundamentally *dis*continuous with the ordinary and normal employment of our words—that is, with the *employment* of our words, as contrasted with whatever it is that we do when we raise and answer the theorist's questions—then there is good reason to worry that our answers to those questions might only *straightforwardly* reveal, at best, how the mind works *when presented with the theorist's questions.*

They *could* also thereby reveal things about how our minds work outside the theoretical setting, including what may aptly be called "the application of concepts," but through a theoretically contaminated lens, not in the sort of straightforward way that Knobe and Nichols, and other experimental philosophers, have supposed.[35]

---

[35] The following chapters will unpack these last, rather condensed remarks. By way of anticipation, however, consider the experiments that, on Knobe's view, have revealed the way in which moral judgments affect our application of the concept of "intentional action" (and any number of other concepts) (cf. Knobe 2010: 353). The results of these experiments would only seem striking to those who have supposed that words such as "intentional" or "intentionally" (and "know," and "cause," and so on) are first and foremost instruments for recording and communicating classifications of worldly "items"—in the case of "intentional (ly)," human doings—and that those classifications may be effected, recorded, and expressed even apart from any particular context of significant use of those words. The value of Knobe's findings lies in their pointing us away from that conception of language, and toward an alternative conception on which, roughly speaking, our words are instruments for *positioning ourselves significantly* in a world shared with others, and in relation to others. As Carpendale et al. correctly observe, in setting up his experiments and interpreting their findings, "Knobe disregards a whole tradition according to which thinking is rooted in a system of socially embedded processes of which morality is an integral part" (Carpendale et al. 2010: 334). Fully to say how Knobe's findings point us—albeit through a glass darkly—in the direction of that alternative conception of language, would require a very long discussion; but a good place to begin to appreciate how Knobe's experiments, and the broader framework that informs his and others' interpretation of their findings, distort the above truth, would be John Austin's work on excuses—conspicuously neglected in discussions of "the Knobe effect." Presented with Knobe's "harm" and "help" scenarios (Knobe 2004: 191), and considering the question whether I "thought the chairman *intentionally* harmed [helped] the environment" (Knobe 2004: 191), the first thing I find is that the question (and therefore any *straight* answer I might give it) is forced; and I am reminded of Austin's saying that "when it is stated that X did A, there is a temptation to suppose that given some, indeed perhaps *any*, expression modifying the verb we shall be entitled to insert either it or its opposite or negation in our statement: that is, we shall be entitled to ask, typically, 'Did X do A Mly or not Mly?' . . . and to answer one or the other" (Austin 1979: 189). Austin's basic contention is that there needs to be a point to the application of some particular modifying expression, and a particular suitable context that calls for or invites that application (see Austin 1979: 190). The doing in question need not be "morally bad" in order to felicitously be said to be (for example) "intentional"—the dropping of the tea tray may have actually saved the party, and been recognized by the conversants as having done that (see Austin 1979: 176); but there needs to be something about it, and about the situation in which we attend to it, that *invites* the application of "intentional" to it and gives the application *sense*—the meaning of "intentional(ly)" alone does not suffice to fix that sense. (When it comes to Knobe's "chairman" vignettes, matters are further complicated by the fact

Knobe and Nichols' "Manifesto" illustrates rather well the way in which experimental philosophy has extended the method of cases experimentally without doing much to clarify its nature and rationale. At the same time, however, and somewhat ironically, the new movement has been shielded against the force of the most basic questions about the method by the authority of the tradition. What exactly are we asking the subjects of philosophical experiments when we present them with one or another of the theorist's questions? *Well, the same sort of questions that analytic philosophers have been asking themselves in their studies for years.* Why suppose that those questions are clear (enough) and have correct answers (if only relative to some person's or community's concept of x)? *Well, that has always been assumed by philosophers who practice the method of cases.* What is it that our answers to the theorist's questions are supposed to be correct or incorrect *about*? *Well, whatever it is that the answers given by philosophers to those questions have been supposed to be correct or incorrect about.* Why suppose that the (correct) answers to the theorist's questions are somehow key to philosophical (or other) enlightenment? *Well, that has been a working assumption in analytic philosophy for years.* It is time to address these questions in earnest.

that, as applied to those vignettes, "*The chairman* Mly harmed [helped] the environment" sounds forced with almost *any* modifying expression I can think of, even with an expression far more suitable to the case as Knobe describes it, such as "knowingly.") So to Knobe's question, my preferred answer, following Austin, would be "not 'intentionally'" (Austin 1979: 188, fn. 1)—meaning that neither the word nor its opposite or negation quite fits his cases, or more precisely that, given the cases as he describes them, I cannot imagine a context in which the word (or its opposite or negation) could naturally and sensibly be used with reference to either case. Of course, Austin was also well aware of our tendency to be quite sloppy in our use of modifying expressions such as "intentionally" (see Austin 1979: 197), and of the human capacity to see, or guess at—well enough for present intents and purposes—the speaker's intended point, however sloppily or imprecisely expressed. This would explain why Knobe's subjects—though evidently quite unsure of how to answer his questions (see Knobe 2010: 318)—were not *totally* befuddled by those questions, and were able to come up with answers to them, however unsure.

2

Internal Difficulties in Defending the Method of Cases, and the Claim of Continuity

The first chapter raised some basic questions about the method of cases and what it could plausibly be expected to accomplish. I tried to show that the answers that have so far been given to those questions by practitioners of the method—both armchair and experimental—are unsatisfactory. The aim of this chapter is to press and pursue those questions further by way of a close examination of Williamson's and Cappelen's attempts to defend the method. Those attempts, I will argue, ultimately boil down to the claim of continuity between every-day, "nonphilosophical" questions about "empirically encountered" cases and the theorist's questions, or, in other words, between the everyday employment of our words in speech and thought and what-ever it is that we are invited to do with them when we are invited to answer the theorist's questions. The claim of continuity rests, as we will see in Chapter Three, on a particular conception of language—a widely held conception that has also underwritten the minimal assumption. In subsequent chapters, I will question the method of cases by questioning the conception of language that has underwritten it, and by presenting and motivating, both philosophically and empirically, an alternative conception of language on which both the minimal assumption and the claim of continuity are false and the method—as commonly practiced by both armchair and experimental philosophers—is deeply and fundamentally misguided.

2.1 Skepticism about the "Method of Cases" without "Intuitions"

Cappelen presents an understanding of the method of cases that is at the same time meant as a defense of it against extant lines of skepticism.[1] As Cappelen understands it, the skepticism is based on the assumption that "contemporary analytic philosophers rely on intuitions as evidence (or as a source of evidence) for philosophical theories" (PWI: 3). Cappelen calls that assumption "centrality" and argues that it is false (PWI: 3). Since the skepticism relies on "centrality," and since "centrality" is false, Cappelen in effect contends, the skepticism is misguided. This, according to Cappelen, is bad news for experimental philosophers who have sought to make a career out of checking on the philosophical "intuitions" of those without formal training in philosophy, and bad news too for anyone else who has hoped to question much of the work produced by analytic philosophers in the last forty years or so at a foundational level.[2] On the other hand, it is intended to be very good news for all those who have found that work fruitful and exciting, and would be happy to see it continuing along more or less the same lines, without a cloud of skepticism cast over it.

But how could so much hang on whether we use "intuitions" to refer to the answers we (find ourselves inclined to) give to the theorist's questions? Either those answers are fit to do the theoretical work they have been supposed to do, or they are not. Either the theories produced by analytic philosophers in the last few decades have relied on

[1] Though Cappelen does not primarily present himself as seeking to *vindicate* the method of cases in the face of extant lines of skepticism, I do not think I am being unfair in taking him to be seeking to vindicate the method, and in assessing his book *as an attempt to vindicate the method*. As we will see, there *are* responses in his book—albeit not satisfactory ones—to those lines of skepticism.

[2] Cappelen paints a pluralistic picture of contemporary philosophy: "The various activities that get classified together as 'philosophy' today are so classified as the result of complex historical and institutional contingencies, not because philosophy has an essence that ties it all together as a natural kind" (PWI: 21). The implied claim is that since contemporary philosophy is so diverse, any effective criticism of it would have to be local—targeting one sort of activity that is called "philosophy" nowadays, but not others (see PWI: 19–20 and 196–7). Now, as an empirical observation concerning the use of "philosophy" Cappelen's description is undisputable. One would hope, however, that the price of diversification has not been that of philosophy losing its (arguably defining) characteristic of questioning *itself* at the most foundational level (on this, see Kant 1998: A838/B866).

questionable or misconceived support, or they haven't. Surely, what you *call* that support cannot be *that* important.[3] And in fact, it is not. The first thing I will try to show about Cappelen's attempt to vindicate the philosophical "method of cases" in the face of recent skepticism is that it does not *substantively* rely on denying the thesis he calls "centrality"[4]—the thesis according to which analytic philosophers have centrally relied on *intuitions* in their theories. The second thing I will try to show is that it is not clear what remains of Cappelen's defense of the method of cases once the apparent contribution of the denial of "centrality" has been shown to be merely apparent. This is true even when Cappelen's attempted defense of the method is taken in conjunction with Williamson's earlier attempted defense of the method in *The Philosophy of Philosophy* ("PP"), on which it clearly and crucially relies. If anything, a close examination of Cappelen's and Williamson's responses to extant lines of skepticism about the method of cases only underscores the difficulty of answering those skeptical worries in a truly satisfactory manner.

---

[3] It might here be felt that I'm doing Cappelen an injustice. His *main* contention, it might be objected, is *not* that the answers we (find ourselves inclined to) give to the theorist's questions should not be called "intuitions," but rather that those answers—whatever we choose to call them—have not *in practice* been treated as providing independent ("Rock") *foundation* for philosophical theorizing, as many have supposed. I'll come back to this part of Cappelen's understanding of how the method of cases is supposed to work, and will argue that, considered as a response to "calibration" skepticism about the method of cases, it fails. I will also argue that Cappelen's attempted vindication of the method of cases boils down to the claim of continuity—that is, to the contention that our answers to the theorist's questions are expressive of "judgments" not essentially different from the sorts of empirical judgments that we routinely make and express in the course of everyday experience and discourse. So, at least rhetorically, the denial of "centrality" does play a crucial role in Cappelen's attempt to vindicate the method of cases. At the end of the day, however, it does not matter for the purposes of the argument of this book whether the answers we (find ourselves inclined to) give to the theorist's questions are taken to provide more or less independent evidence for philosophical theorizing, or, as Cappelen contends, are taken as "worthless" unless supported by argument (PWI: 223). My argument is against the tendency to suppose that those answers, whether supported by argumentation or not, are, in principle, correct or incorrect, and to further suppose that the "correct" answers are somehow key to philosophical (or other) enlightenment concerning such philosophically interesting subjects as knowledge, causation, intentional action, and so on. And these are two suppositions that Cappelen clearly makes.

[4] It does rely on it *rhetorically*, as I will point out in section 2.4, in that the denial of "centrality" ushers in the claim of continuity, without actually supporting that claim. And it's the claim of continuity that's doing all of the real work in Cappelen's and Williamson's defense of the method of cases.

In order to see that Cappelen's response to the skepticism does not actually rely on his denial of "centrality," we need first to see that the skepticism itself may be articulated without reliance on "centrality." To see *that*, we need first a description of the philosophical "method of cases" that does not rely on the notion of "intuition" and is otherwise uncontentious enough so as not to beg any question in favor of the skepticism to which Cappelen is responding.

The "Method of Cases" without "Centrality." A central occupation of analytic philosophers has been the construction of theories of philosophically interesting phenomena such as knowledge, justification, moral permissibility, causation, necessary truth, intentional action, belief (change of belief), and so on. Let "X" stand for any one of those philosophically interesting phenomena. As a way either of supporting or motivating some theory of X (or some related phenomenon), or of undermining some theory of X, philosophers have centrally used "thought experiments": they have constructed (or simply invoked) philosophically interesting cases—cases designed to bring out, either by themselves or in conjunction with other cases, significant features of X; and then they have invited themselves and others to answer questions of the form "Is this a case of X?" or of the form "Is this a case of X or of Y?" (where Y is supposed to interestingly contrast with X).[5] Call any question of this general form, when asked as a way of testing some theory of X, "the theorist's question." The general working hypothesis has been that the theorist's question has a correct answer and that good theories of X should fit with the "correct" answers to the (relevant) theorist's questions.

Next we need to see that the skepticism about the method of cases to which Cappelen has responded may be articulated without reliance on the notion of "intuition" and so without reliance on "centrality." Here we need to distinguish between two basic forms that skepticism about the method of cases can take, and has taken. The two basic forms of skepticism, which were already mentioned in Chapter One, are not necessarily mutually exclusive, but there is a clear sense in which they compete with each other. It would be useful to keep them separate as much as possible, as we consider Cappelen's argument.

The first form of skepticism about the method of cases is what I have called, following Stich 1988, "cognitive diversity skepticism." It is more

---

[5] As, for example, *merely believing* that such and such presumably relates to *knowing* that such and such, or *changing one's belief* that such and such presumably relates to *still believing* that such and such *but in a different way*.

akin to a form of cultural relativism than to skepticism proper; and many of those who, by my lights, would count among its proponents have actually not regarded it as a form of *skepticism* at all. They have simply regarded it as the only plausible understanding of the method of cases and what it can hope to accomplish. I think the label "skepticism" is nonetheless apt here; but the skepticism is directed not at the legitimacy or even possible truth of analytic philosophers' theories of X, but at a common understanding of those theories' legitimacy and truth—an understanding that Cappelen very clearly shares. Another reason for calling the position I am about to describe "skeptical" is that Cappelen, following Williamson, would clearly regard it as such. Here, then, is how this first form of "skepticism" may be described without reliance on the notion of "intuition."

"Cognitive Diversity" Skepticism about the Method of Cases without "Centrality." In constructing theories of X and testing them by way of "the method of cases," analytic philosophers have wanted to think of themselves as tracking and elucidating some particular phenomenon to which our "x" refers but whose identity and existence do not depend on what *we count* as "x" and under what conditions. But in reality our answers to the theorist's question, and so our philosophical theories of X, at best track and elucidate *our concept* of X or *what counts for us* as "x." As such, those answers, and the theories they support, may well teach us interesting things about ourselves and about *our* world; but it is a mistake to think of them as tracking and elucidating some phenomenon X that is there independently of the categorizations *we* have come to effect, record, and communicate by means of the word "x." In other words, if our philosophical theories elucidate anything at all, they elucidate "what governs our classificatory practices" (Jackson 1998: 36–7); and insofar as the answers we give to the theorist's question are correct, they are correct, and can only be correct, "relative to the contents of the concept as it exists in the subject's head" (Goldman 2007: 15). Furthermore, it is quite possible and perhaps even necessary that people sufficiently unlike us have concepts different from ours. Those people may speak the same language we do (or not); but even if they do, their "x" (or the word in their language that most closely translates "x") may not mean the same as our "x"—the categorization they mark by means of it may be different more or less significantly from the categorization we mark by means of it; and there is no reason to assume that *our* concept is somehow "truer" to the world, or otherwise superior to theirs.

Henceforward, I will refer to any proponent of the above, broadly characterized view as "a proponent of cognitive diversity skepticism," even if that philosopher does not regard the view as skeptical of the method of cases (as many proponents of the above view do not).[6]

The second form of skepticism is more clearly skeptical. It originates from Cummins 1998 and, following Cummins, I will call it "calibration skepticism." It can come in various sub-forms and degrees, but here is a generic and barebones version of it that does not rely on "centrality":

"Calibration Skepticism" about the Method of Cases without "Centrality." Analytic philosophers have constructed and argued for theories of philosophically interesting phenomena, and they have used the method of cases (thought experiments) to either support or undermine those theories. Thus, answers to versions of the theorist's question have played an important role in the formation and assessment of philosophical theories. But we have no way of telling that the answers analytic philosophers have taken to be correct really are correct. If we think of ourselves as X-tracking instruments, the point can be put by saying that we have no way of calibrating these instruments—no way of ascertaining that we reliably track X (as opposed, for example, to mere pictures of X that we have formed for ourselves, or to philosophical constructions that, however compelling, are more or less illusory). In this, answers to the theorist's questions are different from empirical observations, which may be calibrated in various familiar ways, and the theories supported by the former are therefore crucially different from scientific theories.

The reason I said that "cognitive diversity" skepticism and "calibration" skepticism are not necessarily mutually exclusive is that one could hold *both* that answers to the theorist's question could only reasonably hope to capture *our concept* of X, as opposed to X as an independently existing worldly "item," *and* that there is reason to worry that those answers are not even reliably tracking *that*. If the argument of this book is on the right track, this is at least a real worry. For now, however, we will keep the two forms of skepticism separate. As already noted in Chapter One, the new movement of experimental philosophy has drawn motivation from both forms of skepticism, with some experiments primarily designed to reveal cognitive diversity, and others primarily designed to reveal "non-truth-conducive" factors that affect the answers people give to the theorist's questions. As we will see, one striking feature of Cappelen's attempt to vindicate the method of cases is that it takes neither form of skepticism very seriously.

---

[6] Jackson and Goldman are two clear examples of proponents and practitioners of the method of cases who accept what I'm here calling "cognitive diversity skepticism" but do not regard this understanding of the method as *skeptical*.

2.2 Cappelen's Response to "Cognitive Diversity" Skepticism about the Method of Cases

The aim of this section and section 2.3 is to find and assess whatever arguments there are in PWI against either "cognitive diversity" or "calibration" skepticism. Since both forms of skepticism may be put without reliance on "centrality," the denial of "centrality" had better play at most an auxiliary role in those arguments. What are Cappelen's arguments?

One thing Cappelen does, following Williamson, is to charge all those philosophers who have been happy to describe themselves as relying on intuitions in their theorizing with "psychologizing evidence" (PWI: 114, and 203–4; see also PP: 3–5). Psychologizing evidence is what philosophers do when they "judge" that p, but then, instead of taking p as evidence for their theories, they take their evidence to only be *their believing* that p, or (even worse from Williamson's and Cappelen's perspective) *their inclination* to believe (or "judge") that p.[7]

The charge that philosophers have tended to psychologize their evidence may be heard as a response to either "cognitive diversity" skepticism or "calibration" skepticism. Let "p" be some indicative sentence of the general form "This is a case of X" or "Cases of *this* sort are cases of X."[8] Proponents of "cognitive diversity" skepticism would presumably be guilty of psychologizing evidence because, having "judged" that p, instead of taking p as evidence for theories of X, where X is supposed to be some "feature of the world" (PWI: 188) that does not depend for its identity or existence on *what we count as "x"* (and how, and under what conditions), they take their judgment or belief that p to reveal something about the meaning of "x"—about what *they* mean by "x," *their concept* of X.

---

[7] I put "judge" in quotation marks to register my worry that the term, as used by Williamson and Cappelen, is a technical term that may cover up an important difference between what ordinarily and normally goes by the name of "judgment" and whatever it is we do when we attend to the theorist's question and come up with an answer to it. I will come to this possible difference later on.

[8] As Malmgren nicely shows (Malmgren 2011), it is actually not easy to specify precisely the content of an answer to one of the theorist's questions, let alone specify it in such a way that such answers would seem capable of carrying the philosophical weight they have been supposed to carry.

By contrast, proponents of "calibration" skepticism take the meaning of "x" ("know," "cause," "free"...) or the concept of X (knowledge, causation, freedom...), to already be clear, or at any rate clear enough for "p" to be (expressing something) clear enough and either true or false. The psychologization of evidence in *their* case would be a matter of denying that we can know whether *p*, and insisting that all we can know and legitimately use as evidence for our theories is that *we believe* or are *inclined to believe* that *p* (or that not *p*). And the move from *that* evidential basis to a theory of *X* (thought of as an independently existing worldly item) seems hopeless (see PWI: 89; see also PP: 211 and 243).

In both Williamson and Cappelen, the charge of "psychologizing evidence" is sometimes directed at the "cognitive diversity" skeptic, sometimes at the "calibration" skeptic, and sometimes indistinctively against both at once. But whether directed at the "cognitive diversity" skeptic or at the "calibration" skeptic (or at both), the charge, taken by itself and apart from some *argument* against the skepticism it is directed at, does no more than dogmatically beg the question against the skeptic. It is true that it is often hard in philosophy to decide where the burden of argument lies, and when it comes to traditional forms of skepticism, the sense has often been that the burden of argument is on the skeptic. But I think it is fair to expect of someone who wishes to dismiss the widespread view that the method of cases centrally aims at analyzing or elucidating our concepts—a view to which Jackson has referred with right as "the conventional wisdom" (Jackson 2009: 105)—to do more than insist that philosophers have mostly and primarily been investigating *knowledge, meaning, freedom, causation, and so on,* as contrasted with *our concepts* of these "objects." More than two hundred years after Kant, the tendency among philosophers to imagine themselves investigating things as they are in themselves—as opposed to phenomena that are shaped by human sensitivities, capacities, needs, interests, and practices, as articulated in our concepts—is surely no evidence that this is what they actually are doing, or indeed that there is anything clear to be done that fits that self-image. Moreover, given the evident elusiveness of these philosophically interesting "objects," it seems fair to expect an argument from someone who wishes to assume that we are reliable trackers (and theorizers) of those objects. Thus, if there is an *argument* against either "cognitive diversity" or "calibration" skepticism in PWI, it must be sought elsewhere than in the charge of "psychologizing evidence."

Beyond the charge of "psychologizing evidence," is there anything in PWI that could be taken as an argument against "cognitive diversity" skepticism? It might be thought that Cappelen's repeated questioning of the philosophical appeal to "conceptual justification" or "conceptual truth" is such an argument. Proponents of "cognitive diversity" skepticism maintain that answers to the theorist's questions, and philosophical theories of X more generally, can at most reveal features of *our concept* of X, and can only sensibly be assessed in terms of "correctness" or "justification" *relative to our (or to some) concept* of X. Does this not commit them to believing in conceptual truths and conceptual justifications? It all depends on what one means by "conceptual truth" or "conceptual justification."

Cappelen makes three notable claims in connection with the notions of "conceptual justification" and "conceptual truth." The first is that there is no agreement among philosophers on what concepts are, let alone on what conceptual justification or truth might be (PWI: 124). This, Cappelen says, is also true of psychologists, who "disagree widely about just what concepts are" (PWI: 209). For this reason, any philosopher who wishes to say of some claim to the effect that p that it is conceptually justified may reasonably be expected to "tell us what she thinks concepts are, what she means by 'conceptual competence,' how she construes the relevant kind of justification, [and then go on] to show that p satisfies these various conditions" (PWI: 125). Cappelen's second claim is that such a philosopher had better "engage with the results from empirical studies of concept possession, concept acquisition and related topics" (PWI: 207). His third claim is that "excellent" and "forceful" arguments have been offered against conceptual truth or analyticity (PWI: 126 and 210)—Cappelen refers to arguments made by Quine and by Williamson—and that any philosopher who wishes to say of some claim that it is conceptually justified may be expected to "tell us how she has convinced herself" that those excellent arguments "can be overcome" (PWI: 125–6).

Since our focus at this point is on "cognitive diversity" skepticism, the first thing to say, in response to Cappelen's first claim, is that proponents of that form of skepticism actually share a pretty clear understanding of what concepts are, or what they mean by "concept." Roughly, by "the concept of X" they mean something like "whatever it is that *ultimately* guides us in classifying items in the world as (belonging to the category of) X, or not-X, and in distinguishing between correct and incorrect classifications (relative to our concept, of course)."[9] This rough understanding may also be given a linguistic turn: "Our concept of X is whatever it is that ultimately guides us in applying 'x' to cases (or withholding 'x' from cases), and in distinguishing between correct and incorrect applications." This understanding of "concept," however rough, seems clear enough for the purposes of "cognitive diversity" skepticism. Concepts, on this understanding, govern our classifications of worldly items; they are what those classifications are ultimately beholden to.

Furthermore, the above understanding is *very* widely shared among both analytic philosophers and empirical scientists. Even Williamson, who argues much in the spirit of Cappelen against the talk of philosophical "intuitions," on the ground that this talk bespeaks misplaced "skepticism about judgment," contends that the capacity that enables us to tell that the subject in a Gettier situation does not know the proposition in question is "the same capacity to *classify empirically encountered cases with respect to knowledge* as we use when, for example, we classify a politician as not knowing the truth of his claims about terrorists" (Williamson 2004: 112, my emphasis; see also Williamson 2005: 12). Well and good, proponents of "cognitive diversity" skepticism would say in response, but, if so, then our philosophical judgments teach us something about what *we call* or *classify as* "knowledge," not something about knowledge as an independently existing worldly "item" (whatever *that* might be); and it may well be that other people mark more or less significantly different classifications by means of "knowledge" (or by means of the word or combination of words that most closely translates "knowledge" in their language).[10]

All of the disagreements about what concepts are that Cappelen mentions are disagreements *within* the broad framework of the above understanding of "concept." The disagreements are about *what form* is taken by what ultimately guides our classifications of worldly items, or our applications of words to cases—whether it takes the form of rules or

---

[9] The "ultimately" here and below is important, for what *actually* guides us—what we actually go by—in classifying an item as (an) x, may be tangential or accidental from the perspective of (what we regard as) the concept of x.

[10] A possibility that Williamson allows (PP: 190).

necessary and sufficient conditions, or of prototypes or exemplars and ways of measuring an item's similarity to them, or of proto-theories, or of "family resemblance," and so on.[11] Moreover, apart from that broad, shared idea of what concepts are, it would not be possible to so much as even articulate the disagreements Cappelen mentions, let alone construct empirical studies aimed at settling them. That at least some level of clarity about our concept of X (here, clarity about our concept of Concept) is required before any empirical study of X—any study of the item or items *we count* as "x"—could even begin, is at least part of the reason why many "armchair" analytic philosophers have seen a real and important role for what they have called "conceptual analysis" or, more broadly, for the "elucidation of concepts" (Jackson 2009: 101). And as long as one assumes the representationalist way of thinking about concepts sketched above, inviting oneself and others to apply "x" to cases that are carefully designed to bring out key features of our concept of X, would seem the right thing to do for anyone interested in elucidating that concept.

I cannot see how Quine's treatment of "analyticity" over the years is supposed to make any trouble for the above understanding of the method of cases and what it can hope to accomplish.[12] As is well known, Quine's argument against "analyticity," in "Two Dogmas of Empiricism" and earlier in "Truth by Convention," is directed mainly at Carnap's conventionalism-cum-pragmatism and the clear-cut distinction it presupposes between analytic and synthetic statements. Quine's aim is to show that no such clear-cut distinction, of the sort Carnap needs, can be so much as intelligibly presented. As Quine puts it already in "Truth by Convention," his aim is to question "not the validity of the distinction between synthetic and analytic truths, but its sense" (Quine 1976: 250). Quine's discussion is couched against the background of his naturalism, behaviorism, holism, and his deep suspicion of the philosophical idea of meanings (or for that matter concepts) as empirically real entities. But since the notion of "the meaning of 'x'" or "the concept of X" can be

---

[11] For an overview of these various options, see Margolis and Laurence 1999: 3–81.

[12] Though Cappelen mentions several times Quine's "arguments" against "analyticity," he never actually refers to any specific text of Quine's. This is problematic, since Quine's discussions of analyticity over the years are actually difficult to interpret. My aim in what follows is merely to show why Quine is no (obvious) ally of Cappelen when it comes to "cognitive diversity" skepticism.

given what Quine has called "empirical criteria" (Quine 1991: 272) in terms of the disposition to apply "x" to cases or to categorize items in terms of "x" under various circumstances, it is just not clear how anything Quine says in his earlier writings against Carnap's notion of "analyticity" is supposed to make trouble for those who believe that the method of cases can enable us to elucidate our concepts.

An utterance of the same form of words—"This is (a case of) X"—that in one context may be taken to provide (defeasible) information about the world, may in another context be focused on as *a piece of human behavior* that teaches us something, not about the case referred to, but about a subject's disposition to use "x," where that is understood in terms of her disposition to apply "x" to cases. If we came to a foreign country, and we found its inhabitants using some word "x" that did not seem to correspond to any word in our language, and if their attempts at verbal elucidations of the meaning of "x" still left us unclear about that meaning, one thing we could certainly do is construct or point to cases, and contexts of attending to those cases, and invite native speakers of that language to tell us whether those cases would *count as* cases of x in those contexts. Naturally, we would assume that their applications of "x" are *correct* by the criteria governing the use of "x" in their language; but our interest would be not in the nature of the cases—after all, they would typically be cases constructed by us, and we would know everything there is to know empirically about them—but in the meaning of their "x."[13] "Cognitive diversity" skeptics proceed on the basis of the hardly contentious idea that *our* concepts, or the meanings of *our own* words, may sometimes be unclear to us; and they take it that when we theorize by way of the method of cases we simply adopt that kind of investigative attitude toward ourselves, in order to elucidate those concepts, or meanings. And *this* idea, provided it is stripped of all metaphysical baggage untamable by clear empirical criteria, is one that Quine has, and as far as I can see should by his lights have, nothing against. After all, he himself has readily allowed that "It is intelligible and often useful in discussion to

---

[13] I should note that, in many cases, in learning the meaning of "x" we also learn what (sort of thing) X *is*, or the place of X (or Xs) in the world of our, or some other, community (on this, see Cavell 1979: 65ff). But the world we learn in learning (a) language is not a world of things as they are in themselves. It is a world structured and informed by human capacities, needs, interests, and sensitivities.

point out that some disagreement is purely a matter of words rather than of facts" (Quine 1991: 270).

Nor is it clear how Williamson's argument against what he calls "epistemological conceptions of analyticity" is supposed to give trouble to the "cognitive diversity" skeptic.[14] Epistemological conceptions of analyticity, as discussed by Williamson, center on the idea that assenting to certain judgments featuring "x" is constitutive of understanding "x." The idea, in other words, is that assenting to certain judgments featuring "x" is necessary for meaning by "x" what *we*—who posit the truth of some judgment as constitutive of the meaning of "x"—mean by it. Williamson argues that there are no "understanding-assent links" of the sort posited by proponents of epistemological conceptions of analyticity. He argues that for any term "x" and some "p" that features "x" and is supposed to be such that anyone who understands "x" would assent to "p," it is possible for there to be a "thoroughly competent" speaker who by any reasonable standard understands "x" and possesses our concept of X, but who nonetheless judges that not-*p* (PP: 85ff).

Williamson's argument is complex, and some of what it presupposes will emerge later on. But for now all we need is to note that the argument does not by itself undermine the "cognitive diversity" skeptic's understanding of what the method of cases and the philosophical theorizing of which it is part may plausibly hope to accomplish. That skeptic does not need to assume that *any particular* application of "x" by a competent speaker and possessor of the concept of X is *necessarily* correct (relative to the meaning of *our*, or of *that speaker's* "x"). It suffices for her that it is *likely* correct, or most likely correct *ceteris paribus*; and Williamson not only has no objection to the assumption that the judgments of competent speakers are likely correct, but he actually devotes a whole chapter to arguing that the judgments of competent speakers are likely to be not just correct but instances of *knowledge* (PP: 247–77).

In order to generate his counterexamples to epistemological conceptions of analyticity, Williamson typically offers a complex story of what might lead an otherwise competent employer of "x" to apply it "deviantly" in some case or range of cases. That we *must* imagine some

---

[14] Williamson also argues against what he calls "metaphysical conceptions of analyticity," but it is the argument against what he calls "epistemological conceptions of analyticity" that is pertinent here.

such story in order for the deviance not to undermine the competence suggests that there is truth, however holistic, in epistemological conceptions of analyticity. In any case, however, the possible deviances Williamson invokes are *necessarily* "localized" (PP: 97); for if the speaker were to misapply "x" in *most* cases, he would *not* count by "any reasonable criterion" as a competent employer of "x" and possessor of the concept of X (see Williamson 2005: 12).

I conclude that Quine's and Williamson's arguments against analyticity do not in any way undermine the "cognitive diversity" understanding of the method of cases, and of the philosophical theorizing of which it is part. For all that Quine and Williamson have said, they have given us no reason for not taking competent speakers' classifications of cases as cases of X, or not-X, to be revelatory of our (or their) concept of X.

Now, it may be that the representationalist way of thinking about concepts as essentially underwriting point-independent classifications is misguided, and misguided not merely because it fails to capture what we normally mean by "concept," or what you might call "our concept of concept," but because it relies on, and in turn encourages, a picture of our relation to language and to our world that is untrue by the standards of empirical science itself.[15] If so, then the philosophical "method of cases" as practiced by analytic philosophers—both "armchair" and experimental— may not actually be the right or best way to elucidate our philosophically troublesome concepts and the phenomena they articulate. The method may engender confusion and misunderstanding instead of alleviating them. Later on I will argue that this is at least a real possibility that ought to be taken seriously by philosophers and empirical scientists alike. For now I only note that neither Williamson and Cappelen nor proponents of "cognitive diversity" skepticism have taken that possibility seriously, or even so much as considered it.

2.3 Cappelen's Response to "Calibration" Skepticism about the Method of Cases

"Calibration" skepticism concerns the reliability of the answers we give to the theorist's questions. *Assuming* that the theorist's questions are fit

---

[15] As Huw Price forcefully argues in Price (2011) and (2013).

to be answered correctly or incorrectly, truly or falsely—which neither Cummins nor any other critic of the method of cases I know of has doubted—the "calibration" skeptic worries that we have no way of ascertaining that the answers we give are correct, no way of establishing their truth.

To this skeptical worry it is tempting to offer the following quick and easy response: *The theorist's question typically invites us to apply some ordinary word "x," or some ordinary concept X, to some case. As competent speakers of the language in which the question is couched, and more specifically as competent employers of "x" and possessors of the concept of X, we may,* ceteris paribus, *be relied upon to apply "x" correctly to cases or, in other words, to identify cases correctly as cases of X (or not-X).*[16]

There are, as we shall see, good reasons for being suspicious of this response to "calibration" skepticism. Most immediately, it runs into the difficulty that, as a matter of empirical fact, competent speakers sometimes disagree in their answers to the theorist's questions. Analytic philosophers did not have to await experimental philosophy in order to become familiar with this fact. As Ernest Sosa, one of the strongest defenders of philosophical theorizing by way of the method of cases, has recently acknowledged, there is no shortage of examples of cases where even the relatively homogeneous community of analytic philosophers is split over answers to versions of the theorist's question (Sosa 2011: 461).[17] Evidently, competently employing "x" outside philosophy does not ensure answering the theorist's question correctly—assuming, for now, with Williamson, Cappelen, Sosa, and many other "armchair" and experimental philosophers, that the question has a correct answer.

Nor can the skeptical worry plausibly be dismissed by claiming that the disagreement is merely apparent since different answers to the theorist's question simply bespeak different concepts of X. Disagreements in answers to the theorist's questions have emerged, as Williamson correctly notes (PP: 216; and Williamson 2005: 11–12), among people who by any reasonable criterion mean their "x" in the same way (or ways)

---

[16] For this line of argument, see Goldman and Pust 1998: 188; Bealer 2000: 2; and Goldman 2007: 15. Jackson, who makes a similar argument, will be discussed in Chapter Three.

[17] Kornblith makes a similar observation (Kornblith 2015: 157).

and share the same concept of X.[18] To attribute every such disagreement to a difference in concepts would be merely ad hoc. It would also cover up real problems with the philosophical method of cases.

One merit of Williamson's *The Philosophy of Philosophy* is its refusal to acquiesce in the above quick and easy dismissal of "calibration" skepticism. Indeed, as we saw, Williamson's argument against epistemological conceptions of analyticity is based on the idea that it is always possible for a competent employer of virtually *any* word to misapply it in some more or less restricted range of cases without thereby ceasing to be a competent employer of the word and possessor of the concept it expresses. Williamson's problem is that in refusing to accept the quick and easy response to "calibration" skepticism he has left himself with no truly satisfying response to that skepticism. Mostly, he seems to rely on a claim to *expertise* in applying "abstract concepts to complex cases" to remove the skeptical worry, where the expertise is glossed in terms of "being good at philosophy" (PP: 40; see also PP: 191). What the expert presumably has is "a capacity for applying ... concepts that goes far beyond what it takes to possess the concepts in the first place ... " (PP: 189).[19]

The claim to expertise seems merely dogmatic, however, for at least three reasons: first, as Sosa has acknowledged, disagreements in answers to the theorist's questions have emerged "among the experts themselves [read: well-trained analytic philosophers], at the highest levels of expertise" (Sosa 2011: 461); second, Williamson acknowledges and even insists that the judgments of "experts" are sometimes "incorrect" precisely *because* of their attachment to some theory, which raises the worry that philosophical training may not in fact increase one's chances of judging "correctly" (see, for example, PP: 189; see also Williamson 2011: 499–501 and 503); and third, and most importantly, in the face of "calibration" skepticism, the question arises how, in principle, the expertise in question could be established, or acquired.[20]

---

[18] They normally do not become puzzled by each other's employment of these expressions; they normally respond to the other's employment of these expressions in ways that the other does not find puzzling; they never, or hardly ever, have occasion to ask the other "What do you mean by 'know'?" or to protest "This is not what 'knowing' means!"; and so on.

[19] The claim of (or to) philosophical expertise is also made in Hales 2006, Ludwig 2007, Sosa 2009, and Devitt 2011.

[20] See Weinberg et al. 2010 and Machery 2015. Cappelen rejects the claim to (philosophical) expertise (PWI: 228).

The root of difficulty for Williamson's attempted defense of the method of cases is that, by his own lights, he needs *both* to insist that there is "continuity" (PP: 192) between answers to the theorist's question and answers to everyday, "non-philosophical" questions (this alleged continuity allows him to dismiss the talk of "intuitions," and to argue that skepticism about answers to the theorist's questions is an extreme and rather implausible skepticism about judgment *in general*), *and* at the same time to allow, in effect, for substantial *dis*continuity between the two (in order to make room for his counterexamples to epistemological conceptions of analyticity, and to accommodate the undeniable fact that disagreements in answers to the theorist's questions have emerged among people who seem able to communicate smoothly and effectively with each other outside philosophy, and by means of the very same words that give them trouble in philosophy).

This tension in Williamson underscores the difficulty of answering "calibration" skepticism about the method of cases truly satisfactorily. Cappelen, however, seems to assume that he can make the skeptical problem go away just by calling answers to the theorist's question "judgments" rather than "intuitions," and by pressing the skeptic to say how those "judgments" are different from other "judgments," and how skepticism about *them* does not boil down to a rather implausible skepticism about judgment *in general* (see PWI: 224–7).[21] So he is relying on the claim of continuity. I will come back to that claim in section 2.4. Before that, I need to consider one place where Cappelen parts ways significantly with Williamson, on a matter pertinent to "calibration" skepticism.

A common view of the philosophical method of cases is that, other things being equal, our answers to the theorist's question take evidential priority over the theories under consideration: the theories need to accommodate the "judgments" we make about cases, and not the other

---

[21] For reasons already mentioned in Chapter One, I think the title "judgments" is misleading when it comes to the answers we give to the theorist's questions. Those answers are not tied to the rest of our practical life as everyday empirical judgments normally are, and we do not receive the sort of worldly feedback on the former that we normally receive on the latter. In order to bypass this terminological difficulty without seeming to beg any question against Cappelen and Williamson, I will either put "judgment" in quotation marks, to register the fact that I am, in effect, quoting Cappelen and Williamson, or else simply use "answer to the theorist's question," which, like "judgment," may refer either to a human act or to its product.

way around. On this issue, Williamson is in agreement with all of the fans of "intuitions" talk—both armchair and experimental. "Much of the philosophical community allows," Williamson writes regarding the method of cases, "that a judicious act of the imagination can refute a previously well-supported theory" (PP: 179; see also PP: 194). Williamson aims to explicate and vindicate this widely held conception of the common practice, not to question it. A few pages later he elaborates: "[T]he primary direction of support is abductive, from particular verdict to general principle (by reference to the best explanation), rather than deductive, from general principle to particular verdict (by universal instantiation)" (PP: 183).

This widespread understanding of the typical relation between "judgments about cases" and philosophical theories makes the reliability of those "judgments" seem fateful for the viability of the method of cases and the theorizing it informs. If the "judgments" are supposed to provide evidential basis for the theories, and the "judgments" themselves are fundamentally suspect, then the theories are fundamentally suspect as well. This is why Williamson spends the last chapter of *The Philosophy of Philosophy* arguing—by developing a version of Davidson's "principle of charity"—that the judgments of competent speakers are not merely likely to be correct, but likely to instantiate knowledge.[22]

It is in connection with this issue that Cappelen makes the striking move of *denying* that the primary direction of support is typically from particular verdicts to general principles or theories. He argues that a close examination of the actual practice, or at least of some indisputable exemplars of the practice, reveals that philosophers do not give particular judgments about cases the kind of foundational evidential status that Williamson and almost everybody else have attributed to them. "Conflicting judgments about a case are evaluated by evaluating the arguments given for them" Cappelen claims (PWI: 223; see also PWI: 121). "Philosophical practice," he adds, "treats unjustified judgments about philosophical cases as worthless" (PWI: 223).[23]

---

[22] Since Williamson's argument for knowledge maximization only supports the philosophical method of cases on the assumption of continuity, and since I shall question that assumption, I will not further discuss that argument.

[23] Similar claims are made by Deutsch 2015. Some reviewers of PWI have been happy to endorse Cappelen's redescription of the practice. According to Brian Weatherson, Cappelen has shown that "we argue a lot more than we intuit, especially about the famous cases"

This redescription of the practice seems to suggest the following response to "calibration" skepticism: *What tells us what the correct answers are to the theorist's questions, are the arguments given in their support; other things being equal, the answer supported by the better argument is the correct one. And where philosophers have, by way of argument, "established" that not-p they can stop worrying about the reliability of their so-called "intuitions"—either for or against p— altogether* (see PWI: 89).

As a reviewer for Oxford University Press had apparently urged Cappelen again and again to acknowledge (see PWI: 122, 156, 169), a problem for his proposed redescription of the method of cases is that the "arguments" he finds in the papers he considers—arguments in favor of a particular judgment about some case or range of cases—tend to take the form of the very principle or theory that the author is seeking to establish in that paper. If that principle or theory is already solid enough to provide support for some verdict about the case, it is not clear why we need to bother with the case at all.

Cappelen is unfazed by this apparent problem for his account. He points out, I believe correctly, that in some famous philosophical thought experiments the question is, precisely, how to describe the case: no one description, or judgment, is treated as an undisputed theoretical starting point (PWI: 123). Where this is not the case—which means in pretty much all of those cases that have seemed to others as paradigmatic examples of abductive reasoning—Cappelen is willing to accept that "support goes in both directions": the proposed theory or principle and the judgment about the particular case provide mutual support for each other (PWI: 123). Another important concession Cappelen makes is that, whereas earlier in PWI he speaks of philosophers as *establishing* the truth or falsity of some judgment about a case (PWI: 89), later on he acknowledges in a telling footnote that "philosophers don't typically present deductively valid arguments, but rather considerations that in some way lend support to their conclusion" (PWI: 165). This is an important concession. One would be hard-pressed to come up with an

---

(Weatherson 2014: 13; but see note 24 below); and Jonathan Ichikawa takes Cappelen to have shown that in at least some famous philosophical thought experiments "the alleged intuition is carefully argued for, rather than merely stated as obvious" (Ichikawa 2013: 3).

example of a philosophically interesting proposition that has been *established* by way of argument.

So now, suppose we grant Cappelen that, at least in very many cases, the relation between the "judgments" about a particular case or set of cases and the theory under consideration is actually more complex and bidirectional than the simple model of abductive reasoning would have us assume.[24] Have we made any real progress with respect to "calibration" skepticism?

The answer is that we have made no progress at all. For the worry, at bottom, has been that philosophical theorizing in the analytic tradition has failed to make contact with anything real or worth caring about. Cappelen's redescription of the method of cases has done nothing to alleviate this worry; if anything, it has made it more intractable.

The so called "judgments about cases" were supposed to *anchor* our philosophical theorizing, to ensure that our theories are actually beholden to X, or at the very least to our concept of X (or to the meaning of "x"), and not merely to compelling pictures of X that we have formed for ourselves, or to misguided theoretical assumptions to which we have grown attached, whether individually or communally. Recall that Williamson's counter-examples to epistemological analyticity mostly consist of theoreticians who, due to having grown attached to some (misguided) theory, judge deviantly (and according to Williamson typically incorrectly). This is precisely why proponents of the method of cases have worried about what they have called "theory contamination" (see Goldman and Pust 1998)—that is, the contamination of particular "judgments about cases" by the theories to which they were supposed to provide *independent* support. The worry that the "judgments" of professional philosophers have been contaminated by their theories has been part of the motivation of the new movement of experimental philosophy. One of the most striking features of PWI, especially given Cappelen's redescription of the method of cases, is its lack of concern about theory contamination.[25] The

---

[24] Weatherson 2014 points out that there are many cases where the abductive model seems to fit perfectly: the "judgment" about the case is taken to have clear evidential priority over the theory in question.

[25] For a compelling acknowledgment of how prone we all are to theory contamination—and how far and unnoticeably such contamination can sway us in our judgments—see Weatherson (2014). Machery also discusses the way in which the presumed "expertise" of philosophers and linguists biases their "judgments" (Machery 2015: 197).

argument of this book suggests, in effect, that theory contamination begins earlier, and goes deeper, than has hitherto been acknowledged. It begins with the minimal assumption, and with the conception of language that underwrites it.

Cappelen's talk of general theories or principles, on the one hand, and "judgments about cases," on the other hand, providing mutual, and mostly non-deductive, support for each other suggests something like "reflective equilibrium" as the goal of philosophical theorizing, or the measure of its success. However, if the history of philosophy has taught us anything, it is that there is no reflective equilibrium so seemingly far-fetched or outlandish that it could not find smart and serious supporters. Put otherwise, there is no reflective equilibrium, arrived at by smart and serious philosophers, that cannot be found wholly misguided by other smart and serious philosophers.[26]

Unlike Cappelen, Williamson fully realizes that the appeal to "reflective equilibrium" represents "psychologization of evidence" with a vengeance. Accordingly, he writes: "To characterize our method as one of achieving reflective equilibrium is to fail to engage with epistemologically crucial features of our situation. Our understanding of philosophical methodology must be rid of internalist preconceptions" (PP: 5; see also PP: 244). This is why it matters to Williamson that our answers to the theorist's question may stand without the support of theory (cf. PP: 194), and why a significant portion of *The Philosophy of Philosophy* is devoted to arguing that those answers may, on the whole, be relied upon, especially when they are given by those who are "good at philosophy." As I said, I do not think Williamson succeeds in showing that, and how, philosophical theorizing can ensure its staying in contact with the reality it purports to help us better understand. But he does succeed in spelling out very clearly why Cappelen's redescription of the method of cases is no help when it comes to "calibration" skepticism.

This leaves us with nothing by way of argument in PWI against "calibration" skepticism, except for the claim of continuity between

---

[26] Here I speak of reflective equilibrium as a (sought-after) *state*. Michael Mitchell has pointed out to me that reflective equilibrium may also be thought of, and perhaps is *better* thought of, as a *process*. Even so, however, there's the question of what the process is beholden to, or what anchors the process—what ensures that it does not lose contact with anything real or worth caring about.

answers to the theorist's questions and answers to everyday, non-philosophical questions, and the implied claim, originally found in Williamson, that skepticism about the philosophical "judgments" boils down to skepticism about judgment in general (see PWI: 224–7). It is therefore to the claim of continuity that we now turn.

2.4 The Claim of Continuity

Earlier in this chapter I asked, somewhat rhetorically, how anything truly important could possibly hang on Cappelen's denial of "centrality." How could anything truly important hang on how we choose to refer to the answers we give to the theorist's questions? There are two other questions that it would be far more pertinent to ask, it would seem: the first is what philosophical work those answers have been supposed to do; and the second is whether they are fit to do that work. In considering Cappelen's response to "cognitive diversity" and "calibration" skepticism about the method of cases, I have in effect contested the answers he gives to these two questions. More precisely, I have tried to show that his answers, though they come in response to serious challenges to the philosophical method of cases and the theorizing of which it is part, are supported by no arguments.

This critical strategy might seem unfair to Cappelen. For after all, *he* presents himself as primarily arguing against "centrality," not against skepticism about the philosophical method of cases. Moreover, it is fairly clear that by Cappelen's lights the denial of "centrality" *is* already, by itself, a significant contribution to the rightful dismissal of the skepticism: by his lights, referring to answers to the theorist's questions as "intuitions" (or describing them as "intuitive") has obscured the continuity between those answers and answers that we give to everyday, non-philosophical questions; and that, in turn, has made the former seem vulnerable to *special* sorts of skepticism; once we eliminate the talk of intuitions, Cappelen in effect argues, the continuity becomes undeniable and skepticism about answers to the theorist's questions is revealed as, in principle, no more legitimate or well-motivated, and no more worthy of a refutation on its own terms, than skepticism about everyday, non-philosophical judgments would be.

The first thing to say in response to this is that the claim of continuity cuts no ice against "cognitive diversity" skepticism. Most proponents of the idea that the method of cases is first and foremost a method for elucidating our concepts also presuppose continuity between answers to the theorist's questions and answers to everyday non-philosophical questions. It is precisely because they take it that the theorist's question essentially invites us to do something that we routinely do with our words outside philosophy that they believe our answers to that question may reveal features of whatever ultimately guides us in the ordinary and normal employment of our words—they call it "our concepts." Against "calibration" skepticism, on the other hand, the claim of continuity may cut *some* ice; but proponents of *that* form of skepticism proceed precisely from the sense—however imprecisely articulated—that there is some significant *dis*continuity between everyday judgments and answers to the theorist's question.[27]

I have engaged with PWI in the way that I have, because I believe its polemics against "centrality" to be a red herring—it distracts attention from real and difficult problems with the philosophical method of cases. It makes it seem as if all that prevents us from recognizing the continuity between answers to the theorist's questions and the everyday employment of our words in speech and thought is the talk of "intuitions," whereas I would argue that the talk of "intuitions" aptly registers the *dis*continuity between the two. Whether I am right about this or not, it is

---

[27] Weinberg attempts to articulate the discontinuity in terms of a difference between the *sorts of cases* we encounter in everyday life and the sorts of cases analytic philosophers have invoked in their thought experiments. He says that the latter have tended to be "esoteric, unusual, farfetched, or generally outlandish" (Weinberg 2007: 321; see also Machery 2011: 202). But this, as it stands, will not do (and has failed to impress Cappelen (see PWI: 227)). First of all, at least *some* of the cases philosophers have appealed to are as mundane as any— a person's epistemic standing with respect to the proposition that he will not have enough money to go on an African safari next year, for example, or a person overhearing a passenger at the airport saying to another that some flight has a layover in Chicago. Secondly, *on the representational-referential and atomistic-compositional conception of language* that will be discussed in Chapter Three and subsequently challenged, but which Weinberg himself has not challenged, it is not clear why it should matter that the case is somehow esoteric, unusual, far-fetched, or outlandish—it too should presumably either belong or not belong to the extension of "x." On the alternative conception of language that I will present and recommend in Chapters Five and Six, on the other hand, it does matter that a case is unlike any case we have ever had the occasion to describe or talk about. What Weinberg fails to consider, however, is that the discontinuity is *primarily* due not to the peculiar nature of the theorist's *cases* but to the peculiar nature of his *context*. In an important sense, we are not *using* our words when we give our answers to the theorist's question; and on the conception of language that I would recommend, words have no determinate sense apart from a determinate use.

the claim of continuity itself that ought to have been at the focus of discussion, not the talk of "intuitions." Hence, showing that PWI's attempted vindication of the method of cases rests entirely on the claim of continuity has been one of the main goals of the first three sections of this chapter.

Some work has already been done to undermine the claim of continuity, or at least to throw it into question. In section 2.3, we saw that though the claim is absolutely essential to the argument of *The Philosophy of Philosophy*, Williamson must in effect retract it no sooner than he had made it, in order to make room for his counterexamples to epistemological conceptions of analyticity, and in order to account for the fact that people—including philosophical "experts"—who are capable of communicating smoothly and effectively with each other outside philosophy by means of the philosophically troublesome word "x" and who, by ordinary criteria, mean the same thing(s) by "x" and share the concept of X, turn out to disagree with each other in their answers to the theorist's questions.[28]

In Baz 2012a and 2012b, I argue against Williamson's claim of continuity by way of (a form of) ordinary language philosophy: I invite the reader to consider a range of contexts of everyday, non-theoretical encounters with an actual Gettier case, and I show that no question about that case that would naturally arise in any such context would be the theorist's question—the question, that is, that has elicited the Gettier intuition in many (but not all) people. The reason for this, I propose, is that questions that arise naturally and intelligibly in the course of everyday experience are tied to our practical needs and interests, and more broadly to the rest of our life and world, as the theorist's question is not. This is why the use of either "judgment" or "belief" (or even "inclination to believe" or "near-belief") to refer to what we express when we give our answers to the theorist's question is problematic, and

---

[28] Kukla also points out the striking fact that disagreements in answers to the theorist's questions have emerged among people who seem to have little trouble communicating smoothly and effectively with each other in their "epistemic practices" (Kukla 2015: 203). This leads Kukla to deny, in effect, the claim of continuity between our "epistemic practices" and our "meta-epistemic discussions" (Kukla 2015: 203). In thus presenting the discontinuity, however, Kukla seems to me insufficiently attentive to the sorts of considerations, and the conception of language, that have led practitioners and defenders of the method of cases to presuppose and insist on its being continuous with our normal and ordinary epistemic practices.

question begging when made in the context of trying to defend the method of cases against forms of skepticism that proceed from the sense that our answers to the theorist's questions are problematically *unlike* our answers to questions that arise naturally in the course of everyday experience.

The claim of continuity also stands in tension with Cappelen's more recent proposal that many philosophically interesting or troublesome words might be nonsensical in the mouths (or texts) of philosophers (Cappelen 2013). Among those words, Cappelen lists "knowledge" (Cappelen 2013: 45). But he also insists, in line with the claim of continuity, that when philosophers are interested in knowledge, "they are interested in the phenomenon ordinary speakers of English talk about when they say things like 'John knows that Samantha is in Paris'" (PWI: 27). And this seems to commit him to the (to my mind) patently implausible and arguably incoherent view that "knows" as used by competent English speakers in sentences such as "John knows that Samantha is in Paris" might be nonsensical as well.

In the following chapters I will argue that the claim of continuity is underwritten by a conception of language that Cappelen and Williamson, together with most of the fans of "intuitions" talk, assume without argument or evidence; and I will argue for an alternative conception of language on which the claim of continuity is false. This would suggest a hitherto unrecognized form of skepticism about the philosophical method of cases—a form of skepticism significantly more radical than either "cognitive diversity" or "calibration" skepticism.

3

The Method of Cases and the Representationalist Conception of Language

The theorist describes (or otherwise invokes) a "case" and then asks by means of perfectly familiar words a question that has the general form, "Is this (or would such a case be) a case of "x"?" and gives his answer to that question or collects the answers given by others; or else he simply theorizes on the basis of some tacitly assumed answer to some such question. In proceeding this way, he assumes that the question has a clear (enough) sense and may be answered correctly or incorrectly. He also assumes that, as competent speakers of the language, we—that is, his audience—ought at the very least to understand the question and be in a position to answer it correctly, just on the basis of our familiarity with the words and with the case as he describes it. This is what I have called "the minimal assumption." The assumption, as we have seen, is shared by all of the parties to the recent debates concerning the method of cases. My aim is to show that the assumption rests on a conception of language that is philosophically and empirically challengeable—I will call it, for short, "the representationalist conception," whenever further specification seems unneeded. My broader aim is to invite an examination of the method of cases at a more fundamental level than that at which it has hitherto been examined. An even broader aim is to bring out the intimate link between how we view and understand language and how we view and understand philosophical work, and philosophical progress.

What exactly is the conception of language that (according to me) underwrites the minimal assumption and therefore also underwrites the philosophical method of cases in either its armchair or experimental version? Here I could have simplified things for myself considerably by answering that, for the purposes of the argument of this book, it could be *any* conception of language on which the minimal assumption is true; since I am going to present and motivate, both philosophically and empirically, a conception of language on which the minimal assumption is false, any conception of language on which it is true will thereby be shown to be, at best, philosophically and empirically challengeable. This would have saved me from having to navigate among all of the more or less subtly different ways of conceiving of language that might seem to entitle one to the minimal assumption. It would also have saved me from seeming to some participants in the debate concerning the method of cases to have missed or mischaracterized *their* conception of language.[1]

And yet I think that it would be worth our while to consider in some detail *one* broadly characterized conception of language that could be

---

[1] I am not sure, for example, where exactly Davidson's views about language would put him with respect to the minimal assumption. The relation of reference between words and independently existing worldly "items" does not play the foundational role on his account that it plays on the conception of language I'm about to discuss. And he does seem to advocate an extreme version of contextualism about linguistic meaning, or understanding, which would appear to lead naturally to suspicion about the minimal assumption (see Davidson 2006). At the same time, however, he takes the assessment of sentences in terms of truth and falsity to be key to an understanding of linguistic meaning, and takes words to make stable and systematic contributions to the truth-conditions of (an individual's or a community's) sentences (cf. Davidson 2001: 18–22); and though he seems to advocate an extreme form of contextualism in some of his writings, his contextualism is typically cashed out in terms of *translation* from one language or idiolect to another: "so and so's 'x' means (our, or my) y, or 'y'" (Davidson is not consistent in his use of quotation marks for the "translating" terms (see Davidson 2006: 253 and 262), which seems to me to be a symptom of deeper confusion in his account: are we *using* "y" in order to *explicate* what so and so means by "x" *here*, or are we saying that the word "y," in our idiolect, would in *general* be the best or closest translation of so and so's "x"?). The sort of contextualism that more clearly gives trouble to the minimal assumption, by contrast, is evidenced in those moments when I know full well (or anyway take it for granted) that your "x" has the same meaning— that is, has *all of the same general "powers"* (Davidson 2006: 261–2)—as my "x," but I'm *still* not sure *what you mean by it*, or *how* you mean it, *here and now*: the circumstances (as I see them) seem to leave open more than one way, or no plausible way, of understanding your "x." Also, Davidson, holding on as he does to a representationalist (truth-conditional) view of language, tends to overlook what Price has called, following Wittgenstein, the "*functional plurality*" of language (Price 2011 and 2013), which I will emphasize later on and which seems to me to render the minimal assumption even more deeply problematic than it would appear just from the contextualist-but-still-representationalist perspective that will be discussed in Chapter Four. Finally, Davidson tends to speak as though the range of what our words *could* mean—call it the range of our concepts—is essentially fixed, whereas I will emphasize the open-ended plasticity of linguistic meaning, which is yet another reason for taking the minimal assumption to be misguided.

taken to support the minimal assumption. In one version or another, that conception is shared by at least very many in contemporary analytic philosophy. Moreover, as we will see in this chapter, some proponents of the method of cases have appealed to that conception, more or less explicitly, in the course of trying to defend the method. In making those appeals, they have in effect acknowledged that the method of cases presupposes a particular conception of language. The significance of *that* has thus far been missed by all of the participants in the debates concerning the method of cases, and for the simple reason that they tend to take the conception in question for granted—so much so, that it may actually have presented itself to them as nothing but a set of truisms, rather than a *particular conception* of language that may well have viable alternatives. One important benefit of trying to articulate the conception in some detail is that it will make it clear that, far from consisting of a set of truisms, it actually involves substantive, and therefore challengeable, assumptions—not merely about language use and acquisition, but also, at the same time, about the world of which, and in which, we talk (or write).

3.1 The Representationalist Conception of Language in Williamson's and Cappelen's Defense of the Method of Cases

Williamson gives the gist of the conception of language that underwrites the minimal assumption, and which is taken for granted in the recent debates about the method of cases, in the following passage: "[E]xpressions refer to items in the mostly non-linguistic world, the reference of complex expressions is a function of the reference of its constituents, and the reference of a sentence determines its truth value" (PP: 281). According to Williamson, this basic way of looking at language originates from Frege (PP: 280). This attribution is at most partially true, for while Frege's work has played an important role in the origination of truth-conditional semantics, his well-known "context principle," as introduced in the *Groundwork of Arithmetic* and developed later in his career, goes against the grain of the atomistic-compositional element of the conception of language articulated by Williamson, and anticipates—though still from within a representationalist perspective—the alternative conception of language that will be presented in Chapter Five. Frege wrote, "I . . . do not begin with concepts that I put together into thoughts or judgments. Rather, I obtain thought-components [*Gedankenteile*] by analyzing [or decomposing, *Zerfällung*] thoughts" (Frege 1979: 253). This seems to imply that, on Frege's view, the words composing the theorist's question cannot be relied upon to ensure its sense, for they themselves are not expressive of determinate concepts, or thought-components, unless the theorist has succeeded in expressing a clear question (or thought) by means of them.

Setting aside the question of Frege's relation to atomistic-compositional and truth-conditional theories of semantics, it should next be noted that Williamson's account of language is supposed to apply *generally* (as Williamson makes clear in PP: 127). In particular, it is supposed to apply not only to philosophically innocent, or seemingly innocent words like "cat" and "gold," but also to the philosophically troublesome words that the theorist's questions have invited us to "apply" to cases: "know," "think," "cause," "free," and so on. Each of these words too is supposed to have an "extension," or "a set of things to which it applies" (PP: 127); they too are supposed to refer to items in the world: states (or relations) of *knowing* or of *thinking* this or that, relations of *causation*, states of *being free*, and so on.[2] Thus, for example, when two people give conflicting answers to the question whether someone in a Gettier situation knows the proposition in question and we wonder whether they mean the same thing by "knowledge" and are in genuine disagreement or mean different things by that word and therefore are not really disagreeing, then, according to Williamson, "the central question [we should ask] is whether they use the word 'knowledge' with the same reference" (Williamson 2009: 130). Williamson contends that *that* is a question about what "knowledge" has come to refer to in the public language they (presumably) both speak, not a question about what *they* might each believe, possibly idiosyncratically, the word refers to. For present purposes, however, all that matters is Williamson's assumption that the meaning of "knowledge," and equally of "know" and its cognates, is essentially a matter of what worldly item, or set or type of worldly items, it refers to. This is why the question whether the person in the Gettier situation knows the proposition at issue is, for Williamson, not primarily the question whether *we* would, or should, *count* that person

---

[2] For a clear expression of this commitment, see Williamson 2009: 130–1.

as knowing that proposition, but rather the question whether that person *knows*, which for Williamson is equivalent to the question whether his epistemic relation to the proposition falls within the extension of "knowledge" (see Williamson 2009: 131). What we learn from the Gettier thought experiment is, according to Williamson, not primarily something about *our concept* of knowledge. Rather, we learn that not all *justified true belief* is *knowledge* (Williamson 2009: 131), which on Williamson's way of thinking is no more learning something about our concepts of knowledge, belief, justification, and so on, than learning that not all swans are white would be learning something about our concepts of swan and whiteness.

Cappelen gives clear expression to the same basic picture of how our words relate to our world when he writes:

> Consider "think" in "I think she is out of town" given as an answer to "Why didn't Louise come to the meeting yesterday?". Here "think" denotes the psychological state people are in when they think. On one simple story, the semantic content is the proposition that the speaker stands in the thinking relation to the proposition *that Louise is out of town.*   (PWI: 38)

I suppose there could be different accounts of how the items referred to ("denoted") by our words come into (and out of) existence and what constitutes their identity over time as the particular items they are; and different accounts too of how particular words have come to refer to ("denote") particular items. But it's worth noting that such accounts have not been forthcoming, and that the ones that have been offered have tended to be very sketchy.[3] What's fairly clear is that the "items" to which our words are supposed to refer are taken to be (or not to be) there

---

[3] Williamson outlines an account of the second sort in very broad strokes in PP: 121–30, and repeats it with minor additions in Williamson 2011, where he acknowledges that what he offers is only a sketch (Williamson 2011: 503). The account he offers presupposes without evidence or argument the existence of the items to which our words presumably refer, and proposes that "the referential properties of expressions supervene on lower-level facts, for example about causal connections between uses of those expressions and objects in the environment" (Williamson 2011: 503). Unless Williamson's "objects" means to refer to such worldly "items" as knowledge, causation, meaning, and so on, it is not clear how this passage is supposed to give us even a sketch of an account of how words such as "know," "cause," and "mean" come to have the referents that, on Williamson's view, they have. But on the other hand, if "items" such as knowledge, causation, and meaning *are* supposed to be the "objects" that stand in causal connections to uses of words such as "know," "cause," and "mean," then Williamson seems to me to have offered even less than a sketch of an account. As I will propose a little later, the only reason for assuming the existence of those "items" (or

anyway, independently of particular contexts in which human beings might successfully refer to them in speech or thought; and the relation of reference between some particular word and some particular item (or set of items), once somehow established, is taken to hold independently of particular human acts of *using* words *significantly* in one way or another in speech or thought. The imaginary speaker in Cappelen's example above only needs to utter the sentence "I think she is out of town" in whichever context, meaning it in whichever way it may be meant in that context, and her "think" will refer to the (type of) item to which presumably it always refers, at least when used "literally and seriously"—namely, "the psychological state of thinking" or "the thinking relation."[4] The meaning of "think" is supposed to consist, essentially, of this relation of reference, and to determine—essentially by itself—the contribution the word makes to the overall sense, or "semantic content," of basically *any* ("serious and literal") utterance of a sentence that features this word. The sense or "semantic content" of a sentence (or utterance) is supposed to be cashable, in turn, in terms of its "truth-conditions."[5]

The representationalist conception, as Williamson describes it, also makes no mention of there being different types of sentences and different types of uses of sentences. It might plausibly be responded that proponents of the conception do not deny that there are, of course, different types of sentences and different types of uses of sentences. They

---

"objects") is that the representationalist conception of language requires them. Moreover, I worry that Williamson's sketch relies on a pre-Kantian, and indeed even pre-Humean, understanding of causation.

[4] I added the parenthetical "type of," because it seems to me that Cappelen can't mean that the tokened word, "think," denotes a particular item—the speaker's thinking that Louise is out of town. For the speaker may not actually think that, and that presumably would not change the denotation of the tokened word. So Cappelen must mean that the tokened word denotes a *type* of item—which may or may not be instantiated on that occasion. I point out this added complication without further discussion, because I am not sure what exactly Cappelen means.

[5] That the sense of uttered sentences should ultimately be understood in terms of "truth-conditions," and that the sense of uttered words should therefore ultimately be understood in terms of their contribution to the determination of those "truth-conditions," is one of the most widespread and pervasive assumptions in contemporary analytic philosophy. So much so, that authors commonly *begin* with that assumption and feel no need to argue for, or even motivate it (see, for example, Lewis 1980: 79; and more recently Schoubye and Stokke 2016: 759). I will question that assumption in Chapters Five and Six, and on behalf of Austin in section 4.2 of Chapter Four.

do, however, take the descriptive or informational ("representational") use of language to be somehow fundamental to language;[6] and they take it that anything else that we can do with words somehow depends on our being able just to say true or false things by means of them—to produce elements of what Davidson calls "the indicative core" of language (Davidson 2001: 121). This—*just* saying something true, or something false, by means of our words—is what the theorist's question is supposed to invite us to do.

On the representationalist conception, saying true or false things about cases is essentially a matter of "classifying" or "categorizing" those cases; and this is just what the theorist's questions are taken to invite us to do: classify cases as belonging or as not belonging to the extension of the philosophically troublesome words (or concepts)—something that, presumably, we routinely do outside philosophy. Thus, as we've already seen in Chapter Two, Williamson contends that the capacity that enables us to tell that the subject in a Gettier situation does not know the proposition in question is "the same capacity to *classify empirically encountered cases with respect to knowledge* as we use when, for example, we classify a politician as not knowing the truth of his claims about terrorists" (Williamson 2004: 112, my emphasis; see also Williamson 2005: 12). "We assent to the Gettier proposition," Williamson writes, "on the basis of an offline application of our ability to classify people around us as knowing various truths or as ignorant of them" (PP: 188).

In both the philosophical context and the non-philosophical context, it is thought, there is a particular item under consideration—in the case of "know(s)," for example, a particular person's epistemic relation to some proposition. When I say, or think, in *whichever* context, of a politician that he does not know that a certain group of terrorists has weapons of mass destruction or is trying to acquire them, the thought continues, I *classify* the politician's epistemic relation to the proposition in question as one of *not knowing*—as a case to which "knows" does not

---

[6] Here is Lewis: "The foremost thing we do with words is to impart information" (Lewis 1980: 80). And here, more recently, are Schoubye and Stokke: "Discourses [are] goal directed activities whose fundamental aim is discovering what the actual world is like" (Schoubye and Stokke 2016: 767). Schoubye and Stokke say they are following Robert Stalnaker in taking *that* to be the fundamental aim of (all?!) discourses (Schoubye and Stokke 2016: 767).

apply.[7] And this, again, is something I am supposed to be able to do, and do mostly correctly, just on the basis of my possession of the concept of knowledge, or my mastery of "know," and my familiarity with the case. Nothing else is supposed to be required; just as nothing else is supposed to be required when I give my answer to the theorist's question. In this way, the minimal assumption goes hand in hand with the claim of continuity, and both are underwritten by the representationalist conception of language.

As I have already noted, Williamson is walking a very thin line here. He needs to insist that the answers given to the theorist's questions by competent speakers are mostly correct; for otherwise we fall, on his view, into "skepticism about judgment (*in general*)" (see PP: 220ff). At the same time, he needs to insist that those answers are *only mostly* correct, and are certainly not *necessarily* correct (see PP: 85–98); for this enables him to reject epistemological conceptions of analyticity, and account for the undeniable empirical fact that people who by every reasonable criterion share the relevant concept(s), or mean the same things by the relevant words, nonetheless sometimes disagree in their answers to the theorist's questions. What Williamson never doubts is that the theorist's questions are, in principle, in order, and that the answers people give to them are either correct or incorrect.

3.2 The Representationalist Conception of Language in Jackson's Defense of the Method of Cases

Williamson and Cappelen represent those who see the method of cases as primarily used for clarifying the nature of worldly "items," or "features

---

[7] As I have already noted, on Williamson's way of looking at things, what a particular speaker's "know(s)" means is a matter of what it means in the language she shares with others. And what the common word means is, for Williamson, essentially a matter of what item(s) in the world it refers to. Thus, if two speakers give different answers to one of the theorist's questions, and we wonder whether this is due to their having different concepts of X or to their being in genuine disagreement about whether the case is a case of X—in which case, on Williamson's view, at least one of them would have to be wrong—we need to consult their overall employment of "x." And if, by ordinary criteria, they both mean the same thing by "x," then, on Williamson's view, "they use the word...with the same reference" (Williamson 2009: 130); and then the question is whether the case with which they were presented instantiates the reference of their (common) "x."

of the world," where those items or features are taken not to depend, for either their nature or their existence, on how the terms "referring" to them function in discourse, or indeed on those terms having any function at all. Jackson, on the other hand, represents those who take the method of cases to be primarily aimed at the "elucidation of concepts" (Jackson 2009: 101). Despite this *seemingly* significant disagreement (in section 3.4 I will argue that it is far less significant than it seems), Jackson's defense of the traditional, armchair version of the method of cases—of which according to him experimental philosophy is but an extension (see Jackson 2011: 468 and 476–7)—essentially relies on the same conception of language (and hence of speaking and thinking) on which Williamson's and Cappelen's defense of the method relies. Jackson refers to this conception as "the representational view of language," and usefully identifies this view explicitly as underwriting the method of cases. Similarly to Williamson and Cappelen, Jackson talks of sentences as having "representational contents" and says that "how [a sentence] represents things to be is a function of the representational contents of its parts and how they are combined" (Jackson 2011: 472). And where Williamson speaks of us as classifying cases with respect to some concept, or term, Jackson similarly speaks of words as instruments for the "categorization of items." "A person's concepts," he writes, "are the categorizations they have mastered. When they use a word for that concept, the categorization they effect with the word will be to place the item in the relevant category" (Jackson 2011: 469, fn. 3). Again there is the idea that the theorist's question invites us to do nothing essentially different from something that we routinely do with our words outside philosophy—namely, categorize items. And it is therefore clear that the items in question are supposed to be not only the sorts of items that may be categorized by means of words such as "table," "chair," or "cat," but also the sorts of items that may presumably be categorized by means of philosophically troublesome words such as "know," "cause," "morally responsible," and so on; for otherwise, the talk of words as instruments of categorization would not have lent any support to the philosophical method of cases. Thus, one crucial assumption that Jackson makes, and makes explicit, is that there is no significant difference (pertinent to the viability of the method of cases) between words such as "tree" or "car" and philosophically troublesome words such as "know" or "cause" (see Jackson 2011: 471). The latter, just like the former, are for Jackson instruments of categorization; and categorizing items by means of these words is taken to be something we competent speakers should be able do just on the basis of our possession of the relevant concepts and familiarity with the items.[8] This—*just* categorizing, or classifying, an item—is what the theorist's question is supposed to invite us to do; and the method of cases is taken to aim at the elucidation of "what governs our classificatory practices" (Jackson 1998: 36–7). If we could not be relied upon to understand the theorist's questions and answer them correctly, Jackson argues, that would mean that we do not know "which situations our words apply to" (Jackson 2011: 472); and that, on Jackson's way of looking at things, would mean, absurdly, that we do not know "what we are talking or writing about" (Jackson 2011: 472)—not only in philosophy, but whenever we use the words in question. Thus, Jackson's defense of the method of cases relies on what I have called "the claim of continuity" in much the same way that Williamson's and Cappelen's defense of the method relies on that claim.

In order to reinforce the link that he sees between the representational view of language and the method of cases, Jackson offers a story about how words—including the philosophically troublesome ones that feature centrally in the theorist's questions—are learned. The story is pretty much what one would expect, given Jackson's adherence to the representational view of language; but it helps to underscore a striking feature of Jackson's, Williamson's, Cappelen's, and many other armchair and experimental philosophers' commitment to that view: that while it is a commitment to substantive empirical, and therefore empirically challengeable, assumptions about language use and acquisition, it is not in fact supported by careful and systematic empirical observations, but rather is taken, in effect, to be true a priori.

According to Jackson, while some words are learned by looking them up in a dictionary or being given a more or less rough definition, "children learn most of their words through interaction with, on the one hand, objects, events, and properties, and with their parents, teachers, and other children, on the other" (Jackson 2011: 473). Jackson continues:

Everything in this area is highly contentious but *one thing is clear*. At some crucial stage in the process, we latch onto the relevant pattern. We recognize the pattern and *use the word for it* . . .

[8] See also Goldman 2007: 15 and Weinberg 2007: 320 for the idea that all it takes to be able to understand and answer the theorist's question is possession or mastery of the relevant concept(s) and familiarity with the case.

How did we acquire the word "knowledge"? We came across lots of examples. We were told a bit about what mattered. Perhaps we were simply instructed that if it is false, it cannot be knowledge. At some point we latched onto the pattern.

(Jackson 2011: 473–4, my emphases)

In this way, for each competent speaker, words such as "knowledge" become instruments for the categorization of worldly items, according to Jackson.[9] And this is what is then supposed to put competent speakers in a position to understand and answer (mostly) correctly the theorist's questions—for example, the question of whether the protagonist of some story knows this or that. The theorist's question, on Jackson's view, simply invites competent speakers to tell whether the worldly "pattern" that they must have learned to recognize in acquiring the word in question is present in the case at hand. And our answers to that question are supposed to help us become clearer about that pattern.

How does Jackson know that this in fact is how children come to master the word "knowledge," and I suppose also other words that have featured centrally in the theorist's questions—words such as "understand(ing)," "mean(ing)," "free(dom)," "intention(ally)," "cause," and so on? Is he basing his account on empirical observations? Has he followed children in their early years and found that this in fact is how they come to master such words? Has he consulted the work of others who have done so? It is safe to say that the answer to these questions is that Jackson relies on no empirical observations or studies,

---

[9] Jackson's story is strikingly similar to Saint Augustine's story in his *Confessions* of how, as a child, he learned to use words to express his desires. I will return to this similarity at the opening of Chapter Six. Jackson's story is also strikingly reminiscent of John Locke's story of "how children learn languages": "If we observe how children learn language, we will find that, to make them understand what the names of simple ideas or substance stand for, people ordinarily show them the thing whereof they would have them have the idea; and then repeat to them the name that stands for it, as 'white', 'sweet', 'milk', 'cat', 'dog' etc." (Locke 1975: Book 3.IX.9). An important difference between Jackson's story and these two other stories—a difference that makes the former all the more problematic—is that the latter *might* not have been meant to apply to philosophically troublesome words such as "know," "mean," or "cause," whereas the former explicitly does. I do not mean to say that the broadly empiricist story of how we come to understand and be able to employ our words is wholly unproblematic in the case of words such as "white" or "dog." But I do mean to question the widespread assumption that a general story that *might* be true, or at any rate unproblematic for *some* purposes, when it comes to words such as "white" or "dog," would *ipso facto* also be true of words such as "know" or "cause."

and safe not merely because Jackson cites no empirical observations or studies to support his account, and not merely because he clearly takes the truth of the account to be self-evident, but also because, while there certainly are observations and studies that *presuppose* the representational view of language as characterized by Jackson, and interpret empirical findings in its light, there are, as I shall argue in Chapter Six, no observations or studies that support that view *as against some alternative view*— certainly not when it comes to philosophically troublesome words such as "know" or "cause."

Like many others in contemporary analytic philosophy, Jackson *thinks* his story is true because he thinks it *must* be true. He cannot see how a child could come to master a word such as "knowledge" in any other way but that of coming to recognize some particular worldly pattern and to use the word, as a label, for *it*. An important task of the following chapters will be to show that there is an alternative account to be given of the acquisition of such words—an account that is informed by an alternative conception of language and which, furthermore, is actually supported by empirical studies of first language acquisition.

3.3   A Closer Look at the Representationalist Conception, Part I: Williamson's and Cappelen's Referents as (at Best) Theoretical Posits

In Williamson and Cappelen on the one hand, and in Jackson on the other hand, we find, despite seemingly fundamental disagreements about the method of cases and what it may reasonably be expected to accomplish, the assumption of the same basic conception of language and a similar attempt to defend the method of cases on the basis of that conception of language. On both accounts, the theorist's questions basically invite us to categorize worldly items (cases, things) as belonging, or not belonging, to the extension of some philosophically troublesome word (or expression);[10] and this is something that, on both accounts, we routinely do in the course of everyday speaking and

---

[10] Goldman and Pust have proposed that these answers express "singular classificational propositions" (Goldman and Pust 1998: 182).

thinking. On both accounts, words in general, and philosophically troublesome words in particular, are taken to refer to (denote, name, pick out) worldly items whose presence (or absence) and identity are taken to be fully determinate independently of how and under what conditions we use those words. On both accounts, this relation of reference ensures the "semantic (or representational) content" of the words, which in turn ensures, in principle, the "semantic (or representational) content" of syntactically well-formed sentences in general, and of the theorist's questions and our answers to them in particular. On both accounts, all this is supposed to ensure the theorist's success in asking a clear question that has a correct answer, and that competent speakers should in principle understand and be able to answer (mostly) correctly, just on the basis of their familiarity with the case and their mastery of the words in which the theorist's question is couched.

Thus, an important contribution of these recent attempts to defend the method of cases is the more or less explicit recognition that the method presupposes a certain conception of language. The main premise of the argument of this book is that this presupposition is fateful, as far as the soundness of the method of cases is concerned. Beginning in Chapter Four, and then more systematically in Chapter Five and Six, I will argue against the method of cases as commonly practiced, not primarily by way of direct criticism of the conception of language that underwrites it, but rather by presenting and motivating—both philosophically and empirically—an alternative conception of language on which the method as commonly practiced is fundamentally misguided and unfit to deliver on its promises. In the remainder of this chapter, I would like to stay with the representationalist conception, and underscore the fact that it rests on substantive assumptions that are, at best, far from obvious.

I keep saying "at best" because—though I mostly speak about it as an intelligible conception (or view) of language, albeit one that is widely and pervasively adhered to on the basis of very poor evidence— I suspect that, at the end of the day, the representationalist conception cannot really be made sense of.[11] It is certainly not a well thought-out

---

[11] As I note in Chapter Five, I take this to be the upshot of Wittgenstein's remarks on rule following.

empirical theory.[12] As I have noted, and will note further below, there are basic elements of that conception that its proponents have barely just sketched.

Do we truly understand the representationalist conception? There is no denying that it is informed by a compelling *picture* of the essence of language, as Wittgenstein puts it (Wittgenstein 2009 (henceforth "PI"): 1); but do we really know how the picture is supposed actually to apply to our language?[13] In particular, do we know what we are talking or thinking about when we talk or think, with Williamson, Cappelen, and Jackson, about the worldly "items" to which our words are supposed to refer, and which our words—including philosophically troublesome words such as "know" or "cause"—are supposed to enable us to classify or categorize?

Immediately when we put the question this way, it becomes apparent that "item(s)" has been doing double duty in our discussion thus far: following Williamson, I have used the word to refer to what our words presumably "refer" to; following Jackson, I have used it to refer to what our words are supposed to enable us to categorize or classify. How are these two sorts of "items" supposed to relate to each other?

Let us take up this question first with respect to Williamson's and Cappelen's way of looking at things. Williamson and Cappelen say things like, "'know' refers to *knowledge*," "'think' refers to *the thinking relation*." They also talk about the extension of a word, which Williamson glosses in terms of "the set of things to which the word applies." If we put these two together, we seem to get the idea that *knowledge*, for example, is a *kind* or *type* of thing,[14] and that kind or type is *instantiated* by all of the things that belong to the extension of "knowledge," which by Williamson's and Cappelen's lights is no different from the extension of "know" (and its cognates). A *case*—here, the relation of some potential knower to some (presumably true) proposition, as that relation is

---

[12] Price aptly, but perhaps still overly charitably, refers to the "representationalist" conception of language he is arguing against as a *proto*-theory (Price 2011: 5).

[13] It is a recurrent theme in Wittgenstein's later work that pictures (as he mostly uses this term) are not by themselves harmful, or wrong. The problems begin when we try to "apply" them—that is, when we theorize philosophically and rely on a picture to ensure the sense of our words and guide us in their use (see PI: 422–6).

[14] Referable to, perhaps, as "the most general factive stative attitude" (Williamson 2000: 34). On Kornblith's view, knowledge is a "natural kind" (cf. Kornblith 2002: 29).

presented to us by the theorist or "encountered" outside philosophy—belongs to the extension of "know" just in case it instantiates *knowledge*, just as a piece of rock, or some portion of it, may belong to the extension of "granite" and instantiate the type *granite*. This, I take it, is the basic picture.

On Williamson's and Cappelen's way of looking at things, (instances of) knowledge, causation, freedom, intentional action, and so on, are Kantian "things in themselves," in the sense that these "items," or types of "items," are supposed to be there anyway, fully determinate in their identity or nature, independently of our referring to them with words, and, more broadly, independently of our putting the words—"know," "cause," "free," "intentional(ly)," and so on—to some significant use or another, under conditions suitable for that use. The world according to Williamson and Cappelen is populated by items to which our words refer, but which do not depend on our use of those words for either their existence or their identity as the particular items they are (and the types they instantiate). When philosophers ask questions about meaning, knowledge, causation, freedom, and so on, they are supposed to be asking questions about those (types of) items and their "nature" (PP: 206), in much the same way that natural scientists ask questions about (kinds of) natural objects (PP: 206).[15] Thus, for example, Cappelen asserts that when philosophers are interested in knowledge, "they are interested in the phenomenon ordinary speakers of English talk about when they say things like 'John knows that Samantha is in Paris'" (PWI: 27). Again there is the assumption that there is some one (type of) thing, or set of things—here, presumably, a mental *state*, or a *relation* that sometimes holds between potential knowers and facts (or true propositions)—that "knows" and its cognates refer to or denote, that speakers

---

[15] Kornblith too sees his work as not essentially different from that of the natural scientist: "Just as the folk physical faculty may play a role in explaining how it is even possible for us to begin theoretical investigation of the physical world, a folk epistemology faculty might play a role in explaining how it is that we are able to begin a theoretical investigation of the nature of knowledge. But in neither case would such a faculty obviate the need for that theoretical investigation... [E]pistemology must go beyond the deliverances of intuition and engage with the phenomenon of knowledge itself" (Kornblith 2015: 158). As noted earlier, however, Kornblith's way of identifying "knowledge itself" is philosophically contentious in several respects. Collecting "samples" of knowledge, in order to subject them to "experimental scrutiny" (Kornblith 2015: 161), is importantly unlike collecting samples of water and subjecting them to experimental scrutiny.

are talking *about* whenever they use these words in everyday life, and that philosophers may identify and investigate *directly*—that is, not by way of investigating the ordinary and normal functioning of "know" in discourse. (Here I must note the oddness of saying of someone who utters "John knows that Samantha is in Paris," meaning it in whichever way it may naturally be meant, that she is talking *about (the phenomenon of) knowledge*. The oddness would not have mattered if it were clear what Cappelen *meant* in saying that; but it isn't. There is a pretty clear *picture* in play; but pictures do not ensure sense.)

This is why, for Williamson and for Cappelen, the bulk of the work of philosophy falls to the hands of *metaphysicians*, whose job is to "discover what fundamental things there are and what properties and relations they have" (PP: 18–19), and for whom language is no more than an "instrument" for representing or describing those things (PP: 6; see also PWI: 191). On Cappelen's way of looking at things, the semanticist, who studies linguistic meanings, can mostly just tell us that "know" denotes *knowing*, and it is then the job of the metaphysician to tell us what knowing consists in, and *thereby* to clarify for us the meaning of "know." And the same presumably goes for most other philosophically interesting or troublesome words, and phenomena.[16]

But how exactly is the metaphysician supposed to study *knowledge*, if not by way of studying the ordinary and normal functioning of "know" and its cognates? Why even assume that there is anything of the envisioned sort for the metaphysician to study? Let me clarify and press these questions by way of a brief discussion of Hume and Kant on causation. Hume observed his billiard balls moving and hitting each other and could identify nothing corresponding to "cause" or "necessary connection" in what he (thought he) actually saw. From this he mostly concluded that it is not *reason* that tells us that the billiard balls will behave in the future as they have hitherto behaved. At other moments, and in faithfulness to the empiricist picture of how words come by their meaning, his conclusion seems to be that the term ("cause" or "necessary power" or "necessary connection") has been used by us "without meaning or idea" (Hume 1993: 13; see also Hume 1993: 49). But how could Hume sensibly deny *both* that we have an experience of causation *and*

---

[16] This is one of the central claims in Cappelen and Lepore 2005 (see especially 155–75); see also Cappelen 2013: 30, fn. 2.

the meaningfulness of "cause"? The presumed intelligibility and truth of his claim that we have no experience of causal relations, it would seem, should have led Hume to the realization that his empiricist picture of how, in general, words come by their meanings is misguided.

Now, it is quite clear that Kant thought that in looking for the meaning of "cause," and for what legitimizes our employment of that word, Hume was looking in the wrong place. But where exactly should Hume have looked, on Kant's proposal? In *When Words Are Called For*, I propose that while the first *Critique* seems to offer more than one answer to this question, the most compelling answer is that Hume ought to have looked at how the principle that "everything that happens has a cause" guides and informs our practice of empirical inquiry. Extrapolating from Kant's basic insight, I there propose that if Hume wanted to become clearer about the meaning of "cause," he ought not to have looked for *causation* ("as it is in itself"). Rather, he ought to have examined the *practice* of employing "cause" (and related words)—in different ways, in different types of situations, and for different intents and purposes.[17] And if he wanted to see what *legitimizes* our use of that word—that's Kant's "quid juris" question—he ought to have looked not for some once-and-for-all legitimization from a perspective altogether external to the practice, but rather should have examined the ordinary and normal ways in which speakers entitle themselves to the use of "cause" in different contexts, and the various types of commitments that using that word ordinarily and normally exacts of its users, together with the ordinary and normal ways of discharging those commitments.[18]

---

[17] Including uses of "cause" that Kant does not consider. A perspicuous presentation of the functioning of "cause" (and related notions) in *legal* contexts may be found in Hart and Honoré 1985. And Köhler discusses *experiences* of causation, as when "a particular attitude is experienced as arising "because of" an equally particular event or object" (Köhler 1947: 199). Hume, of course, was apt to suppose that even such experiences of "understandable connection" (Köhler 1947: 191) would ultimately need to be understood mechanistically, as arising from the regular concomitance of happenings that, as far as we know, are only *externally* related to each other.

[18] I note that this is emphatically not *Kant's* way of answering his *quid juris* question. Like Hume, Kant is still looking for an answer to that question that comes from outside the perspective of our practice with the word. On my proposal, by contrast, the *quid juris* question boils down to the *quid facti* question, in the sense that the legitimation establishable *within* the practice is all the legitimation we need and can reasonably hope for. But in order to see this, we will need to realize that the *quid facti* question is not the question of what sounds we tend to utter under certain objectively establishable circumstances, but

This practice-based approach to the philosophical elucidation of "cause," and *thereby* of causation, is what Huw Price calls for in Price 1996 and 2001. In what I take to be an echoing of Kant, Price argues that *causation* may not plausibly be thought of as part of "the furniture of the world" in the way that rocks and dogs, for example, or even electrons may be thought to be, and that it may not be studied by using the standard tools of empirical science, for the simple reason that the principle of causation is one of the constitutive principles of empirical science. More recently, Price has proposed along the same lines that if we want to understand, not this or that particular causal relation or law, but *causation*, we should "study *talk* of causation" (Price 2011: 143). This proposal fits within Price's (Wittgenstein-inspired) broader pragmatist, anti-representationalist understanding of language. It is also in broad agreement, as we will see in Chapter Six, with Michael Tomasello's "usage-based" or "social-pragmatic" theory of the acquisition of all (first language) words, for which he has argued on the basis of numerous empirical studies (Tomasello 2003, 2008, and 2009).[19]

Now let us go back to Williamson's argument against "epistemological conceptions of analyticity," which we discussed in Chapter Two. The argument proceeds on the basis of the eminently plausible thought that "understanding words in a natural language has much to do with the ability to use them in ways that facilitate smooth and fruitful interaction with other members of the community" (PP: 97). This is why, according to Williamson, no *particular* judgment about a case (or some limited range of cases) is, by itself, criterial for an understanding of the word in question. Elsewhere Williamson proposes, in connection with the same line of argument, that native speakers of English, who are not classified as incompetent by other native speakers of English, "understand the word 'know' and possess the concept *know*," "by any reasonable criterion"

---

rather the question of what makes (what) sense, and how, and under what conditions. And *that* is not a straightforward empirical question.

[19] As I said in the Introduction, though I believe there is much truth in it, I choose to remain silent in this book about Price's "*global* expressivism," and to focus just on the words that have featured centrally in the theorist's questions. I agree with Price (and Tomasello) that not even "dog" or "rock" may aptly be thought of as an instrument for recording and expressing context-independent and practice-independent categorizations. At the same time, it seems clear to me that thus thinking about words such as "dog" or "rock" is not liable to get us into the sorts of deep philosophical difficulties that it has gotten us into with words such as "know" or "cause."

(Williamson 2005: 11–12); and this too is wholly uncontentious. But then, having argued that there is no one judgment or inference that all those who understand the word *must* accept—this, in essence, is the argument against epistemological conceptions of analyticity—Williamson turns to ask, "[H]ow should we picture meaning the same thing [by a word]?" (PP: 127). And it is here that he makes the fateful and, as far as I can tell, unsupported move of proposing to answer this question, first and foremost, in terms of the extension of a word—"the set of things to which it applies" (PP: 127).[20]

However, what if our ability to use philosophically troublesome words such as "know" or "cause," in ways that facilitate smooth and fruitful interaction with members of our community, could be explained without positing the sort of items presupposed by Williamson and Cappelen?[21] Even if it were a clearly thought-out empirical theory, which I'm trying to show it isn't, and were well-supported by the evidence, which I shall argue it isn't, the representationalist conception of language could not plausibly be expected to escape the fate of all such theories of being underdetermined by the data and empirically challengeable. Surely, the mere fact that we can say, in English, of two or more people that they mean the same thing by a word does not mean that there is literally some one *thing* (or set of things), of the envisioned sort, that they all somehow mean by that word.[22] In Chapter Six, I will propose a model of the acquisition and use of "know" and cognates on which the metaphysician's *knowledge* plays no role. The same thing is true of the metaphysician's *causation* on Huw Price's non-representationalist account of the functioning of "cause" in the natural sciences (Price 1996 and 2001).

---

[20] *How* exactly the extension of a word gets fixed is a question that Williamson only answers very sketchily. (He himself acknowledges that his answer to this question is no more than sketched (Williamson 2011: 503)). And his answer simply presupposes the existence of the items to which each word supposedly refers. For these reasons, and for the further reason that an answer to that question would only seem philosophically urgent on the assumption of the representationalist conception of language, I will not further pursue that answer.

[21] As Chomsky has proposed, "It is possible that natural language has only syntax and pragmatics; it has 'semantics' only in the sense of 'the study of how this instrument, whose formal structure and potentialities of expression are the subject of syntactic investigation, is actually put to use in a speech community'" (Chomsky 1995: 26).

[22] I elaborate on this point in section 6.3 of Chapter Six.

Williamson and Cappelen presuppose without argument or evidence the existence of the items to which philosophically troublesome words presumably refer, and which philosophers are supposed to study. I will go as far as to say that the only reason to suppose the existence of those items is that the representationalist conception of language requires their existence. And this means that those items are, at best, posits of what may turn out to be a bad theory of language.[23] At worst, they are nothing more than shadows cast by the ways we talk, to use Price's apt image (Price 2011: 319). Insofar as our employment of words such as "know" and "cause" may satisfactorily be explained without invoking the sort of referents Williamson and Cappelen envision for those words, we have no good reason to suppose the existence of those referents.[24]

[23] Compare Davidson: "I suggest that words, meanings of words, reference, and satisfaction are posits we need to implement a theory of truth" (Davidson 2001: 222). Williamson's and Cappelen's idea that philosophers should study philosophically interesting "objects" directly, rather than by way of studying our concepts of those "objects" is a manifestation of what Price calls "object naturalism." About object naturalism Price says that it "rests on substantial theoretical assumptions about what we humans do with language—roughly, the [representationalist] assumption that substantial 'word-world' semantic relations are part of the best scientific account of our use of the relevant terms" (Price 2011: 190). Price argues, however, that "by the naturalist's own lights, the [representationalist's] proto-theory ought to count as an hypothesis about what it is right to say about language itself, from a naturalistic standpoint. If it turned out to be a bad hypothesis—if better science showed that the proto-theory was a poor theory—then the motivation for the Naturalist's version of the matching game [of words and worldly items] would be undermined" (Price 2011: 5; see also Price 2013: 4, 14, and 25).

[24] In a recent paper on the "metasemantics" of singular reference, Ori Simchen discusses David Lewis's invocation of "reference magnetism" in response to Putnam's model-theoretic argument for indeterminacy of reference. In his response, Lewis appeals to what he calls "the objective joints in nature" (Lewis 1984: 227), which Simchen glosses in terms of "the structure that already inheres in the world itself" (Simchen forthcoming: 3). Simchen notes that the idea that "the world has its own structure independently of our conceptual involvement in it" would strike "those with Kantian leanings" as "spooky and unillumin-ating" (Simchen forthcoming: 3–4). But then he sets the worry aside and assumes throughout—not only in his discussion of reference magnetism, but in arguing for the priority of subsentential-reference over sentential-truth-conditions—that the world is composed of ready-to-be-referred-to things-in-themselves. Simchen should be applauded for at least mentioning, before setting aside, the Kantian worry, which does seem less pressing as long as one focuses, as he does, on such referents as apples and planets, as contrasted with the supposed referents of philosophically troublesome words such as "know," "cause," "intend," and so on.

3.4 A Closer Look at the Representationalist Conception, Part II: Jackson's Patterns as (at Best) Theoretical Posits

It is here that Jackson's way of looking at the method of cases may appear to have a significant advantage over Williamson's and Cappelen's way of looking at it. For Jackson, it would seem, is not committed to the existence of knowledge, causation, freedom, and so on, as "things in themselves." On Jackson's account, the method of cases aims not at the study of the nature of such elusive "objects," but rather at the elucidation of *our concepts* of knowledge, causation, freedom, and so on, as those reveal themselves in our "applications" of the relevant words. The philosopher's primary data, on Jackson's account, are not such metaphysically elusive "truths" as that *cases of **this** sort—where the content of "this" is given by the description of a case—are (are not) cases of knowledge.* Rather, the philosopher's primary data, on that account, are fairly easily establishable facts such as that competent speakers (are inclined to) count some descriptively given case as a case of knowledge (or absence of knowledge), or (are inclined to) say of the protagonist of some story that she knows (or does not know) that such and such. In being, in a sense, considerably less ambitious in its aims, the method of cases as Jackson thinks of it would seem to be considerably less vulnerable to skepticism. Indeed, it would seem that *on the assumption of the representationalist conception of language* it is very hard to find anything wrong with the philosophical method of cases as Jackson thinks of it. *If* our words, including our philosophically troublesome words, are first and foremost instruments for classifying empirically encountered cases; and *if* the classifications they ordinarily and normally enable us to effect, record, and communicate require nothing more than familiarity with the cases under consideration and mastery of the words; *if*, in particular, the classifications are such that they may successfully be carried out apart from any particular context of significant use of the words and apart from any particular non-merely-theoretical needs or interests; then what better way could there be for elucidating whatever underwrites or ultimately guides our ordinary and normal classification of cases as cases of X—call it "our concept of X," or call it "the meaning of 'x'"— than constructing theoretically significant cases and inviting competent speakers to tell us whether they are cases of X? This, in essence, is what Jackson contends when he submits that "what we use 'knowledge' for is something that calls for investigation . . . But if this is right, what sort of evidence is appropriate? Surely part of the answer lies in what a user of the word says about its application or non-application to various possible cases" (Jackson 2009: 104).

The above are very big ifs, however. One way of challenging them is to take them to be expressive of clear enough empirical assumptions, and challenge those assumptions empirically. This will be the main task of Chapters Five and Six. Right now my question is whether we so much as understand the above set of assumptions, or truly know what they come to. In order to press *this* question, I note that once we grant these assumptions—as both intelligible and true—the supposedly important difference between Williamson's and Cappelen's way of thinking about the method of cases, on the one hand, and Jackson's (and many others') way of thinking about it, on the other hand, collapses. For how exactly does the *pattern* that, according to Jackson, (English-speaking) children must learn to recognize, and to use "knowledge" for, differ from the *item* that Williamson and Cappelen take themselves to be referring to when they say things like "'Knowledge' (or 'know(s)') refers to *knowledge*"? Surely, Williamson and Cappelen would not mind calling knowledge, for example, "a pattern" rather than "an item." Putting what is essentially the same question differently, what is the difference between the idea that the method of cases aims at clarifying the nature of knowledge, causation, and so on, and the idea that it aims at clarifying our concepts of knowledge, causation, and so on, *if our concepts are simply whatever it is that ultimately guides us in classifying empirically encountered cases as cases of knowledge, causation, and so on, and if the classifications are such that they may be effected even apart from any context of significant use of "know," "cause," and so on*? After all, if we are to learn anything about, for example, our concept of knowledge by means of the method of cases, we would presumably need to be able to characterize somehow the type of cases to which competent speakers (in our community) do, and the type of cases to which they do not, "apply" the word "know." And it is not clear how *that* would be essentially different from what Williamson and Cappelen would regard as a characterization of *knowledge*. On both accounts, the characterization is of some constellation that is there in the world independently of our employment of "know" and its cognates, and to which these words have simply come to refer.[25]

Going back to the list of "ifs" above, I can now summarize our most recent finding in the following way: *if* our words, including our philosophically troublesome words, are first and foremost instruments for classifying empirically encountered cases; and *if* the classifications they ordinarily and normally enable us to effect, record, and communicate require nothing more than familiarity with the cases under consideration and mastery of the words; *if*, in particular, the classifications are such that they may successfully be carried out from anywhere, so to speak, apart from any particular context of significant use of the word(s) and from any particular non-merely-theoretical needs or interests; then it does not matter much whether we say that the method of cases aims at the clarification of (the nature of) *knowledge, causation, meaning,* and so on, or we say that it aims at the clarification of *our concepts* of knowledge, causation, meaning, and so on. The former may sound more ambitious than the latter, and closer to a certain popular picture of how science relates to and studies its objects, but the two come to the same thing.[26]

The upshot of all of this is that if the items to which words such as "know," "cause," "mean," and so on, are supposed to refer on Williamson's and Cappelen's view may turn out to have been, at best, posits of an empirically unsupported, and misguided, theory of language, then so may Jackson's patterns. But if so, and if the method of cases is designed to reveal and clarify the patterns that are presumably associated with philosophically troublesome words, as Jackson suggests, then the method of cases may turn out to have been fundamentally misguided as well. The main task of Chapters Five and Six will be to substantiate this worry.

---

[25] Both ways of looking at the method of cases can make room for *mistaken* (false) answers to the theorist's question by drawing a distinction—as Williamson explicitly does—between what a community's "x" means or refers to and what some particular member of *that* community calls "x" on a particular occasion (or set of occasions).

[26] Williamson and Cappelen more or less acknowledge this. When they charge philosophers such as Jackson with "psychologizing their evidence," their point is that there has been nothing wrong, in principle, with how the method of cases has been practiced, but only something wrong with how philosophers have tended to conceive of that practice.

4

Contemporary "Contextualism" and the Twilight of Representationalism

In the following chapters I will question the philosophical method of cases as commonly practiced by questioning what I have called "the minimal assumption"—the assumption, namely, that the theorist's question has a clear enough sense that competent speakers may be expected to see, and a correct answer that competent speakers may be expected to give. And I will question the minimal assumption by way of presenting and motivating a conception of language on which that assumption is false. On the alternative conception that I will offer, the theorist cannot rely on his words alone (together with his description of the case) to ensure the sense of his question—where, by design, there is nothing *else* in his peculiar context that could contribute to fixing a determinate sense for his question.

Put this way, my contention may seem similar—and indeed, at a sufficiently high level of abstraction it *is* similar—to a contention made by proponents of the position known in contemporary analytic philosophy as "contextualism."[1] For this reason, it would be useful to consider

---

[1] It should be noted that I will be using "contextualism" (and "the contextualist") throughout to refer to the particular position that goes by that name in contemporary analytic philosophy (and to its proponents), and not to just *any* position that takes context to play an essential role in fixing the sense of utterances. The alternative conception of language that will be presented and motivated in subsequent chapters is also contextualist in this broader sense, but it is different in important respects from contemporary contextualism.

at this point contextualism, its relation to the representationalist conception of language, and how it bears on the philosophical method of cases. Becoming clearer about the respect in which contemporary contextualism challenges the representationalist conception of language, the respect in which it does not, and—most importantly—how it points to a radical break with that conception without actually following through with that break, will prepare the ground for the presentation of the alternative conception of language in Chapters Five and Six.

4.1 Contemporary "Contextualism" and the Representationalist Conception of Language

The contemporary contextualist still takes it—together with proponents of what I have called "the representationalist conception of language"—that our words, including philosophically troublesome words such as "know" and "cause," are first and foremost instruments for the classification of "empirically encountered cases." He argues, however, that the classification is beholden not only to the encountered case itself, but also to the context in which the encounter takes place, and more precisely to the context in which the question of whether the case is a case of "x" has arisen, or is being answered. On the contextualist picture, when it comes to some context-sensitive term "x"—as on some contextualist accounts all general terms are[2]—there is no context-independent fact of the matter whether some case is a case of x, so no context-independent correct answer to the question whether some case is a case of x. What contribution "know" (for example) makes to the sense of an utterance—where that sense is still primarily thought of by contextualists in terms of truth-conditions, or more broadly in terms of suitability for assessment in terms of truth and falsity—depends in part on the context of the utterance, says the contextualist; and this means that the contextualist rejects

---

[2] Cappelen and Lepore (2005) argue that all contextualists should be what they call "radical contextualists"—that is, contextualists with respect to all general terms. They take Charles Travis to be one of the main proponents of radical contextualism; and it is indeed true that Travis (1989, 1997) has principled reasons—stemming from Wittgenstein's rule-following considerations—for thinking that all general terms are context-sensitive in his sense. Robyn Carston has been another important proponent of radical contextualism. "*No sentence*," she says, "ever fully encodes the thought or proposition it is used to express" (Carston 2002: 29, my emphasis).

what I have called "the minimal assumption," and thereby objects, in effect, to the method of cases as commonly practiced by armchair and experimental philosophers alike. Given that contextualism, in one version or another, seems to have been winning more and more adherents in contemporary philosophy of language, it is striking that its (potentially radical) implications for the method of cases have not, on the whole, been recognized in the recent debate concerning the method of cases.[3]

If, as Lewis says, the sense of an utterance (which, like other contextualists, he still understands in terms of "truth-conditions") depends, among other things, on "the audience, the standards of precision, the salience relations, [and] the presuppositions" of the context (Lewis 1980: 86), where those are in turn "determined, if they are determined at all, by such things as the previous course of the conversation that is still going on at the context, the states of mind of the participants, and the conspicuous aspects of the surroundings" (Lewis 1980: 86), then there is every reason to expect that the theorist's question—raised, as it is, apart from *any particular* constellation of such contextual features—would be indeterminate in its sense and unfit for being answered correctly or incorrectly. When one is presented, for example, with a case of some proposition *p* which is assumed to be true and some person N who takes it that *p*, and is then asked, apart from any particular context in which the question may be found to express some particular interest in the case, "Does N know that *p*?" the correct answer, according to contextualists (with respect to "know(s)") would be that the question is not yet determinate enough to be answered correctly or incorrectly—at least when raised about many ordinary cases, or types of cases.[4] And this, even before we bring into consideration the context-sensitivity of 'p'.

No contextualist has pressed this last point more forcefully than Charles Travis. The failure to appreciate the dependence of sense on (suitable) context, Travis has argued, is responsible for any number of traditional philosophical impasses, with skepticism (as Travis understands it) being

---

[3] There *have* been some experiments designed to test *contextualism itself* empirically (see, for example, Buckwalter 2010; Hansen 2013; and Hansen and Chemla 2013).

[4] As I note later in this section, the contextualist can allow that *some* cases may be such that they would truly or appropriately count as cases of "x," or as cases of "not x," in *every* context, or in all *conceivable* contexts. The theorist's question would then *still* be importantly indeterminate in what it asks, but it would be determinate *enough* to be answered correctly or incorrectly.

chief among them. "A speaking sensitive account of knowledge explains how philosophical perplexities arise," he writes, "they do so when 'language goes on a holiday'; when we are not speaking in surroundings where we would actually express a thought in saying N to know F, but suppose that we must be expressing one anyway. It thus also details precisely what misunderstanding skepticism is" (Travis 1991: 246).

In emphasizing the *pervasive* role context plays in the determination of linguistic sense, contemporary contextualism constitutes an important move away from the representationalist conception of language as presented in Chapter Three, and poses a serious challenge to the minimal assumption.[5] At the same time, however, the contemporary contextualist is still committed to a representationalist view of the functioning of words—including philosophically troublesome words such as "know" or "cause"—in ordinary and normal discourse.[6] He therefore has no problem with the idea that the meanings of context-sensitive terms are first and foremost a matter of what cases (or items) in the world they (truly) refer to, and what contribution they thereby make to the truth-conditions of utterances. He only insists that the set of those cases is context-dependent: a case that in one context truly and appropriately counts as a case of "x," may in another context truly and appropriately count as a case of "not x." The contextualist with respect to "know" or "cause," for example, has no problem with the idea that the primary function of the word is to enable us to classify (or categorize) "empirically encountered cases"; he only insists that *what* classification the word

[5] The emphasis here is on "pervasive," because proponents of the representationalist conception do not deny that context plays *some* role in fixing the contribution made by *some* words—for example, indexicals, demonstratives, and "ambiguous" words—to the overall sense of utterances in which they feature.

[6] Thus, Lewis still thinks of the sense of an uttered sentence in terms of its truth-conditions (Lewis 1980); Carston speaks of the sense of uttered words in terms of "the thought or proposition" expressed (Carston 2002: 29); Lakoff and Johnson talk about "*categories* [that] are not fixed but may be narrowed, expanded, or adjusted relative to our purposes and other contextual factors" (Lakoff and Johnson 2003: 164, my emphasis); Recanati is happy to describe his position as "truth-conditional pragmatism" (Recanati 2010); and Travis argues that "the role of a sentence . . . is *not* to be the expresser, in its language, of such and such thought, but rather to be usable in many different circumstances for expressing any of many thoughts, each with its own condition for truth" (Travis 1991: 242). In this way, contextualists have all participated in what Lance and Kukla call "the declarative fallacy" (Lance and Kukla 2009: 11). For a recent discussion that underscores these representational-referential commitments of the contextualist, see Camp 2016: 115 and 119.

is fit to effect or record depends not on its meaning alone but also on the context in which the classification takes place.

Precisely because contemporary contextualism still holds on to a representational-referential conception of language, it might seem that, at the end of the day, it does not pose any *fundamental* challenge to the philosophical method of cases. It might seem that the method could fairly easily be adjusted to accommodate (as well as test) the truth of contextualism. There are two ways this adjustment could be, and has been, made. The first way would be to consider not just the case, but a context in which someone encounters a case and calls it "x" (or "not-x"); and then to ask, not "Is the encountered case a case of X?" but rather "Did the protagonist say something true in calling the case "a case of x" *in that context?*"[7] The second way would be to describe a case and then to invite oneself, or one's audience, to imagine an encounter with that case *in some particular context*; and then to ask oneself, or one's audience, whether, *considered in that context*, the case should count as "a case of x," or whether, *in that context*, it would be true to say that the case is "a case of x."[8] In *When Words Are Called For*, I argued that because contextualists tend to ignore the Austinian question of what's *done* with the words—*presupposing*, as they tend to do, that the words are used simply for "imparting information" (Lewis 1980: 80)—the difference between the first and second way of arguing for contextualism has been rendered insignificant. Put otherwise, since those who argue in the first way invariably ignore the question of what's done with the words, or treat it as irrelevant to their argument, it would seem that they might as well have argued in the second way, which does altogether without (the consideration of) *utterances* or *speech acts*. For the contextualist, the speech act itself is really just a way of "placing a sentence at a context," and making sense of a sentence-at-a-context is not a matter of making sense of *the speaker*—of seeing how she positions *herself* significantly by means of words.[9] With the traditionalist ("invariantist"), the

---

[7] This is how contextualists such as Travis (1989, 1997), Lewis (1996), Cohen (1999), and DeRose (1992, 1995) tend to proceed.

[8] For this way of arguing, see Schaffer (2004, 2005, 2006).

[9] In Baz (2012a), I consider a range of contextualist "examples" of everyday utterances featuring "know" or one of its cognates, and I show that either the utterances cannot truly be made sense of as *human acts* under the circumstances as described by the contextualist, or, where we *could* imagine the context in such a way that they make sense, they actually

contextualist still thinks of our words as essentially speaking for themselves—over our heads, as it were—and of language as a system of significant signs that does not depend on speakers (and listeners) for its ongoing maintenance.[10] I'll come back to this issue in sections 4.2 and 4.3, and at greater length in Chapter Five.

Not only would it seem that the method of cases could fairly easily be adjusted to accommodate contextualism, but it may also seem that for the purpose of answering at least some philosophical questions about some philosophically interesting subject X, such an adjustment would be unnecessary even if "x" *were* context-sensitive in the contextualist's sense. For example, even if "know" is context-sensitive in the contextualist's sense, it *may* be that *in no context* would a merely reliably true belief truly and appropriately count as "knowledge"; and *if* that is the case, the method of cases *as traditionally practiced*—that is, without the contextualist's "semantic ascent"—could still legitimately be used to undermine "externalist" conceptions of knowledge. Or again, even if "know" is context-sensitive in the contextualist's sense, it *may* be that *in no context* would *any* Gettier-type relation to a true proposition truly and appropriately count as "knowledge"; and *if* so, the method of cases *as traditionally practiced* could still legitimately be used—as in Gettier 1963—to undermine the justified-true-belief analysis of knowledge.

In the case of other philosophical subjects or questions, on the other hand, the method of cases as traditionally practiced may seem problematic, and precisely because it fails to take into account the context-sensitivity of the terms in question. For example, it *may* be that the method of cases *as traditionally practiced* gives rise to the traditional problem of skepticism, as Travis and other contextualists have proposed, and that *here* the contextualist amendment to the method—his "semantic ascent"—may enable us to dissolve the (apparent) problem.[11] But

---

point us away from the contextualist's, and equally the traditionalist's, representational-referential understanding of language.

[10] It is something like this understanding of language, I think, that Davidson means to question when he says that "there is no such thing as a language, not if a language is anything like what many philosophers and linguists have supposed" (Davidson 2006: 265).

[11] As has been argued by Travis (1989, 1991, 1997), Lewis (1996), DeRose (1995), and Cohen (1998, 1999). In Baz (2012a and 2014) I argue that while contemporary contextualism of the sort advocated in these works may appear adequate diagnosis and dissolution of skepticism of *a very certain form*—at least for someone who accepts the representationalist conception of language—it clearly misses the mark when it comes to

again, even in cases such as these, the contextualist amendment may plausibly be seen as just that—an amendment to the traditional method of cases, not a rejection of it; and this, I propose, is precisely because contemporary contextualism has not truly broken with the representational-referential conception of language that has underwritten the method of cases as traditionally practiced.

4.2 J. L. Austin's Anti-Representationalism and Contemporary Contextualism

Since contextualists such as Travis (1989, 1991, and 1997) and DeRose (2002 and 2005) have taken themselves to be following Wittgenstein and/or Austin, it is worth noting that there are good reasons for thinking that neither Wittgenstein nor Austin would have been happy with the contextualist's commitment to the representational-referential and truth-conditional view of language. Wittgenstein will be discussed in Chapter Five. Austin's work will not be focused on later in this book; so let me say why I think it is a mistake, or at least importantly misleading, to call him contextualism's "granddaddy," as DeRose has done (DeRose 2002: 196). To regard Austin as a forerunner of contemporary contextualism is to fail to appreciate the radicalness of his break with the representationalist view of language.

At the opening of *How to Do Things with Words* Austin draws our attention to "performative" utterances that, despite having a "declarative" form, he thinks are obviously unsuitable for assessment in terms of truth and falsity (Austin 1999: 6); and then, in "Other Minds," he compares "I know"—at least in *one* of its uses (a use, I note, that is actually quite uncommon)—and the performative "I promise," and argues that the former too is not a "descriptive phrase" (Austin 1979: 103).[12] "Even if some language is now purely descriptive," he adds, "language was not in origin so, and much of it is still not so" (Austin 1979: 103). Towards the

---

other traditional forms of skepticism, such as Cartesian skepticism about the "external world," Humean skepticism about induction, or skepticism about "other minds."

[12] In Baz 2012a, I say what I think is insightful and useful in this comparison of "I promise" and *one uncommon* use of "I know." Those who rushed to point out the differences, I there propose, have missed the broader and deeper lesson it points to—though admittedly *only* points to.

end of *How to Do Things with Words*, Austin professes an inclination to "play Old Harry with the true/false fetish" (Austin 1999: 151); and in a footnote to "A Plea for Excuses," having said that ordinary language—as it reveals itself in an examination of "what we should say when, and so why and what we should mean by it" (Austin 1979: 181)—should provide "the first word" for philosophy, he implores his readers to "forget, for once and for a while, that other curious question 'Is it true?'" (Austin 1979: 185).

DeRose, having proposed that Austin may be seen as "contextualism's granddaddy," cites the above footnote from "A Plea for Excuses" and says that he finds it "troubling" (DeRose 2002: 196). It is clear why DeRose should find this footnote troubling: contemporary "contextualism" is *essentially* a theory about the truth-conditions of "assertoric" ("declarative") sentences.[13] DeRose notes, however, that the footnote is actually consistent with Austin's writings on epistemology, in which Austin "avoid[s] issues of whether our epistemological claims (especially claims about what is and is not known) are true or false" (DeRose 2002: 196).

And that is true. In "Other Minds" Austin says things like the following:

> If you say "That's not enough" [as a way of challenging a claim that such and such and the basis given in its support, AB], then you must have in mind some more or less definite lack . . . If there is no definite lack, which you are at least prepared to specify on being pressed, then it's silly (outrageous) just to go on saying "That's not enough." (Austin 1979: 84)

He also says that what's enough will be a matter of what is "within reason," and will depend on "*present* intents and purposes" (Austin 1979: 84). One could see in these passages of Austin's all of the main ingredients of contemporary contextualism about "knowing (that such and such)"; except that he seems content to speak in terms of when we would be "right" to say we know (Austin 1979: 98), or "justified" in saying this (Austin 1979: 101), and, as in the above quotation, in terms of what would or would not be "silly" or "outrageous" or "within reason" to say. He never asks when it would be *true* to say of someone, who has asserted that there is a goldfinch in the garden, that he knows there's a

---

[13]   Grice, whose theory of "implicature" is premised on the possibility of separating the truth-conditional content of an uttered sentence from what, in the Austinian sense, is being done with it, also complains about Austin's footnote (Grice 1989: 13).

goldfinch in the garden. He never says that if the knowledge claimer has said enough for all intents and purposes to support his claim, then he just *knows*, or at any rate has claimed something *true*.

Similarly, Austin cashes out the infallibility of knowledge—"when you know you can't be wrong" (Austin 1979: 98)—not in terms of the metaphysical constitution of *knowledge*, nor in terms of the truth-conditions of knowledge ascriptions, but rather, once again, in terms of the felicity-conditions, so to speak, of knowledge claims: "*If you are aware* you may be mistaken, *you ought not to say* you know" (Austin 1979: 98, my emphases). I would argue that the so-called "factivity" of knowledge—"If N knows that *p*, then *p*"—should similarly be understood in terms of the felicity-conditions, rather than truth-conditions, of knowledge claims and ascriptions: you ought not to claim to know that such and such, or say of someone else that she knows that such and such, when you do not think, or are not sure, that such and such. Not because there is some particular type of mental state denoted by "know" and its cognates, which, as a matter of metaphysical fact, is factive; but rather because that's how we, competent adult speakers, normally use that word (as opposed to words such as "think" or "believe"). If you use it differently, you are liable to be misunderstood, and to mislead.[14]

The representationalist—whether "invariantist" or "contextualist"—is bound to find Austin's anti-representationalist pronouncements, and his seemingly systematic avoidance of the question of when knowledge claims and ascriptions would be *true*, or else *false*, difficult to accept, or even understand. Chapters Five and Six of this book, though not focusing on Austin, may be seen as an attempt to vindicate theoretically his anti-representationalist pronouncements and practice. I am not going to

---

[14] It is interesting to note that (normally) we also only say of someone that she does *not* know that such and such, when we ourselves take it for granted that such and such (for empirical studies of when, and to what extent, young children come to know this, see Dudley et al. 2015). "To know that such and such," in such contexts, normally just means something like "to have already gotten the information (learned, found out, figured out ...) that such and such." It does not mean, as it normally does in philosophy, "to have arrived at some special epistemic position with respect to (the proposition that) such and such, which allows one to rule out all (relevant) doubts as to such and such." As I note below, it is a rather peculiar *philosophical* speech act, motivated by the representationalist conception of language, to insist that someone does not (or did not) *know* that such and such, or said something *false* in saying "I know ...," because knowledge is factive and (evidently) it is not the case that such and such.

argue, and do not think, or think Austin thought, that the assessment in terms of truth and falsity is *never* in place, or never in place when applied to utterances featuring "know." Sometimes it clearly is, and sometimes it isn't. My proposal, and here I believe I am in agreement with Austin, will only be that the assessment is not *always* in place—not even in the case of utterances of sentences in the indicative—and that it should not be taken as somehow holding *the key* to an understanding of linguistic meaning. It's the insistence that it is *always* in place and does hold the key to an understanding of linguistic meaning that seems to me to be responsible for any number of philosophical difficulties and impasses. It also seems to me to reflect, and at the same time encourage, a false picture of what making sense with our words involves and requires.

Let me briefly illustrate the way in which contextualists get themselves philosophically entangled because of their commitment to representationalism and their failure to heed Austin's imploration to forget, for once and for a while, the question, "Is it true?"[15] This would also provide some indication of the direction I will be going in Chapters Five and Six.

Take a contextualist account such as Lewis's (1996) or Travis's (1989, 1991, and 1997), on which "know(s)" truly applies to some pair of propositions assumed to be true and a potential knower who believes that proposition, just in case the potential knower (or "her experience," or "her evidence") has ruled out ("eliminated," "discharged") all *relevant* alternatives (Travis says "real (as opposed to mere) doubts")—where what alternatives are relevant is context-dependent.[16]

---

[15] Again, I do not say that the method of cases with (or even without) the contextualist amendment would *always* get us into theoretical trouble. It *might* be that with *some* sorts of words—not, I think, the sorts of words that have tended to exercise and puzzle philosophers—the method of cases with (or even without) the contextualist amendment would be innocuous. As I go on to propose in the text, when it comes to philosophically troublesome words such as "know," "cause," free," "think," and so on, it is likely to lead us astray; and in some cases it has already been leading philosophers astray because of its representationalist commitments.

[16] There are also contextualist accounts on which the perceived *stakes* in p being, or not being, true, affect the truth-conditions of utterances of the form "N knows that p" (see DeRose 1992 and 2011; and Cohen 1999). These accounts are more vulnerable to the anti-contextualist charge that the contextualist intuitions are affected by the pragmatics ("assertability conditions"), rather than semantics ("truth-conditions"), of "know" and its cognates. A significant advantage of the "relevant-alternatives" contextualist account—besides the fact that, as I point out below, it does get *something* right about the ordinary and normal functioning of "know" in *some* contexts—is that it is supported, not merely by intuitions about cases, but also by the serious difficulty faced by the invariantist of coming up with a

One worry about this account—and equally about other contextualist accounts of "know"—is that it's not clear that it succeeds in offering a satisfying response to traditional skepticism, as it purports to do. Both Travis and Lewis build the requirement that *p* be true into the elimination-of-relevant-alternatives requirement. Lewis simply says that "the possibility that actually obtains is never properly ignored" (Lewis 1996: 554), and then adds that a possibility that "saliently resembles actuality" may not properly be ignored either (Lewis 1996: 557). Travis puts the idea this way:

If there are facts to make this a case of F's not obtaining, then for any claim that A knows that F (or, equivalently, any occasion for judging whether A knows that F), there are some facts which show some doubt to be real for that claim or on that occasion which A has not discharged. (Travis 1989: 162; see also Travis 1989: 173)

But in thus building the so called "factivity" of knowledge (If you know that such and such, then such and such) and its infallibility (If you know, you [somehow epistemically] can't be wrong) into their account of what makes alternatives (or doubts) relevant (or real)—and *thereby* (departing from Austin) into their account of the truth-conditions of knowledge ascriptions—they undermine their ambition to offer a satisfying response to the skeptic. For though on their account we *may*—if we are (epistemically) lucky!—"know a lot" (Lewis 1996: 549), we cannot (truly be said to) *know* that we know those things. And this is because there are, presumably, for any would-be knower and any empirical proposition *p*, skeptical alternatives to *p* that, while seemingly far-fetched, have not actually been eliminated by that person (or by anyone else for that matter). And should *any* of those alternatives happen to be actual—a possibility that by hypothesis has not actually been eliminated—it would, by Travis's and Lewis's light, *be relevant*, in *any* context, and therefore be an alternative that *would* need to actually be eliminated by the would-be knower if she is to truly count as "knowing that *p*." This may seem like a merely technical difficulty for the contextualist, but it actually points to a fundamental problem with *any* attempt

context-insensitive way that is at once *principled* and *plausible* of drawing the distinction, within all of the countless alternatives to *p* that a would-be knower has not eliminated, between those that need to be eliminated by her and those that need not be eliminated by her in order for her to truly count as "knowing that *p*" (see Travis 1989: 168 and 1991: 245).

to respond to some version or another of traditional skepticism—as analytic philosophers have tended to do—by way of a theoretical account of when (it would be true to say) someone *knows* something.[17]

Another problem with the "relevant-alternatives" contextualist account of "know," and one that bears more directly on the main argument of this book, is that, though there seems to be an undeniable truth in the idea that some distinction between relevant and irrelevant doubts or alternatives is at least sometimes pertinent to our use of "know" and cognates, no clear and truly satisfying story has been offered by anyone about how exactly the distinction gets effected on particular occasions in which those words are used; nor has a clear and truly satisfying story been offered about how, or in what sense, relevant alternatives, or doubts as to *p*, get "eliminated" or "discharged" by N, or by N's "evidence" or "experience."[18]

The good news is that we do not really need such a story in order to know all there is to know about the ordinary and normal use of "know" and its cognates. The story would only appear needed on a representationalist conception of what using our words intelligibly involves and requires—a conception on which there need to be truth-conditions (context-sensitive or not) for every "application" of "know," and a truth-value to each such "application" that is establishable from the theorist's perspective; and that conception is not actually vindicated by our practice of employing this word. As I note in *When Words Are Called For*, the distinction between relevant and irrelevant alternatives normally belongs in the same sorts of contexts in which the "How do you know?" question—the question on which Austin focuses in "Other

---

[17] In Baz 2014, I argue that essentially the same problem plagues Sosa's attempt, in Sosa 2007b, to overcome Cartesian "dream skepticism" by way of an "apt belief" account of knowledge. Cartesian skepticism, I there propose, calls for a rethinking—à la Merleau-Ponty—of our relation to the world, to our body, and to others, not for a theory of knowledge, or of "knowledge." And I also propose that Wittgenstein and Austin, whose work has typically been taken by analytic philosophers to bear on the latter sort of project, may be read as actually participating in the former sort of project.

[18] Travis offers no account, as far as I can tell, of how the distinction between real and mere doubts gets effected on particular occasions, or of what "discharging" a doubt requires. Lewis too is silent about how one's "experience" is supposed to "eliminate" an alternative; and he notoriously proposes that an alternative becomes relevant whenever it is "attended to" (Lewis 1996: 559), which would make it *extremely* easy to disown any unwanted piece of knowledge—for example, when one is *charged* with having known something one ought to have done something about, but hasn't.

Minds"—normally belongs. In those contexts, someone asserts that such and such, or assures someone else that such and such, and then tells the other—either in response to her "How do you know?" or without her prompting—what his basis is for taking it, and for asserting, that such and such. And, as Austin reminds us in "Other Minds," not just any doubt or alternative to such and such could *then* reasonably or competently be invoked to challenge that person's assertion or basis; and, moreover, alternatives that in one context would reasonably be taken to be relevant, could in another context reasonably be dismissed as irrelevant.

This is the truth in (context-sensitive) "relevant alternatives" accounts of "knowledge." But it is *not* a truth about what philosophers have called "truth-conditions." It is a truth about what may generally be called *reasonableness* in the employment of our words. (I have earlier spoken about it, following Austin's *How to Do Things with Words*, in terms of felicity-conditions.) And *one* crucial difference between the Austinian question of reasonableness and the question of truth and falsity as the theorist understands it, is that the former is not just context-sensitive, but importantly also allows (within reason) for no-fault disagreements, whereas the latter is supposed to have one, and only one, objectively establishable correct answer (on which theorists have not been able to agree).

Austin's deep insight in "Other Minds" is that if we truly are interested in a "restatement of our common knowledge about our practices of linguistic communication" (Lewis 1980: 79), and interested specifically in reminding ourselves of how "know" "functions in talking" (Austin 1979: 79), then *the truth about reasonableness is all the truth we need*. If you assure me or otherwise assert that such and such, and give me your basis for taking it that such and such, *and I accept your basis* as good enough "for present intents and purposes," and do not or cannot raise further reasonable doubts, and then all goes well, and such and such turns out to be the case, then that's the end of the story—as far as the work "know" has done for us goes.[19] Whether or not you *knew* that such and such, or said something *true* in saying you knew (assuming you

---

[19] And if I do *not* accept your basis as giving us *sufficient* assurance that such and such, then *that*—that is, whether your basis is good *enough* (for present intents and purposes) for us to proceed as if such and such, rather than whether you (may truly be said to) *know*—is the issue on which we disagree. And *this* sort of disagreement, once again, is one that allows for cases in which neither party is wrong, or mistaken.

actually said "I know"), is a question that makes no contact with the normal practice in such situations and has no bearing on that practice. And if not all goes well, and it turns out that, by some turn of events *neither* of us has expected, it is not the case that such and such, then, under normal circumstances, *I would have no grounds for complaint against you*; and *that* is what matters—as far as our use of "know" is concerned—in *such* moments. The insistence that, in that case, the assurer didn't (couldn't) really *know* that such and such, because knowledge is "factive," would then be an expression, once again, not of part of our common knowledge about our practices of linguistic communication, but of representationalist theoretical commitments extraneous to the practice itself.

And yet, for all of these ways in which the contemporary contextualist still thinks from within the framework of those representationalist commitments and entangles himself in difficulties that are due entirely to those commitments, in recognizing the role of context in fixing the contribution words make to the overall sense of utterances, contemporary contextualism points toward a more radical break with the representational-referential conception of language than it itself has accomplished, or envisioned. Before I try to say more precisely how it does so, however, I need to say something about the notion of "context"; for it seems to me that the notion, as used in contemporary analytic philosophy, stands in need of elucidation.

4.3 What Is the Context of an Utterance?

Let "the meaning of a word" refer to whatever it is that the word carries with it from one use to another and makes it fit (given suitable conditions) for certain uses but not others. And let "the meaning of a sentence" refer to whatever it is that the particular grammatically well-formed string of words carries with it from one use to another and which makes it fit (given suitable conditions) for certain uses—or, if you will, for the expression of certain contents—but not others.[20]

---

[20] Lewis (1980) refers to what I am here calling "word-meaning" and "sentence-meaning" as a word's or a sentence's "semantic value." "The semantic value of any expression," he writes, "is to be determined by the semantic values of the (immediate) constituents from which it is built, together with the way it is built from them" (Lewis 1980: 83).

Contextualism may then be said to concern the relation between the meaning of a sentence and the sense of an utterance of it, where "the sense (or content) of an utterance" is sometimes explicated in terms of "the proposition (or thought) expressed," sometimes in terms of "what is said," and on the whole is taken to be cashable in terms of "truth-conditions." Later on I will question this representationalist understanding of "sense," and the need for a broader understanding of the term will become clear. The sense of an utterance, I will propose, may aptly and usefully be understood as the correlate of a proper understanding of it—as that understanding manifests itself in how one responds to the utterance— which leaves open the question of whether, in each case, that proper understanding is best understood in terms of truth (conditions, value), or in other, non-representational terms. For now, however, the representationalist, truth-conditional understanding of "sense" will do.

However exactly we understand "the sense of an utterance," "the sense (or content) of an uttered word" may usefully be taken to refer to the contribution the word makes, on some occasion, to the overall sense of an utterance. The general tendency has been to think of the sense (or content) of a word (on some occasion of its employment) in terms of its "reference" or "extension" (on that occasion).[21]

Given the above understanding of "the meaning of a word," "the meaning of a sentence," "the sense of a word (on some occasion of its employment)," and "the sense of a sentence (on some occasion of its employment)," the contextualist's central contention may now be put thus: meaning alone is insufficient for determinate sense. "The context of an utterance" is then supposed to refer to whatever needs to combine with the meanings of uttered words, to endow them, and the uttered sentence, with a determinate sense.

Here it should be noted that I have been talking about the sense of *utterances* and of words composing utterances. In contemporary analytic philosophy, however, and precisely because what is *being done* with the words is typically taken to be separable from, and to presuppose, their sense, or truth-evaluable content, the tendency has been to talk not of utterances, but of "sentences in contexts." The context, in turn, has typically been taken to be a sort of container that is specifiable by

---

[21] For a recent example, see Camp 2016: 115.

specifying a time, a geographical location, and "a world (actual or possible)"; and some would add "agent"—not "speaker"!—to the specification. "World," in this specification of context, is clearly meant to refer to an *objective* world (actual or possible)—a world about which empirical science is (or would be) authoritative.[22] Plug a (context-sensitive) sentence into the container, the representationalist thought goes, and you'll get a determinate sense (and truth-value).

This representationalist way of thinking has run into difficulties whenever it was recognized that the speaker's *intention*, or what her intention is most reasonably taken to be, is at least sometimes needed in order to fix the sense of certain context-sensitive terms—Kaplanian "true demonstratives" ("this," "that"), for one, but also Kaplanian "pure indexicals" such as "here" or "now," and many other words as well. I will ultimately suggest that what the speaker's intentions are most reasonably taken to be is *always* essential to the proper understanding of what she is saying with her words. But in order to see this, we would need to move away from a Gricean understanding of "intention" ("speaker meaning") as referring to an inner representation that is essentially separable from its outer expression. We would need to understand intentions as *embodied* in, and *inseparable* from, their (linguistic or other) expression.

In Chapter Five we will see Merleau-Ponty criticizing empiricist and rationalist theorists of language for giving no significant role in their accounts to *speakers*—that is, to human beings who, finding themselves in some humanly significant situation or another, are moved to speak, to position themselves significantly by means of words and thereby contribute to the (re)shaping of their situation. In light of what I have just said, I think the same complaint could with equal justice be made about many contemporary semantic theorists, contextualist and anti-contextualist ("invariantists") alike.[23] Thus, for example, in presenting the contextualist position (with which he ultimately disagrees),

---

[22] As contrasted with what phenomenologists have called "the phenomenal world"—the world *as perceived and experienced* by us, and which may be (found to be) more or less shared with others. I will come back to this important distinction in the Appendix.

[23] As Lance and Kukla note, "philosophers of language never deny that language is communicative, in that we *use* it in order to have effects on particular other people, through our interactions with them. However, according to traditional, impersonalist pictures of language, this function is strictly speaking external to the linguistic act itself. On such a picture, bits of discourse have their identities independent from their use in conversation . . ." (Lance and Kukla 2009: 171).

Hawthorne writes that "a sentence can be true at a context even if it is not asserted at [that] context" (Hawthorne 2004: 83).

Since I really do not know what it could possibly mean for a sentence to *be at* a context when nobody *uses* it (even if only for formulating a thought one keeps to oneself), and since I will ultimately question the idea that words may have a determinate sense apart from being put to some particular *use* (in a context suitable for that use), I will continue to talk about *utterances*—that is, about words *in use*. In recognizing the role of context in fixing the sense of an utterance, contemporary contextualism has made an important step toward the recognition that the sense of words depends on their being *put to some particular use or another* (in a context suitable for *that* use), which in turn may lead us to recognize the *variety* of uses—some truth-assessable, some not—to which we may put our words. But, as we have seen, contextualists have tended to overlook, or seriously downplay, this important implication of their position.

Setting that issue aside for now, what is it exactly that is taken to combine with the meaning of a (context-sensitive) sentence in order to endow it with a determinate sense? One problem is that if "context" is supposed to refer to an objectively existing, container-like entity that is fully specified by specifying a time, a geographical location, a world, and maybe also an agent, then it seems clear that the context of an utterance includes countlessly many features, as David Lewis has noted (Lewis 1980: 85), and that most of those features would play no role whatsoever in fixing the sense of the uttered words—as the current weather conditions in New Zealand play no role in fixing the sense of what I have just written (but may well play a role in fixing the sense of many other utterances). Even more importantly, the notion of "context" thus understood is of very limited use to us when we wish to *understand* the way in which contextual features interact with whatever the words carry with them from one context of use to another to generate the sense of an utterance.

Alternatively, then, we could use "context of an utterance" to refer to what is, or could be found, *relevant* for a proper understanding (and the alleviation of misunderstandings) of the utterance. This, unsurprisingly, is how empirical scientists studying language use and comprehension have tended to use "context,"[24] and this is how I will come to use that

---

[24] See, for example, Giora 2003: 53 and 63. As far as I know, only philosophers have found (*intra*disciplinary) use for "context" understood in terms of world, geographical location, and time.

term; and the first thing to note about "context" *thus* understood is that *it is itself a context-sensitive term*: there is no context-insensitive final and complete list of all that is or could be found relevant for the proper understanding (and for the alleviation of all possible misunderstandings) of some given utterance. The context of an utterance is therefore better understood, not as something that is objectively there, independently from the utterance and how it is understood, but rather as *the correlate of an understanding*—whether one found proper, or not—of the utterance. A particular understanding and *its* context come into view (or not) *together*:[25] come to understand an utterance differently, and you will come to see differently its context. (This should begin to indicate why I find problematic the tendency to think of the context of an utterance in objectivist terms.) This does *not* mean that we can understand any given utterance however we want, or choose. We are no more able to do *that* than we are able to perceive a given situation however we want, or choose. But it *does* matter that we do normally have the power to perceive things, and therefore also to understand a given utterance, in more than one way.[26]

Failure to appreciate the context-sensitivity of "someone's (or an utterance's) context" renders various theoretical uses of the notion problematic, or even ultimately unintelligible. Consider, for example, "subject-sensitive invariantist" accounts of knowledge such as those offered by Fantl and McGrath 2002, Hawthorne 2004, and Stanley 2005. On those accounts, whether some particular person knows some particular proposition that is true and taken by that person to be true, depends not just on "her evidence" but also on whether that evidence is "good enough for knowing" (Fantl and McGrath 2002: 67) in *her* context. This account of knowledge is meant as an alternative to contextualist accounts of "know" and cognates, on which whether someone correctly counts as knowing a proposition that is true and taken by that person to be true depends not just on her evidence and circumstances but also on the context in which *the counting* takes place.

---

[25] This is how Sperber and Wilson 1986/1995 have proposed that we think about the relation between the understanding of an utterance and the context of that understanding.

[26] I'll say a little more about perceptual indeterminacy in the Appendix. I discuss that issue in detail in Baz (forthcoming).

By "a person's context" the subject-sensitive invariantist clearly means something more specific than what is specified when just a world, a time, a place, and an agent are specified. It may include, for example, the subject's practical interests and what is at stake for her in p being, or not being, the case. But for the subject-sensitive invariantist too, "context" is supposed to refer to something like a container that is objectively there, uniquely attached to an individual or a group of individuals at a time. Plug a person's evidence, beliefs, and so on, into that container and, on the subject-sensitive invariantist account, you'll get either her knowing that p—for any given p—or her not knowing it.

But how are we to determine what a person's context is at some particular time? Here *internal* problems arise for those who wish to think about context as an objectively existing, unique container that is attached to a person (or a group of people) at a time. To see this, consider one of the cases presented by Stanley in his argument for subject-sensitive invariantism. The case is a variation on DeRose's much discussed "Bank" example (DeRose 1992). Hannah and her wife Sarah are driving home on a Friday afternoon with paychecks that they would like to deposit. It is very important (for them) that they deposit the checks before Monday. The lines at the bank are long and the couple deliberates about whether they should go home and come back the next morning. They worry, however, that the bank might not be open on Saturdays. (As is the custom in such discussions, Stanley assures us, his readers, that the bank *will be* open on Saturday, and thereby puts us in an epistemic position that earthly agents rarely if ever occupy in relation to future contingencies.) Hannah then calls up Bill on her cell phone and asks him whether the bank will be open on Saturday. Bill replies, "Well, I was there two weeks ago on a Saturday and it was open." But after reporting the discussion to Sarah, Hannah "concludes that, since banks do occasionally change their hours, 'Bill doesn't really know that the bank will be open on Saturday'." They decide to get in line and deposit the checks then (Stanley 2005: 5).

Now I should note, and have argued at some length in Baz (2012a), that Stanley's case, like so many other cases that have featured in the debates between contextualists and anti-contextualists (of various stripes), is an example of nothing real. It is hard to imagine two real people in similar circumstances behaving quite like Hannah and Sarah, and hard not because people do not, as a matter of empirical fact, behave that way, but rather because anyone who behaved that way under the circumstances Stanley describes would be very hard to make sense of.[27] In particular, it is *very* hard to make sense of Hannah's final utterance in Stanley's story—to see how she means, or is supposed to mean, the words Stanley put in her mouth. I mean, it is easy enough to form a fairly good idea of what she is, or could be, *trying* to say, given the rest of Stanley's story;[28] the difficulty is to see why she chose *those* words ("Bill doesn't really know that...") to say it. And the answer, I'm afraid, is that she is Stanley's protagonist, and says what he needs her to say given his theoretical goals. I have already remarked, in my discussion of Hawthorne's "lottery puzzle" in Chapter One, on the tendency among contemporary analytic philosophers to rely in their arguments on imaginary stretches of human discourse that are quite unnatural and sometimes truly unintelligible. This tendency is not unrelated to the overall argument of this book; but I will here set it aside and focus on Stanley's problematic understanding, and use, of "context."

On Stanley's subject-sensitive invariantist account, Sarah and Hannah are in a "high-stakes" context, so the (presumed) fact that Bill was at the bank two weeks earlier on a Saturday and it was open then is not enough, in *their* context, for *knowing* that the bank will be open the following day. Bill, on the other hand, is in a "low-stakes" context, so the fact that he was at the bank two weeks earlier on a Saturday and found it open *is* enough, in *his* context, for knowing that the bank will be open the following day. So, on Stanley's account, when Hannah says "Bill doesn't

---

[27] Why did Hannah decide to call Bill, rather than call the bank, or stop the car and quickly inquire inside? What sort of an assurance did she think he would be able to provide her? He told her the bank was open on Saturday two weeks earlier. She is worried that it has changed its hours since then. Was there anything he could have told her that would have eliminated the possibility that the bank has changed its hours since then, or since the last time he checked? Perhaps with enough ingenuity one could imagine the situation in a way that would allow for plausible answers to these questions; but my prediction is that one would thereby only push the lump in the rug of Stanley's story elsewhere.

[28] Roughly, I suppose, "Bill says he was there two weeks ago on a Saturday and it was open. But I don't know... Banks sometimes change their hours. (Sigh.) Let's not take a chance and get in line." There is no reason for Hannah to say anything about Bill's *knowing*, or not *knowing*, that the bank will be open the next day. The question for her and Sarah is what they should do next, or what would be most reasonable for them to do, given what they've just learned from Bill. And *this* is a question that—unlike the theorist's question of whether (it would be true to say) Bill *knows* that the bank will be open tomorrow—normally allows for faultless disagreements (within reason, of course).

really know ... " she is saying something false, but understandable: What she really wants, and ought, to say is that Bill's evidence is not good enough for knowing that the bank will be open on Saturday for someone in *her* (and Sarah's) context; that the evidence is good enough for *him* to know that the bank will be open on Saturday, given *his* context, is not what concerns her at the moment, and this leads her to speak falsely (Stanley 2005: 102).

But now, why isn't the fact that a great deal hangs for two of his friends on whether the bank will be open the next day part of *Bill's* context, especially given that those friends have decided to call him for help? Shouldn't it be? Stanley's way of determining the different contexts in this case is either extremely, and I would even say troublingly, individu- alistic, or else guided by nothing more than a picture of contexts as spheres surrounding individuals (or groups of individuals), and fitting quite tightly. The problem, however, is that once we allow that Bill's context may be partly constituted by other people's projects, concerns, needs, and so on, it is not clear why it should not also include his and other people's *possible*—and why not even *counterfactual?*—projects, concerns, needs, and so on. In short, it is unclear, at the end of the day, how to tell what belongs and what does not belong to a person's context- understood-as-an-individually-assignable-and-objectively-existing unique container, if at the same time we wish the invocation of context to be *illuminating* in a way that talk about "world, time, and location" is not.

This problem *never* arises in the ordinary and normal use of "so and so's context," and for the simple reason that this expression—just like "the context of an utterance"—is itself context-sensitive. Normally, when we speak of "so and so's context (or situation, or circumstances)," what we mean or refer to—how that expression as we use it is to be (properly) understood—depends on the context (situation, circumstances) in which we use it.[29] The ordinary use of "context" (and similar expressions) therefore does *not* commit us to the idea that there is, for every person at a particular moment in time, *the* context she is in at that moment.

---

[29] One thing this means is that, thought through, subject-sensitive invariantism boils down to (some version of) the contextualism for which it was meant to be an alternative. If a person's knowledge depends on her context, but what is meant by "her context"—what it refers to—depends on the context in which *it* is used, then "a person's knowledge" is itself context-dependent in what *it* means, or refers to.

It therefore does not entangle us in the hopeless project of trying to determine that context, or to decide theoretically and context-insensitively what should, and what should not, count as belonging to it.

Coming back to contemporary contextualism, since it is agreed on all sides that contexts-understood-as-all-encompassing-containers include much that is irrelevant to the proper understanding, or determination of sense, of utterances made in them, the real challenge, for the semantic theorist, is to give a satisfying account of how what *is* relevant for the proper understanding of an utterance gets determined, and how it contributes to the determination of sense.

Among semantic theorists, there are the optimists who take it that what needs to be combined with the uttered words, or with their mean-ing, in order to endow them with a determinate sense may fully be specified by specifying a relatively short list of parameters or, as Lewis calls them, "coordinates" (Lewis 1980: 86).[30] *Which* parameters need to be specified is supposed to be fixed straightforwardly by, or be "encoded" in, the meaning(s) of the expression(s) in question.[31] Thus, for example, the relevant context of "I am here"—that is, what is supposed to combine with the meanings of the context-sensitive components of the sentence to generate sense, or truth-evaluable "content"—may be fully specified, on the optimist's view, by specifying the speaker, the geographical location, and the time of utterance. In the case of other kinds of sen-tences, the list of parameters would be somewhat different: for example, a variable would need to be added for the object or person gestured toward ("demonstrated") in the case of demonstratives, or for the person addressed in the case of second-person pronouns, and so on. But in all cases, the list is taken to be relatively short, and to be a function of the meanings (Kaplanian "characters") of the expressions making up the sentence in question: if you know the meaning of a word, then, on this way of thinking, you know, *in advance*, which contextual elements are going to affect its sense on an occasion of its use, and how.

From the perspective of contemporary semantic contextualism as championed by Travis—and this much it shares with the conception of language that will be presented and motivated in subsequent chapters—the optimistic position described above is misguided. It proposes recipes

---

[30]   A major source of inspiration for this way of thinking has been Kaplan 1989.

[31]   This brand of optimism may be found in Stanley (2000).

where no recipes—as contrasted with more or less heuristically useful generalizations based on current (normal) practices—may be had.[32]

Take "I am here," as uttered by a person speaking on her cell phone at an airport, for example. On the Kaplanian understanding, her "I" refers to her, her "here" refers to her geographical location (however precisely specified), and the "am" indicates that she is talking about the present moment. On this understanding, the speaker is saying of herself that she is, at the time of utterance, where she is. Thus, the Kaplanian content of her utterance—or for that matter of any other "serious and literal" utterance of "I am here"—is trivially true, and uninformative.

But of course, if an utterance of "I am here" is competent, or truly intelligible, it may well be informative to its audience; and it may also have an *expressive*, non-*informative* sense. For example, it may (be meant to) inform its audience that the speaker has arrived at the airport.[33] In *that* case, the "here" would mean "at the airport" (where exactly at the airport would presumably not matter, and would not be part of what she means, and says). But if that same speaker, at that same location, were to call out across the crowded hall "I am here" to a friend who has been looking for her, her "here" would not mean "at the airport," but would rather mean something like "at *this* end of the hall," or perhaps "where you'd need to look in order to see me." And if that same person, at that same location, were to call out "I am here" to someone who has been anxiously waiting for her and is looking at her running through the door, then her "here" could perhaps mean something like "at the gate, with you." I do not take my paraphrases of "here" in these examples to be very precise; and ultimately I will suggest that what individual words mean— the contribution they make to the sense of whole utterances—is inseparable from the sense of the utterance taken as a whole; and it is *this* that competent paraphrases need to capture, or make the audience see. My paraphrases here were only meant to bring out the way in which what the

---

[32] As Camp has recently put it, against the traditional tendency on the part of both philosophers and linguists to "[assume] a model of language closely allied to formal logic, on which arbitrary symbols are assigned stable individual values and combined into larger units by determinate rules, and contextual variation is minimal and highly regimented" (Camp 2016: 113), the contextualist has denied the existence of "straightforward rule[s]" that could lead us from some given pair of uttered sentence and context to a proper understanding of the utterance, and has insisted that "the effect of context is messy and ad hoc" (Camp 2016: 115).

[33] This example is inspired by Travis (1989).

optimist understands by "context" is insufficient for fixing the sense of an utterance of "I am here."

And those were relatively simple examples. I once attended a wedding in which the father of the bride, who had just recovered from a life-threatening illness, opened his speech by saying "I am very happy to be here." Everyone who knew his story knew that by "here" he did not mean "at this geographical location." And if the person on the phone, at the airport, utters her "I am here" with the aim of reassuring the other person that she is listening, perhaps after having been distracted by some noise or thought, and perhaps in response to her friend's asking "Are you there?" then what her "I" means—what contribution it makes to the overall sense of her utterance—is different from what it means in any of the other examples we've considered. Knowledge of all that one would need to know on the Kaplanian theory in order to understand an utterance of "I am here" would not suffice for understanding or making sense of her utterance—or, for that matter, for assessing its truth.

What *would* someone need to know or be familiar with in order to understand her utterance? Initially we could say that one would need to know much more than the optimist would have us suppose. Putting together and somewhat paraphrasing two of Wittgenstein's remarks (PI: 19 and 199), we could add: to understand a sentence means to understand a language, and to understand a language means to understand a form of life. But of course, within, or against the background of, any given form of life—whatever *exactly* we take Wittgenstein to mean by "form of life"—there will be different possible senses or proper understandings for any given sentence. Anyone who maintains that those senses are partly affected by context, and that different contexts would endow the same string of uttered words with different senses, had therefore better not identify context with anything as broad and general as what "a form of life" is meant to gesture at.[34] (Here it matters that in PI 199 Wittgenstein talks about the understanding of a *sentence* [*Satz*], not of a particular *utterance*.)

The truth in the above paraphrasing of Wittgenstein is that what *could* turn out to be relevant to an understanding of an utterance—and hence what could properly count as part of its context—may be a general "fact

---

[34] Compare Searle's distinction between "the context of utterance" and what he calls "background assumptions" (Searle 1978: 221).

of nature" such as the fact that people sometimes get distracted during a conversation and fail to pay attention, or a general fact of culture such as the fact that people sometimes call upon other people to be attentive, or a fact of linguistic usage such as the fact that talk of "where someone is" may concern where they are "in their thought" (which often is *not* a *geographical* location), and, at other times, whether that person is dead or alive. As Sperber and Wilson (1986/1995) have urged, we cannot know *in advance* where and how far we would need to go in order to explicate an utterance. That the speaker has recovered from a life-threatening illness, for example, may, but also may not, be relevant for a proper understanding of her utterance of "I am happy to be here"—and specifically for what her "here" means—and in this sense be part of its context.

So what determines what's relevant to an understanding of some particular utterance? The philosopher who is less optimistic but still committed to the traditional project of semantic theorizing would insist that though coming up with the full list of all of the parameters of contextual features that may contribute to the determination of the sense of any given uttered sentence would typically be very hard, or even practically impossible, such a list may *in principle* be had. In other words, this philosopher acknowledges that coming up with a complete *recipe* for finding the sense of some given uttered sentence may be very hard, or even practically impossible, but insists that such a recipe may *in principle* be had. This seems to be the position Lewis ultimately came to hold. Continuing to believe that it should *in principle* be possible for us to come up with "a systematic restatement of our common knowledge about our practices of linguistic communication [that would] assign semantic values that *determine* which sentences are true in which contexts" (Lewis 1980: 79, my emphasis), he came to acknowledge that "we are unlikely to think of all of the features of context on which truth sometimes depends" (Lewis 1980: 79), and that "it would be no easy matter to devise a list of all of the features of context that are sometimes relevant to truth-in-English" (Lewis 1980: 87).

For reasons that will become clearer in Chapters Five and Six, I take even Lewis's dampened optimism—or, if you will, positivistic pessimism—to be unwarranted. Following Wittgenstein and Merleau-Ponty, I will propose that there are no *foundational*, or *constitutive*, principles or rules in the realm of sense, and linguistic understanding therefore cannot, ultimately, aptly be thought of on the model of a recipe, or a machine that "when fed an arbitrary utterance (and certain parameters provided by the circumstances of the utterance), produces an interpretation" (Davidson 2006: 256). As I will propose following Wittgenstein and Merleau-Ponty, it is of the essence of natural language that what words bring with them from one occasion of use to another—call it "their meaning"—leaves open the possibility of more or less creative and yet mutually intelligible expansions of their use; and each intelligible use, as I have suggested, is internally related to the context in which it may be found intelligible—the sense of an utterance and the context in which it may be found to have that sense come into view (or not) together. However far one may go in feeding Davidson's machine with "parameters provided by the circumstances of the utterance," there will always be different ways of interpreting *that*, which means that human *judgment* plays an ineliminable and irreducible role in the determination of sense; and, as Kant has pointed out, there can be no foundational rules of judgment (Kant 1998: A132/B171-3). As I will suggest in Chapter Five, following Merleau-Ponty, Davidson's "understanding machine" would only seem an apt model of linguistic understanding as long as we focus on what Merleau-Ponty calls "sedimented," or habituated speech—as opposed to "originary," or more or less *creative* speech; but, at the end of the day, what makes (what) sense, and under what conditions, is up to competent speakers of the language to *find*, not *calculate* or *compute*. This, I take it, is what Wittgenstein was getting at when he wrote: "I must *begin* with the distinction between sense and nonsense. Nothing is possible prior to that. I can't give it a foundation" (Wittgenstein 1978: part I, section 6: 81). It's also what Kant was getting at, in his third *Critique*, when he argued that our ability to communicate empirical, objective judgments to each other ultimately rests on nothing more (nor less) than a "*sensus communis*" that comes to the fore in aesthetic judgments (Kant 2000: sections 20-2 and 38-40)—an idea that he saw as just the upshot of the "regress on rules (or judgments)" argument from the first *Critique* (Kant 1998: A132/B171-3; see also Kant 2000: 169).[35]

The semantic theorist could still formulate more or less illuminating or useful *generalizations* that capture, more or less accurately, *current*

---

[35] I discuss this point of affinity between Kant and Wittgenstein (as well as some crucial differences) in Baz (2016b).

normal practices (and related "intuitions").[36] Those generalizations *might* have some heuristic value; but they do not have the foundational status the semantic theorizer tends to assume for them. This understanding of what semantic theorizers could reasonably hope to provide would no doubt be unsatisfying to those committed to a *computational* view of linguistic sense and understanding. But if it should turn out that the theoretical demand for a computational, recipe-like transition from what words carry with them from one utterance to another to how they are to be understood in some particular utterance leads to a distorted view of that very transition, the dissatisfaction might be easier to overcome.

4.4 Contextualism and the Non-Representational Relation of Speakers to their World

I can now turn to say why contemporary contextualism poses a deeper challenge to the representationalist conception of language than is typically recognized, even by its proponents. To begin to see this, consider that if we choose to continue to talk about context-sensitive terms as having a reference, that reference cannot plausibly be thought of as an item, or set of items, that may be identified independently of our use of the term, and to which the term—as such, and irrespective of how it is used—refers. If the contextualist with respect to "know" (for example) is right, we cannot identify instances of *knowledge*—thought of as existing in the world independently of our employment of "know" and its cognates—and study those instances directly; for there are no such things to identify and study. With perhaps very few exceptions—and even if we allow, for the sake of argument, that one could identify *facts* context-independently—no relation between a potential knower and an empirical fact, taken by itself and context-independently, constitutes knowledge *simpliciter*, or may truly be said to be, context-insensitively, "a case of knowledge."[37] We can therefore only study what *we* (may properly)

---

[36] My Austinian reminders in section 4.2 should also be seen as an invitation to look differently, non-representationally, at (a portion of) current normal practice.

[37] Travis allows that "I know I exist" may be true in any context in which it is uttered (Travis 1989: 146). But, to the extent that it expresses anything clear, I'm not sure that "I exist," as used by Descartes, for example, is aptly understood to be expressing an empirical fact.

count, in some particular context or set of contexts, as a case of know-ledge. In this way, contemporary contextualism constitutes the latest affirmation of Kant's warning against the idea that our concepts may apply to the world "as it is in itself"—that is, as it is apart from our practices of applying our concepts to it, and apart from the ("transcen-dental") conditions of those practices.

With context-sensitivity, the difference between studying knowledge—thought of as an independently existing worldly item or type of item—and studying our concept of knowledge as it reveals itself in our use of "know" and its cognates, becomes the difference between studying a fantasy and studying something real. But it is not as if contextualism simply vindicates Jackson's idea that philosophy should aim at the elucidation of concepts as Jackson conceives of them. For if "x" is context-sensitive in the contextualist sense, and we think—plausibly, and together with Jackson, Williamson, and many others—of the con-cept of X as the meaning of "x," or as whatever it is that ultimately guides us in our application of "x" to cases, then our concept of X is importantly different from what Jackson (together with many others) takes it to be, and can no longer be thought of purely representationally. And this points in the direction of a truly radical break with the traditional way of thinking, not just about language, but about our relation to our world more broadly.

To begin to see this, ask yourself: Could we sensibly hold on to Jackson's idea that learning the meaning of a word, or "acquiring a word," is essentially a matter of coming to recognize a particular worldly "pattern" and to "use the word for it," while at the same time taking the word in question to be context-dependent in the contextualist's sense? It might seem that we could, if only we let what we call "the pattern" include the contextual factors that—on our favorite contextualist account—affect the contribution the word in question makes to the overall sense of utterances in which it features (where "sense" is still primarily understood in terms of "truth-conditions"). Thus, for example, suppose we accept a "relevant alternatives" contextualist account, on which "know(s)" truly applies to some pair of a true proposition and a potential knower who believes that proposition, just in case the potential knower (or her "experience," or her "evidence") has ruled out ("elimin-ated," "discharged") all *relevant* alternatives to that proposition—where what alternatives are relevant depends on the context of application. And let's set aside all of the serious difficulties, noted in section 4.2, that arise when we try to think this account through from within the perspective of the representationalist conception of language. Then it would seem that we could hold on to Jackson's basic account of how children acquire the word "knowledge" simply by letting the pattern they must learn to recognize include a variable that ranges over all of the alternatives to p that are—or that properly count as—relevant in the context of application, and the requirement that all of *those* alternatives be properly eliminated by the potential knower (or by her "evidence," or "experience"), if she is to count as knowing that p. And so it would seem that the contextualist position could fairly easily be reconciled with Jackson's basic story, or picture, of how children come to master words such as "knowledge."

This proposed reconciliation misses the full significance of contextualism vis-à-vis the representationalist conception of language, however. Once we expand the intended reference of Jackson's "pattern" to include contextual features, or types of features, that affect the contribution some word "x" makes to the overall sense of utterances in which it features, it becomes misleading to say that we use "x" *for* that pattern, or that we use "x" to refer to or represent that pattern. For the intended pattern now includes contextual features that affect what "x" refers to, or how it is to be understood, on some occasion of its employment; and *those* features may not themselves plausibly be thought of as *part* of what "x" refers to, or as represented by "x," on that occasion.[38]

What I'm trying to bring out is that, on the contextualist view, our words—and so *we*, as their (competent) employers—are beholden not only to the world we use them to speak *about*, but also to the world *in* which we use them. And this means that even if we *sometimes* relate to our world in ways that may aptly be thought of in representational terms—which seems undeniable, if only in the trivial sense that it *sometimes* makes sense to ask questions such as "What (or who) are

---

[38] Compare Searle: "representation, whether linguistic or otherwise, goes on against a background of assumptions which are not and in most cases could not also be completely represented as part of or as presuppositions of the representation" (Searle 1978: 219).

you referring to, or talking about, and what are you saying about it?"—our basic relation to the world qua speakers (and thinkers, and rational agents) may not aptly be thought of in those terms. For even in representing things to ourselves or to others, we are necessarily beholden and responsive—on pain of incompetence and incomprehensibility—to a worldly background that is not itself, there and then, *represented* by us or spoken *about*. Our relation to that background is rationally assessable, but not in terms of truth and falsity—or anyway not in terms of truth and falsity as those terms are understood by the representationalist. This, it seems to me, is one of the deepest and underappreciated lessons of Austin's *How to Do Things with Words*.[39]

In this way, contemporary contextualism, thought through, points in the direction of the phenomenological work of Heidegger and Merleau-Ponty, for whom our relation to our world is not to be understood first and foremost in representational terms. "The world," Merleau-Ponty writes in the Preface to the *Phenomenology of Perception*, "is not what I think, but what I live through" (Merleau-Ponty 1996 (hereafter "Phenomenology"): xvi–xvii). And later on he writes, "The Kantian subject posits a world, but, in order to be able to assert a truth, the actual subject must in the first place have a world, that is, sustain round about it a system of meanings whose reciprocities, relationships, and involvements do not require to be made explicit in order to be exploited" (Phenomenology: 129; see also Husserl 1970: 118). But of course, he could equally have said this about *any* utterance, or thought—whether "world positing" or not, whether truth-evaluable or not. And this means that, on his understanding, the relation between our words and our world is not *essentially*, let alone *necessarily*, representational, or assessable in terms of truth and falsity. For our words not to be "frictionlessly spinning in the void," as John McDowell puts it (cf. McDowell 1994: 11), they need not *represent* anything truly or else falsely—their justification (or lack thereof) need not take *that* form. Nor, therefore, should we think of what philosophers have called "judgment" as the fundamental relation between speakers (and thinkers) and their world; not every time that the world draws out or solicits from us a linguistic response that may under the circumstances be found apt (competent, intelligible, reasonable,

---

[39] I discuss this Austinian lesson and its bearing on Cartesian skepticism about the (so-called) "external world" in Baz (2014).

acceptable...), or not, are we aptly described as having judged, or as giving voice to a judgment.[40]

An important task of the following chapters will be to develop and motivate a conception of language that preserves this basic, even if mostly just implicit, contextualist insight, while moving beyond the representationalism of contemporary contextualism.[41] On the alternative conception, the contribution a word makes to the overall sense of an utterance is affected by the utterance's context, just as contextualists have argued, but that contribution need not be thought of solely, or even primarily, in terms of an item or set of items to which it "refers," or may truly "apply"; and the sense of an utterance need not be thought of solely, or even primarily, in terms of truth-conditions. By the light of the alternative conception of language, if we still wish to speak of a "pattern" that children need to learn to pick out and follow, in order to become competent users of (for example) "know" (and its cognates) and possessors of our concept of knowledge, that pattern may no longer be thought of as some general pattern in which *knowledge* presumably consists and to which "know" and its cognates presumably refer—not even context-dependently. Rather, as I will propose in Chapter Six, it would need to be thought of as a pattern, and more precisely several different and variously related patterns, of *usage* of constructions featuring these words, together with the ordinary and normal worldly conditions for, and the ordinary and normal significance(s) of, each pattern of usage. And the basic problem with the philosophical method of cases, even after the contextualist has added to it his "semantic ascent," is not just that it is

---

[40] Here I mean to allude to Travis's (2013) critique of representationalist accounts of perception such as McDowell's. While denying that perceptual experience provides us with truth-assessable representations, Travis still takes McDowell's representationalist question—"How can perceptual experience make the world bear (rationally) *for the perceiver* on what he is to think and do?"—to be "the fundamental question of perception" (Travis 2013: 3). I do not deny that Travis's question is interesting and important. But in calling it *"the fundamental* question of perception," Travis seems to me to betray a misguided adherence to the overly intellectualist tradition of Western philosophy—a tradition that his semantic contextualism actually points us away from.

[41] Michael Williams (2004) has also suggested, for reasons different from (but compatible with) mine, that contextualism should see itself as an ally to the non-representationalism of what Williams calls "neo-pragmatism," and that Travis's residual commitment to representationalism prevents him (Travis) from fully appreciating the non-representationalist upshot of his own position.

unfit for revealing and clarifying patterns of usage and their worldly conditions and significances, but that, in sending us in search of *the* pattern in which *knowledge* (for example) consists and to which "know" and its cognates refer, it actually leads us to misconstrue or else overlook those patterns altogether.

5

The Alternative Conception of Language

The philosophical method of cases, as commonly practiced, presupposes what I have called "the minimal assumption." Those who practice the method manifest commitment to the assumption. Those who have recently tried to defend the method, as well as those who have expressed skepticism about it, have also shown themselves committed to the assumption. To be committed to the assumption is to be committed, in effect, to some conception of language or another on which that assumption is true—a conception, that is, on which the theorist's words and case suffice for ensuring that his question has clear (enough) sense and a correct answer, and on which, as competent speakers, we ought at the very least to understand the question and be able to answer it correctly. As we've seen, recent defenders of the method have made their commitment to some such conception of language more or less explicit.

In taking the meanings of words to be, first and foremost, a matter of what worldly "items" they refer to; in taking words to be, first and foremost, instruments for the categorization of such items and for the communication of such categorizations; and in taking it that the categorization effected or expressed by some combination of words may in principle be separated from what—in the Austinian sense—is being done with the words, or how they are (most reasonably taken to have been) *meant*; those recent defenders of the method of cases have placed themselves in the company not only of the vast majority of analytic philosophers,[1] but also of many in linguistics and cognitive science.[2]

---

[1] As Price puts it: "Representationalism can easily look obvious . . . and is deeply embedded in contemporary philosophical theory" (Price 2011: 11).

[2] Witness, for example, the fact that all of the papers collected in Margolis and Laurence 1999 equate concepts with the meanings of linguistic expressions and, with the exception of Jackendoff's contribution, take it that possessing a concept is a matter of being able to

The tendency, in philosophy and elsewhere, has been to take the meanings of individual words to determine, quite straightforwardly, the proper understanding of an utterance of some syntactically well-formed combination of them. Here, for example, is Paul Elbourne in a fairly recent book that is meant to introduce its readers to the academic field of semantics:

> Suppose you are interpreting an uttered sentence. In a series of extremely intricate processes that are largely subconscious, you access the sentence's words in your mental lexicon and find their meanings; you work out the intended sense of any ambiguous words it might contain; you work out the references of indexicals in the sentence; you work out the sentence's syntactic structure and resolve any structural ambiguities there may be; and *you combine the contents of the words in the compositional semantics* ... If implicit content is not mediated by means of covert indexicals (and thus covered by the second step mentioned above), you add some of this too. *Finally, you have worked out the content of the sentence, as uttered on that occasion.*   (Elbourne 2011: 131, my emphases)

Some such conception of language underwrites the adherence to the minimal assumption, I am proposing, and underwrites as well contemporary semantic theorizing. Elbourne does not so much as even consider that there could be another, and possibly better story to tell about how the meanings of words relate to what may be said by means of them, or to how they are to be understood on some occasion of their employment. He takes it to be obvious that figuring out the overall sense of an utterance is a matter of *first* figuring out the contribution that each of the uttered words makes to that sense—or the sense of each individual word—and *then* combining those separate contributions, or word-senses, to arrive at the sense of the utterance.[3]

---

classify worldly items. Similarly, Paul Elbourne equates concepts with the meanings of words (Elbourne 2011: 29), and asserts: "It seems beyond doubt that normal human beings are equipped with *concepts*. Concepts are mental representations that allow us to classify things we come across and access memorized information about them" (Elbourne 2011: 26). And witness also the live debate in contemporary linguistics about whether thinking is inherently and necessarily dependent on, and (therefore) shaped by, spoken language. For both parties in that debate, thinking is essentially a matter of categorizing items, and language is essentially used for marking, recording, and communicating categorizations. For a survey of the debate, see Gleitman and Papafragou 2005.

[3] It was suggested to me that this particular passage *could be* read non-representationally and so (by my lights) more charitably. This more charitable reading does not fit, however, with Elbourne's identification of word-meanings with concepts (Elbourne 2011: 29) and explication of concepts in terms of "classification of things we come across"

Given the predominance of the representationalist conception of language, it is understandable that defenders of the method of cases have felt no need to argue for it, even as they have more or less explicitly relied on it in their defense of the method. And yet, surely, as an empirical view—and what else could it be?—the representationalist conception of language *is* empirically challengeable. Why, then, has it been taken for granted by philosophers and scientists alike? Is it that empirical evidence has spoken so forcefully and unequivocally in its favor, so much so that it has somehow escaped the general fate of empirical theories of being underdetermined by the evidence?

The answer to this, I submit, is that the representationalist conception of language rests on no empirical evidence.[4] I'm sure many would find what I have just said outrageous, since it would appear that much work has already been done to support that conception; so let me emphasize that all of the empirical and theoretical work in linguistics and philosophy that has *presupposed* the representationalist conception of language is *no evidence for that conception*. As Jerome Bruner has observed, "research on *anything* will yield findings that mirror its procedures for observing or measuring" (Bruner 1990: 104). Empirical evidence for the representationalist conception of language could only have come from studies that recognize a viable alternative to that conception and are designed to test one conception *as against the other*. I am aware of no study of *such* sort that has generated evidence favoring the representationalist conception of language over the alternative I am about to present. In Chapter Six, I will argue that extant studies of first language acquisition have not generated any such evidence.

Resting on no empirical evidence, the representationalist conception of language rests instead on what Wittgenstein has aptly called "a picture." That picture is undeniably compelling and powerful. It encourages us to think that we already understand language, know its essence, *prior to any investigation, empirical or other*. The picture has

(Elbourne 2011: 26). In general, if you take the contribution some individual word makes to the overall sense of an utterance to be something one arrives at, and indeed must arrive at, *before* figuring out (or just seeing) that overall sense, then you are pretty much bound to think of that contribution, at least in the case of most words, as a matter of what the individual word refers to, or represents.

[4] There are influential a priori considerations (often masquerading as empirical) that have been adduced in its support. Those will be discussed in section 6.3 of Chapter Six.

therefore eclipsed other ways of looking at language, and has largely predetermined how we view and interpret the empirical evidence we have. In this way, it has led philosophers to adopt what François Recanati aptly describes as "a stipulating and question-begging stance on empirical matters" (Recanati 2004: 160).[5] Despite being empirically challengeable, the representationalist conception of language has thus been taken by many to have no viable alternative and to be, in this sense, true a priori. My task in what follows is to offer a viable alternative to the dominating conception—an alternative, moreover, on which the minimal assumption is false and the method of cases as commonly practiced is therefore fundamentally misguided.

I should immediately add that I am very far from being the first to question the representational-referential and atomistic-compositional conception of language. Others—both philosophers and scientists—have questioned it before me, and I will be drawing on some of that work in what follows. In questioning the assumption that the meanings of words alone may determine what is being said by means of them even apart from any particular context of significant use—as the theorist's words are supposed to ensure the clear (enough) sense of his question—the conception I will present has an affinity, as I have already noted, with contemporary semantic "contextualism." In questioning the assumption that the meanings of words—including philosophically troublesome words such as "know," "cause," and "mean"—is first and foremost a matter of their "referring" to independently existing worldly items (or patterns) and enabling us to categorize or classify those items, the conception I will present has an affinity with various "pragmatist" conceptions.[6] More so than contemporary "contextualists" and "pragmatists" have done, and following Wittgenstein and Merleau-Ponty, I will emphasize the synchronic and diachronic plasticity of language—the way in which what may be said with a word, or how it is to be understood, may always in principle be expanded creatively but at the same time naturally and comprehensibly, which means that the set of

---

[5] I should say that the same could be said about Recanati's adherence to a truth-conditional approach to linguistic meaning.

[6] As I've noted, I have found particularly congenial Huw Price's pragmatist questioning of the "mapping" picture of linguistic meaning, in Price 2011 and 2013. Another penetrating and systematically thought-out challenge to the representationalist conception of language is offered by Lance and Kukla 2009.

powers with which the history of a word's employment has endowed it and which makes it suitable for certain uses but not others—call it its "meaning"—is not fixed, but rather is best thought of as an open-ended, and never fully determinate potentiality.

While the different elements of the conception I am about to propose and motivate—especially the first and the second—are not new to analytic philosophy, they have rarely been thought of as forming a unity.[7] And for this reason, I think, the tendency has been to suppose that the representationalist conception, though it might still need to be tweaked here and there—for example, along the lines proposed by semantic contextualists—has no real, substantive alternative. This would explain why the representationalist conception has simply been presupposed in all of the recent debates concerning philosophical method. The aim of this chapter and the next one is to undermine this presupposition, by presenting and motivating, both philosophically and empirically, an alternative conception of language—a conception, as I have just said, on which the minimal assumption is false, and the method of cases as commonly practiced is therefore fundamentally misguided.

---

[7] Williams 2004 suggests that though pragmatists such as Davidson have tended not to emphasize the sort of context-sensitivity emphasized by contemporary contextualists, and contextualists such as Travis have tended to hold on to key elements of the representationalist—Williams calls it "neo-Cartesian"—conception of language, contextualism actually fits well with what he calls "neo-pragmatism." For the reasons discussed in section 4.3 of Chapter Four, I think Williams is right about this last point. As for Davidson, however, I think that if he had recognized the sort of context-sensitivity Travis has emphasized, he would have had to rethink his understanding of linguistic understanding as essentially a matter of translation or disquotation. For if, being a fully competent speaker of the language you speak, I'm not clear on what you mean *here* by, for example, "(being) green"—how your "(being) green" is to be understood *here*—it would do me no good to be told (or tell myself) that by "green" you mean green, or (if I am a native speaker of German) *grün*. Another interesting case here is Robert Brandom (1994, 2008), who may be described as offering a pragmatist foundation for the representational, or "assertoric," function of language—which, together with the majority of analytic philosophers, he takes to be both central and essential to anything else we do with words (cf. Brandom 2008: 41–2). Brandom proposes to cash out the "language-game of assertion" in terms of "commitments" and "entitlements"; but since *any* speech act may arguably be defined, or understood, in terms of the commitments it generates for the speaker and her audience, and of what entitles one to perform it—that is, what puts one in a position to *felicitously* perform it—his insistence on language having an *assertoric* "downtown" seems to me misguided. Lance and Kukla challenge the tendency of Brandom and most other analytic philosophers "of any stripe" to proceed "as though the most fundamental, important, and common thing we do with language is use it to make propositionally structured declarative assertions with truth-values" (Lance and Kukla 2009: 10).

The basic elements of the alternative conception may be found in both Wittgenstein's *Philosophical Investigations* and Merleau-Ponty's *Phenomenology of Perception*.

5.1 Wittgenstein and Merleau-Ponty's Vision of Language

Early on in Wittgenstein's *Philosophical Investigations*, words are compared to tools (*Werkzeuge*, work-things—things to do work with) (PI: 11, 14; see also Austin 1979: 181). This comparison, which serves a particular purpose or set of purposes in Wittgenstein's text, must not be taken to imply an instrumentalist view of language—a view that takes language, or its use, to be everywhere a means to the attainment of ends that are identifiable prior to, and independently from, their attainment. There are deep reasons, in both Wittgenstein's work and Merleau-Ponty's, for resisting an overly instrumentalist view of language. Words are, or anyway can be, world-creating, world-expanding, and world-transforming instruments, not merely instruments for getting by in a world that's already fully given.[8]

The comparison of words to instruments is nonetheless useful in that it opens up a new way of thinking about the meanings of words, and how those meanings relate to what may be done with the words. The meaning or significance of an instrument *in use* is a matter of what (work) is being done with it; the meaning or significance of an instrument apart from some particular use is a matter of what *may* be done with it—the work, or works, for which it is fit. In either case, the meaning of an instrument is not some object, or idea, or some set of objects or ideas, that is theoretically

---

[8] Keeping in mind that the world in which we find ourselves and in which our words and acts, as well as our interests and practical goals, have their sense is not the natural scientist's "universe," but rather a world of historically evolving and culturally shaped *meaningful* phenomena, or phenomena of *meaningfulness* (see Phenomenology: 71). As against an instrumentalist view of language, Merleau-Ponty wrote later in his life: "Expressive speech does not simply choose a sign for an already defined signification, as one goes to look for a hammer in order to drive a nail or for a claw to pull it out. It gropes around a significative intention which is not guided by any text and which is precisely in the process of writing the text" (Merleau-Ponty 1964: 46; see also Phenomenology: 196). And compare Wittgenstein's saying that "to invent a language could mean to invent an instrument for a particular purpose on the basis of the laws of nature (or consistently with them); but it also has the other sense, analogous to that in which we speak of the invention of a game" (PI: 492).

separable from the use of the instrument and for which the instrument stands. What we have here, as Merleau-Ponty puts it, is a new meaning of "meaning" (Phenomenology: 146);[9] for the meaning is here inseparable from its vehicle, or from what *has* it (see Phenomenology: 174).[10]

Interestingly, both Merleau-Ponty and Wittgenstein use the example of music, and the understanding of music, to illustrate and explicate this different meaning of "meaning" (cf. Phenomenology: 182–3; and PI: 527). Wittgenstein says that "understanding a sentence is much more akin to understanding a theme in music than one may think," in the sense that "understanding a sentence lies nearer than one thinks to what is ordinarily called understanding a musical theme" (PI: 527). In both cases, he goes on to suggest, our understanding of the piece of music or the sentence is inseparable from the object we understand—it is a way of taking (appreciating) and responding to *it*, rather than a grasping of something *else* of which the piece or sentence is merely expressive.

The immediate aim of Wittgenstein's proposal that we look at words as work-things is to shake the hold of what may be described as a flattened view of language, which leads us to overlook complexities in the functioning of our words, and to ignore potentially significant differences among the ways different words function, or even among the ways in which one and the same word may function in different contexts (see PI: 182).[11] According to the flattened view, or picture, our words—including philosophically troublesome words such as "know(ledge)," "mean(ing)," "understand(ing)," "see(ing)," and so on—name (refer to) objects (items) (see PI: 1), and this is supposed to make them suitable for the one

---

[9] I find this translation of the French better than Donald Landes' "a new sense of the word 'sense'." Here and elsewhere, Landes' choice to always translate the French "*sens*" by "sense" seems to me to result in a translation that does not capture well, or not as elegantly, Merleau-Ponty's intention, or intended point. For this reason mainly, I chose to use Colin Smith's translation of the *Phenomenology* throughout (while consulting the Landes translation).

[10] Wittgenstein also compares words to game-pieces (cf. PI: 31 and 108)—things to make moves with—and the comparison is reinforced by the central notion of "language-game". For a penetrating discussion of this comparison, see Gustafsson forthcoming. In the case of each of the two comparisons, one can find both illuminating similarities and illuminating differences. For simplicity's sake, I focus on the comparison to work-things, but it is important to note that the comparison to game pieces is also effective in weakening the hold of the representationalist conception of meaning.

[11] Price (2011, 2013) has insightfully proposed that Wittgenstein is calling us to recognize the "functional pluralism" of language.

function that is taken to be fundamental to language: namely, communicating information, or "conveying thoughts" (PI: 304).[12] The power of words to refer to items—call it "their meaning"—and the existence and identity of the items themselves, are taken not to depend on whether and how we use the words, on our *meaning* them in one way or another, in a context suitable for meaning them in *that* way. Thus, the conception of language that underwrites the common philosophical practice of theorizing on the basis of the "application" of words to cases is essentially the same conception that Wittgenstein identifies at the opening of the *Investigations* as lying at the root of at least very many traditional philosophical difficulties.

No doubt, there are various and complex reasons why Wittgenstein's questioning of the "Augustinian picture of language" has been ignored in the recent debates about philosophical method. One reason may be that it has rarely been explicitly recognized that something very much like the Augustinian picture of language underwrites the method of cases; and where *that* has been recognized, as in Jackson's case, the Augustinian picture has simply been taken for granted, Wittgenstein's questioning of it notwithstanding. Another reason why Wittgenstein's teaching is mostly ignored nowadays within mainstream analytic philosophy may well be a certain deference to empirical science—a deference, as we will see, that has tended not to show itself *in practice*—and the fact that Wittgenstein's philosophical work has presented itself as anything but scientific.[13] His teaching, he famously says, is not that of a theory (PI: 109). In this respect, Merleau-Ponty's *Phenomenology of Perception* may seem very different from Wittgenstein's *Philosophical Investigations*. Merleau-Ponty has no problem referring to the understanding he offers as a "theory" (cf. Phenomenology: 203); and in presenting and arguing for that understanding he is everywhere conversant with the behavioral-cognitive science of his time. The difference is arguably not as

---

[12] I think it is clear that the thoughts here are *Fregean* thoughts—that is, truth evaluable entities. And even if one immediately adds, following Geach (1960, 1965), that the thoughts need not be asserted or otherwise committed to, but may merely be "entertained," one would not thereby address Wittgenstein's concern.

[13] Which does not mean that it cannot inspire empirical theorizing and research. One important example of Wittgenstein-inspired empirical research of language acquisition and use is to be found in Eleanor Rosch's and Carolyn Mervis' work on prototypes (Rosch and Mervis 1975). It should be noted, though, that Rosch and Mervis' theory of prototypes still falls within the conception of language questioned in this book.

substantive as it appears, precisely because one of Merleau-Ponty's main goals is to show that the scientific way of thinking is inherently incapable of explaining, and in fact necessarily leads to distorted views of, human perception (cf. Phenomenology: 115ff.); and if taking science seriously means appreciating the power and appeal of its way of thinking, as well as its inherent limitations, then Wittgenstein is arguably taking science just as seriously as Merleau-Ponty does. Still, the *method* of the *Phenomenology* is undeniably different from that of the *Investigations*; and the argument of the former is, or anyway should be, harder to dismiss for those committed to the empirical study of language than the argument of the latter. In the Appendix I will further explore the differences between Wittgenstein's method(s), aims, and general approach and Merleau-Ponty's. For now, and for the main purposes of this book, those differences may be set aside.

In his discussion of language, as elsewhere in the *Phenomenology*, Merleau-Ponty positions his account by contrasting it with empiricist-mechanical theories, on the one hand, and rationalist or "intellectualist" theories, on the other hand. In the case of language, he argues, both kinds of theories in effect ignore the speaking subject—the person who, finding herself in some particular situation or other, may find herself moved, *motivated*, to speak (or think).[14] On both traditional ways of thinking about language, what is available at any moment for an individual to say or think has nothing essentially to do with *her*—her history, her cares and commitments, her style of thinking and relating to things, how she sees the situation, and so on; and what an individual *actually* says or thinks on some occasion is taken not to depend on what moved her, or may reasonably be found to have moved her, to say or think it.

---

[14] The notion of "motive" is very important to Merleau-Ponty's avoidance of both mechanistic and intellectualist approaches to the understanding of behavior in general and linguistic expression in particular (see Phenomenology: 48–50). On Merleau-Ponty's way of looking at things, our speech (and behavior more generally) is normally *motivated*, in the sense we that are not merely *caused* mechanically to speak, and in the sense that our behavior manifests an *understanding* of the phenomenal world to which we respond. At the same time, however, we do not normally *choose* to say something that is already somehow present to consciousness independently from whether we put it into words. We *find* what we think, or want to say, *in saying it* (see Phenomenology: 177–8). And this means that normally we do not choose, for a reason, to say what we say, since, until we say it, there is no determinate *it* for us to choose to say for a reason. I elaborate on this point, with special attention to its implications for the philosophy of action, in Baz, forthcoming.

This is very clear in the case of empiricist-mechanical theories of language, on whose understanding of language there is, in effect, "no speaker," but rather only "a flow of words set in motion independently of any intention to speak" (Phenomenology: 175). On that understanding, "[S]peech is not an action and does not show up the internal possibilities of the subject: man can speak as the electric lamp can become incandescent" (Phenomenology: 175).[15]

On the intellectualist picture, language is expressive of thoughts—understood in terms of the "categorization" of worldly items; and individual words are expressive of concepts—thought of as defining or constituting categories. Neither the thoughts nor the concepts are taken to depend on their linguistic expression for their identity as the particular thoughts, or concepts, they are. This means that on this understanding too speech itself—the act of positioning oneself significantly by means of words, in a world shared with others—is not essential to linguistic meaning, or to the "content" of what's said. Nor is whatever may be found to move an individual to position herself in some particular way by means of words taken to be essential to the determination of what she says.

This means that on both ways of thinking about language, the uttered word itself "has no meaning" (Phenomenology: 176):

In the first case [that of empiricist theories of language, AB] this is obvious since the word is not summoned up through the medium of any concept, and since the given stimuli or "states of mind" call it up in accordance with the laws of

---

[15] One is reminded here of contemporary "causal theories of meaning" such as Jerry Fodor's, according to which the connection between a word and the object (or set of objects) it refers to is, essentially, a matter of (a member of) the latter *causing* a "token" of a "mental representation," for which the word is merely the outward sign. This basic "causal" account has required amendments, in order to account for the connection between a tokened "symbol" (mental or linguistic) and the (type of) item to which it refers, when the latter is not perceptually present (see Fodor 1987 and 1999). Even with such amendments, though, the causal account of word-meaning contrasts sharply with Kurt Goldstein's phenomenological-existentialist diagnosis, which had major influence on Merleau-Ponty, of what's missing in the case of patients with a particular type of word-finding impairment:

The patient cannot find the words because *he cannot assume the attitude* in which they normally appear. Even then, if he is able to find the word which belongs to an object, these words have lost "meaning" as analysis has revealed... *The nature of naming is often misinterpreted because one does not differentiate between naming and simple association of a word with an object.* (Goldstein 1948: 61, my emphases)

neurological mechanics or those of association ... It is just the same when we duplicate denomination with a categorial operation [as the intellectualist would have it, AB]. The word is still bereft of any effectiveness of its own, this time because it is only the external sign of an internal recognition, which could take place without it, and to which it makes no contribution ... In the first case, we are on this side of the word as meaningful; in the second we are beyond it. In the first there is nobody to speak; in the second there is certainly a subject, but a thinking one, not a speaking one ... Thus we refute both intellectualism and empiricism by simply saying that *the word has a meaning.*   (Phenomenology: 176–7)

For Merleau-Ponty, the word itself has meaning; but only as an instrument or vehicle of human expression. The spoken word is a gesture, he says, and it "contains its meaning" in just the way that a non-linguistic gesture does (Phenomenology: 183). We learn the meaning of a word in much the same way that we learn the use, and significance, of a tool, he says: not by coming to see, or form, a mental representation that is theoretically separable from it and for which it stands, but rather "by seeing it used in the context of a certain situation" (Phenomenology: 403).

It is important to see that thinking of words as work-things, whose meaning is a matter of what is, or may be, done with them, under suitable conditions, leaves it perfectly open that some of them may aptly be said to name objects in the world and some of their uses may aptly be characterized as "representational" or "descriptive." One thing the comparison of words to work-things is meant to help us see, however, is that our words have uses that may neither aptly nor theoretically fruitfully be thought of as representational, and that they *need not* do anything aptly describable as "naming items in the world" in order to be fit for their different uses.

One significant difference between words and the sorts of work-things typically found in a toolbox is that what makes such a "work-thing"—a hammer, say—fit for certain uses, but not others, are its physical properties;[16] whereas what makes the word suitable for certain uses but not others—call it "its meaning"—is its history, or in other words "former acts of expression" (Phenomenology: 186). "Strictly speaking," Merleau-Ponty writes, here contrasting his view with that of the intellectualist, "there are no conventional signs, standing as the simple notation of a

---

[16] Which does not mean that its physical properties by themselves *determine* its significance, context-insensitively. Apart from contexts of certain actual or possible projects, and the broader background of a human world in which those projects have *their* significance, or sense, the hammer would not have the significance(s) it now has, or could have.

thought pure and clear in itself; there are only words into which the history of the whole language is compressed" (Phenomenology: 188).[17] "It is because it has been used in various contexts that the word gradually accumulates a significance which it is impossible to establish absolutely," he writes (Phenomenology: 388).[18]

Thus, the basic unit of linguistic sense or intelligibility, for Merleau-Ponty as for Wittgenstein, is not the isolated word or combination of words, but the speech act as performed by an individual human being within some particular context—"the total speech act in the total speech situation," as Austin puts it (Austin 1979: 148). Going against the grain of the representationalist and atomistic-compositional view of language— as captured, for example, in the above quotation from Elbourne— Merleau-Ponty writes:

> In order that I may understand the words of another person, it is clear that his vocabulary and syntax must be "already known" to me. But that does not mean that words do their work by arousing in me "representations" associated with them, and which in aggregate eventually reproduce in me the original "representation" of the speaker. What I communicate with primarily is not "representations" or thought, but a speaking subject, with a certain style of being and with the "world" at which he directs his aim.   (Phenomenology: 183)[19]

In taking not the individual word, nor the sentence-type, but the historically situated human utterance to be the basic unit of linguistic sense or intelligibility, wherein alone the meanings of individual words "stabilize" (Phenomenology: 389), Merleau-Ponty is following both Gestalt psychology and Kurt Goldstein's "organismic" view of language—a view that

---

[17] Compare Tomasello: "[W]hen a child learns the conventional use of linguistic symbols, what she is learning are the ways her forebears in the culture found it useful to share and manipulate the attention of others ... And because the people of a culture, as they move through historical time, evolve many and varied purposes for manipulating one another's attention (and because they need to do this in many different types of discourse situations), today's child is faced with a panoply of linguistic symbols and constructions that embody many different attentional construals of any given situation" (Tomasello 2003: 13).

[18] This way of looking at things has some affinity with the "meaning eliminativism" that Recanati considers (still from within a representationalist framework), in Recanati 2004: 146ff.

[19] "World" is in quotation marks in this passage to signal that it refers not merely, or even primarily, to the physical world, but to the phenomenal world—the world *as perceived and responded to prior to any theoretical reflection*. And the phenomenal world is "a world of meanings," as Merleau-Ponty puts it elsewhere (see Phenomenology: 193). I'll say more about this in the Appendix.

Goldstein contrasts with "atomistic" theories of language and which is itself greatly influenced by Gestalt psychology. Similarly to Merleau-Ponty, Goldstein (1948) argues against both mechanistic and intellectualist theories of language. In particular, he argues that neither of these approaches is adequate when it comes to understanding and treating aphasia. Neither approach, he claims, can enable us to see aright the variety and uniqueness of individual speech abnormalities; for whatever the underlying physiology taken in isolation might be, and whatever the individual's cognitive capacities taken in isolation might be, both the symptomatology of some individual's speech impairment and the effectiveness of some particular therapeutic intervention or course of therapy are going to depend on the personality of that individual—her existential "style," her way of looking at and responding to things—and on the particular circumstances in which she finds herself, at any given moment and over time.[20]

The primacy of the particular, historically situated speech act means that *languages*, in the sense of "constituted systems of vocabulary and syntax, empirically existing 'means of expression'," are best thought of as "the repository and residue of acts of *speech*" (Phenomenology: 196–7). And this suggests that the subject matter of contemporary semantic theories—call it, if you will, "conventional meaning"—while not exactly unreal, is at best an abstraction that has a derivative existence and does not play the foundational role semantic theorists have tended to assume for it.[21]

---

[20] I'm not an expert, but as far as I know, Goldstein was just right about this.

[21] Giora's "salient meanings" (Giora 2003) are a different matter. Those may well be psychologically real, but they do not operate at the right level to ensure the clear (enough) sense of the theorist's questions. For example, let's say that the "solid" meaning of "firm" is more (or for that matter less) salient than its "strict" meaning (Giora 2003: 111); and let's say that the more salient meaning is "accessed" whenever a sentence featuring "firm" is heard, even when the context clearly calls for the other meaning (Giora 2003: 24). Still, the first thing to note is that, even on Giora's view, the salient but contextually "irrelevant" meaning will ultimately be "dampened" and not participate in fixing the sense of the utterance (Giora 2003: 50), which means that, salient meanings notwithstanding, the context does have final say, so to speak, when it comes to fixing the sense of an utterance; and this in turn means that when the context is unsuitable for fixing the sense of an utterance—as I'm going to propose is typically the case with the theorist's context—that sense is indeterminate, sometimes fatefully so. Even more importantly, the sort of context-dependence that matters most for our present purposes has to do *not* with the selection among a word's "meanings"—as Giora uses that term—but with the determination of a word's *sense* even when its relevant *meaning* (in Giora's usage) has already been

The conception of language that has underwritten the assumption that the theorist's questions have clear enough sense and correct answers takes the meaning of a word, and hence the (sorts of) contributions it could make to the overall sense of utterances, to be essentially fixed—at least at any given point in time—and relegates whatever creativity language affords to the level of the *combination* of words.[22] For Merleau-Ponty, by contrast, the history of a word makes it fit for certain uses, but does not foreclose more or less creative uses: though language *may sometimes* become dead, or merely repetitive of its past, there is always the possibility of "authentic," or "first-hand," or "originating" speech (see Phenomenology: 178–9, 197, and 389)—in which the individual draws upon existing linguistic resources to say, or think, something new and, in doing so, contributes to the evolution of the meanings, or expressive powers, of those resources.[23]

This basic thought is echoed in Wittgenstein's saying that our use of words "is not everywhere circumscribed by rules" (PI: 68); but this way of putting the point is arguably too weak, as Wittgenstein himself later suggests (PI: 84; and see also Wittgenstein 1981: 440). For the upshot of Wittgenstein's remarks on rule following is that we do not really know what it could mean, hence what it would be, for our use of words to be everywhere circumscribed by rules—in such a way that no room would be left for more or less creative and yet mutually intelligible expansions

---

determined: even when it's obvious that "firm" is used, on some occasion, to refer to a character trait, say, rather than to a physical property, it may *still* not be clear what, here and now, is meant by, or ought to count as, (a person's) "being firm."

[22] One notable recent exception is Ludlow 2014. Ludlow argues that word-meaning is "dynamic"—in the sense that *what someone means* by some given word, or how someone means it, changes from conversation to conversation and even within a single conversation. He also argues that word-meaning is "underdetermined" or "open-ended"—in the sense that what could be meant by a word, or how it could be meant, is not predetermined by anything like a rule, and may not be known in advance. All this fits well with the conception of language presented in this chapter. At the same time, Ludlow's account, just like other contemporary contextualist accounts and unlike the conception presented in this chapter, is squarely representational-referential, in that the flexibility he argues for is wholly a matter of the categorization (that could be) effected by a word, on an occasion of its employment; and accordingly Ludlow believes that the pervasive flexibility he identifies is compatible with truth-conditional semantics (Ludlow 2014: 102ff.).

[23] Compare Giora, who describes the human mind as "constantly in search of novelty" (Giora 2003: 179), and the ways in which linguistic innovation plays with "routines," or "fixed expressions whose meanings and forms have been conventionalized and lexicalized," which are "prey for our novelty-craving mind" (Giora 2003: 180).

of that use, and the difference between sense and nonsense would not ultimately depend on *our sense* of what makes (what) sense, and under what conditions (see PI: 241–2). As Stanley Cavell has argued in his "Excursus on Wittgenstein's Vision of Language" (in Cavell 1979), an individual lacking in the capacity to project words more or less creatively into new contexts and uses would never become a competent speaker of (anything recognizable as) a natural language.

I said above that the semanticist's proposed rules are, at best, abstractions—more or less useful generalizations based on habituated, "sedimented" speech (Phenomenology: 190)—that do not have the foundational status the theorist tends to attribute to them. And now we can add that the semanticist's abstractions are bound to miss, and cover up, the *open-endedness*, or *indeterminacy*, of linguistic (as well as any other kind of) meaning, and the *creativity* that is necessarily involved in the acquisition and use of a natural language. "Taking language as a *fait accompli*—as the residue of past acts of signification and the record of already acquired meanings," Merleau-Ponty wrote later in his career, "the scientist inevitably misses the peculiar clarity of speaking, the fecundity of expression" (Merleau-Ponty 1964: 85). It is therefore no wonder that counterexamples may be found for virtually any semantic "rule" offered by the theorist (see Horwich 2012: 4). As Wittgenstein puts it, describing the repeated frustration that his earlier self and Russell encountered in their attempts to come up with the one, final analysis, of *everything* we might say: "Our experience was that language could continually make new, & impossible, demands; & in this way every explanation was frustrated... Again and again an application of the word emerges that seems not to be compatible with the concept to which other applications have led us" (Wittgenstein 1980c: 35).

The plasticity and open-endedness of language means that understanding the "authentic," non-merely-automatic speech of another is not a matter of simply putting together the already-fixed meanings of her words, but rather is, ultimately, a matter of coming to see her *point*— of being able to follow, and follow upon, her act of articulating and taking up a position in an interpersonal world, orienting herself by means of words (see Phenomenology: 193).[24] And it should further be noted

---

[24] Let me emphasize that by "a speaker's point" I do *not* mean to refer to a speaker's *purpose* in saying this or that, or to a speaker's *reason* for saying this or that. "A speaker's

that, on this way of looking at things, understanding uncreative ("routinized") speech is also not a matter of simply putting together the already-fixed meanings of the words, but rather is a matter of finding the speaker's intention-as-embodied-in-her-speech-act wholly familiar, utterly unsurprising—as if not just the combination of words, but the total speech act has become an idiom. Habituated, routinized speech may naturally encourage the idea of word-meanings separable from use; but it is no evidence for such meanings (see Phenomenology: 184, 188, and 190).

As long as we are unable to see the other's point—that is, the overall sense of her utterance, her intention as embodied in her speech act—we may still know the meanings of her words, in the sense of being familiar with their ordinary and normal range of use(s) as indicated by a good dictionary; but we will not know what each of her words means there and then—what particular contribution they each make to the overall sense of her utterance.[25] We cannot know what determinate contribution each of a person's words makes to the overall sense of her utterance as long as we are unable to see that overall sense:

> In understanding others, the problem is always indeterminate, because only the solution will bring the data retrospectively to light as convergent.
>
> (Phenomenology: 179)

> Speech is . . . that paradoxical operation through which, by means of words whose meaning is given, and by means of already available significations, we try to follow up an intention which necessarily outstrips, modifies, and itself, in the last analysis, stabilizes the meanings of the words which translate it.
>
> (Phenomenology: 389, translation modified)

For this reason, Merleau-Ponty suggests, we get ourselves into endless trouble when we try to analyze an utterance on the assumption that its sense—what is said in it, how it is to be understood—is essentially a

---

point," as I'm using this term, is roughly equivalent to "utterance meaning" (as commonly used in philosophy), and therefore does not refer—as "purpose" or "reason" normally do—to something that is separable from (the content of) what is said. I use the notion of "point" in order to register the connection between the content, or sense, of an utterance and its (perceived) *value*—its being expressive of what the speaker cares about, and how. I'll say more about this in section 6.3 of Chapter Six.

[25] In section 6.3 of Chapter Six, I'll say more about the difference, and relation, between, on the one hand, the meaning of a word and, on the other hand, how it is meant, or what is meant by it, on an occasion of its employment.

function of the already-determinate meanings of the words, and is therefore separable from the act of expression and its context:

> Expression is everywhere creative, and what is expressed is always inseparable from it... The act of speech is clear only for the person who is actually speaking or listening; it becomes obscure as soon as we try to bring explicitly to light those reasons which have led us to understand thus and not otherwise... I may say that "I have been waiting for a long time"... and I think I know what I am saying. Yet if I question myself on time... there is nothing clear in my mind. This is because I have tried to speak about speech, to re-enact the act of expression which gives significance to the words, to extend the brief hold on my experience which they ensure for me.   (Phenomenology: 391)

Merleau-Ponty may be seen as applying here to speech, while at the same time inflecting existentially, a fundamental insight of Gestalt psychology—the insight, namely, that the sense of a perceived whole is not something we arrive at by combining the already determinate senses of its elements. Nor *could* we thus arrive at the sense of the whole, since, for the perceiver (speaker or audience), the elements only acquire their determinate sense—that is, the particular contribution they each make to the overall sense of the utterance—when that overall sense has been perceived. This basic insight may be illustrated by means of the famous "duck-rabbit" (as long as we keep in mind that perceived meaning in general, and linguistic meaning in particular, is *indeterminate* when considered apart from a suitable sense-fixing context, rather than simply *ambiguous*).[26] We don't come to see the duck-rabbit as a rabbit, say, by *first* seeing that *these* are the ears, *that's* the mouth, and so on; for the two elongated appendages are not seen as ears, and the small bend is not seen as a mouth, until the whole is seen as a rabbit. Until we see the duck-rabbit as a rabbit, or as a duck, the elements of the drawing are *indeterminate* in their perceived sense, and therefore cannot serve as the *reason*, or otherwise rationally *explain*, why we see the rabbit, or the duck.

   This same idea, as applied to the perception of linguistic meaning, is central to the *Investigations* as well. What Merleau-Ponty says in the above passage about "time," is strikingly echoed in Wittgenstein's saying, following Augustine, that time is the sort of phenomenon "we know when no one asks us, but no longer know when we are supposed to give an account of it" (PI: 89). The way to clarity, according to Wittgenstein,

---

[26] See Williams 2004: 120.

requires reminding ourselves of contexts in which the word "time" is used significantly (see PI: 90).

The idea that words only have a determinate sense when contributing to a significant utterance within a suitable context plays an important role in Wittgenstein's diagnosis of traditional philosophical difficulties. At the root of those difficulties, Wittgenstein suggests, is the assumption that the meanings of our words alone suffice for endowing our utterance with clear sense—clear enough for generating precisely those traditional philosophical difficulties, for example. Wittgenstein questions this assumption:

You say to me: "You understand this expression, don't you? Well then—I'm using it in the sense you are familiar with."—As if the sense were an atmosphere accompanying the word, which it carried with it into every kind of application.

If, for example, someone says that the sentence "This is here" (saying which he points to an object in front of him) makes sense to him, then he should ask himself in what special circumstances this sentence is actually used. There it does make sense.   (PI: 117)

When engaged in the sort of "philosophizing" that is the main target of Wittgenstein's critique, we imagine that the meanings of our words alone ensure the sense or intelligibility of what we are saying or thinking. We imagine that there is something our words mean, all by themselves, and that in uttering them we could simply mean or commit ourselves to *it*.[27] Both Wittgenstein and Merleau-Ponty are arguing, in effect, that the relation actually goes in the opposite direction: what our words (may reasonably be found to) mean, on some occasion, is a matter of what *we* (may reasonably be found to) mean by them on that occasion. But it matters crucially that meaning this or that with one's words, or meaning one's words one way or another, *has its conditions*: how we *could* (reasonably be found to) mean our words on some particular occasion, given our and their history, is not up to us to choose or decide.[28] And the

---

[27] See Conant 1998. What often helps us to sustain the illusion that our words by themselves ensure the sense of what we are saying, Wittgenstein suggests, is a picture that we have formed for ourselves and come to associate with them (cf. PI: 115, 295, and 426). Another thing that helps to create the illusion of sense is that we can easily enough imagine a context in which our words *would be* used intelligibly (see Wittgenstein 1969: remark 10).

[28] So I am *not* proposing to "blur the distinction between speaker's meaning and literal meaning" (Davidson 2006: 252). What I'm proposing, rather, is that the *latter* may not aptly or usefully be thought of as a function of the already determinate meanings of the words

basic problem with so much philosophizing, both traditional and contemporary—the basic problem with the method of cases as commonly practiced, for example—is that the philosopher either takes his words to mean something clear even apart from *his* meaning something clear by means of them, or else takes himself to be able to mean his words in some determinate way, even though the conditions for *thus* meaning his words are missing in his particular context and cannot be created by a sheer act of will, or by concentrating one's mind in some special way.

5.2 Another Look at Cappelen on Philosophical "Intuitions"

Before I turn to consider, in Chapter Six, empirical studies of first language acquisition and the evidence they provide in support of Wittgenstein's and Merleau-Ponty's understanding of language, I'd like to take a moment and reconsider, in light of that understanding, Cappelen's argument against the tendency on the part of contemporary analytic philosophers to describe themselves and others as relying on "intuition," or else as giving voice to "intuitions," in giving their answers to the theorist's questions.

Recall that "centrality," as defined by Cappelen, is the thesis that "contemporary analytic philosophers rely on intuitions as evidence (or as a source of evidence) for philosophical theories" (PWI: 3). Cappelen's primary question is whether "centrality" is *true*. Just as he takes the theorist's questions to be inviting us to apply terms to cases, Cappelen invites us to consider whether "intuition" truly applies to the answers philosophers have given to the theorist's questions. In other words, by Cappelen's lights, his argument against "centrality" is a *particular*

(their "conventional meaning") and how they are put together, and as having nothing to do with how *the speaker* may (most reasonably) be found to make sense—to position herself in some particular way—with her words. What's (literally) said should rather be seen as a matter of how—given the ordinary and normal use(s) of the words, the circumstances of their utterance (which include the history of their utterer), how they are put together, and importantly also including (in the case of oral speech) the utterer's facial expression, bodily gestures, and tone of voice—the utterer is most reasonably taken to mean her words. This leaves ample room for cases in which the utterer means (to be saying) one thing, but is most reasonably taken to be meaning (and saying) something else.

application of the very philosophical method—the method of cases—that he is trying to vindicate in PWI.

As Cappelen sees things, for "intuition" to be used non-"defectively" in either philosophy or everyday life, there has to be some *thing* (or set, or type, of things) it "denotes" (PWI: 27). An utterance of an indicative sentence featuring "intuition" is true, according to Cappelen, if and only if the "denotation" of the word is indeed present in the case the speaker refers to and presumably means to describe. In "centrality," as Cappelen understands it, "intuition" is intended "to denote a kind of judgment or mental state that serves as evidence or a source of evidence" for philosophical theorizing (PWI: 25); and the central question for him therefore becomes whether that intended denotation of "intuition" is found in those cases in which analytic philosophers employ the method of cases. Cappelen argues that it is not.[29]

If the representationalist conception of language is misguided, however, Cappelen's argumentative strategy is misguided as well. On the alternative, Wittgensteinian-Merleau-Pontian conception that I have presented in this chapter, the first question to ask is what has led competent speakers of English to refer to their own and other people's answers to the theorist's questions as "intuitions."[30] After all, we are not inclined to refer to our answers to everyday, similarly worded but non-philosophical questions as "intuitions," or to describe them as relying on intuitions. What is it about the theorist's context that has called for *that* word? My own proposal is that philosophers' use of "intuition" in connection with the method of cases registers rather well their sense of lacking sufficient *orientation* in the theorist's peculiar context—the kind of orientation that, *pace* the representational-referential and atomistic-compositional conception, the theorist's words (and case), by themselves, cannot provide. Since our response to the theorist's question—just like the question itself,

---

[29] As I later note in the text, one added complication to the story is that, as Cappelen sees things, "intuition" is typically "defective" when used by contemporary analytic philosophers, since there is nothing clear it denotes when they use it; and this, for Cappelen, means that those uses of the word are "strictly speaking meaningless" (PWI: 59). Accordingly, Cappelen proceeds charitably, by working with what he takes to be *the most plausible intended denotation* of "intuition" as used by contemporary analytic philosophers in connection with the method of cases.

[30] Cappelen is happy to answer *that* question by saying that the talk of philosophical intuitions is no more than a "tick" or "virus" (PWI: 22), or else a dispensable hedge (PWI: 47 and 83).

but unlike competent answers to similarly worded questions about cases, when those questions arise in the course of everyday experience—is neither called for nor guided by a significant situation in which it is responsive and answerable to particular salient non-merely-theoretical interests, all that is left for us to do is look "inside" ourselves for guidance, or tuition.[31]

Whatever has led philosophers to use "intuitions" to refer to the answers they find themselves inclined to give to the theorist's questions, to ask the further question, "Is it *true* (that philosophers have centrally been relying on intuitions)?"—a question that Cappelen takes to always be in place when raised about an utterance of an indicative sentence, and to always have a correct answer—is in this case to ask one question too many. It is like asking, now that "feeding" has become—naturally *and* contingently—the customary way (in the US) of referring to the act of putting quarters into parking meters (with the aim of buying parking time and avoiding parking tickets), whether it is *true* that those who put quarters into parking meters are *feeding* them.[32]

Cappelen contends that much of the contemporary philosophical use of "intuitions" is defective, because that word is used without any clear reference or denotation (PWI: 59–60). It seems to me, however, that "intuitions," as used by the philosophers Cappelen criticizes, actually has a pretty clear reference: it refers to the answers we find ourselves inclined to give to the theorist's questions. And those answers *have* widely been taken as evidence for philosophical theorizing (even if not always in quite the straightforward way suggested by the abductive model).

I am proposing that the use of "intuitions" to refer to the answers we find ourselves inclined to give to the theorist's questions is *neither* exactly an instance of any of the ordinary, non-philosophical uses of that word, *nor* a technical use that does not rely in any way on its ordinary, previous uses (see PWI: 27). As so often happens in the life of a language, the use of a word has here been extended (not technically but) *naturally*: a new situation has given rise to a new need, for which the word, carrying as it

---

[31] The use of "intuition" no doubt also connects with the rationalist tradition in philosophy, and specifically with its account of our knowledge of a priori philosophical truths.

[32] The "feeding" example is taken from Cavell's discussion of the "projection" of words into new contexts/uses (Cavell 1979).

does its history of employment, has been found fitting. The use of "intuitions" to refer to the answers we find ourselves inclined to give to the theorist's questions, I am proposing, is neither correct nor incorrect, neither true nor false; for the word "intuitions" is not here used to *describe* those answers, or to say (assert, claim) *that* they are intuitions. It is used simply to refer to those answers. And that is a natural extension of the use of "intuitions," which is clear enough for all (pertinent) intents and purposes. On the alternative conception of language presented in this chapter, the word "intuition" has no denotation, or extension, or intension, or anything else for that matter, that determines *in advance* and all by itself how speakers may come to mean it, or what they may come to mean by it, under more or less novel circumstances and given more or less novel needs. All it has is a history of use that constrains, but does not foreclose, more or less creative new uses.

The use of "intuitions" to refer to the answers we find ourselves inclined to give to the theorist's questions is only problematic when it is taken to express some sort of *understanding* of the nature and provenance of those answers, and of the method of cases more broadly. It does not. Calling the answers we find ourselves inclined to give to the theorist's questions "intuitions" no more clarifies their nature and philosophical significance than calling the insertion of quarters into parking meters "feeding" clarifies *that* practice and all that must be in place for it to work as it does. There are, as we have seen, real difficulties in understanding the philosophical method of cases and how it is supposed to work. The talk of "intuitions" does nothing to remove the difficulties. *Pace* Cappelen, however, it has not created them either; and avoiding it will not make them go away.

6

Acquiring "Knowledge"—An Alternative Model

Introducing a study that closely followed the process of language acquisition in two boys, from the ages of three and five months to the ages (respectively) of 18 and 24 months, Jerome Bruner claims, referring to the very same passage from Augustine's *Confessions* that opens Wittgenstein's *Investigations*, that "a look at children as they actually acquire language shows Saint Augustine to be far, far off target" (Bruner 1983: 31). "It is one of the mysteries of Kuhnian scientific paradigms," he says a little later on, "that [the] empiricist approach to language acquisition has persisted in psychology (if not in philosophy, where it was overturned by Frege and Wittgenstein) from its first enunciation by Saint Augustine" (Bruner 1983: 32). As we have seen, however, and despite the efforts of Bruner and others, the broadly empiricist picture of how words relate to the world and become fit for their various uses still holds sway more than thirty years after Bruner wrote these words—and in mainstream analytic philosophy no less than in psychology or linguistics.

Go back to Jackson's story of how we each have acquired the word "knowledge." Essentially, acquiring the word—which here can only mean coming to be its competent employer—is for Jackson a matter of "latching on to the pattern" (Jackson 2011: 474), where the pattern is some worldly (cum-mental) constellation in which knowledge consists: the item, or set of items, to which "knowledge" presumably refers. This, I submit, is not only what Jackson *seems* to be saying, but also what he *must mean*, for otherwise his story could not plausibly be taken to support the method of cases as commonly practiced, which is clearly what it is meant to do.

Since the representational view of language as characterized by Jackson bears striking affinity to the so-called "Augustinian" picture of language that Wittgenstein identifies in his *Philosophical Investigations* as lying at the root of any number of traditional philosophical difficulties, it is no accident that Jackson's account of how children come to master words such as "knowledge" bears striking affinity to Augustine's account in his *Confessions* of how he, Augustine, learned his first language. On both accounts, the acquisition of words is essentially a matter of coming to associate them with independently existing (types or categories of) worldly items that are identifiable apart from how those words are used. This, Wittgenstein suggests, *may* be more or less correct, and philosophically harmless, when it comes to words such as "table," "chair," and "bread," to people's names, and (though possibly less straightforwardly) to names of certain actions and properties (PI: 1). The whole of the *Investigations* may be read as an attempt to show that, and how, that view of language is inapt, and leads us into trouble, when it comes to words such as "know," "understand," "mean," "pain," and so on.

I have asked how Jackson knows that this is how the word "knowledge" is acquired—what his evidence might be. And one thing I've said is that his claim rests on no *empirical* evidence. I now turn to substantiate this claim, by examining studies of first language acquisition.

It might seem impertinent to the main argument of this book how words such as "know" are *acquired*. Can't the representational-referential and atomistic-compositional conception be true of the language of competent adult speakers—and so of those who have been invited to respond to the theorist's questions—regardless of how they have *acquired* their competence? Can't it be that, regardless of how we come to be their competent employers, "know" and its cognates (for example), as used by competent speakers, always refer to some worldly pattern in which *knowledge* consists, and which competent employers of those words ought to be able to detect even apart from any context of significant use of them?

The first thing to say to this is that yes, our primary concern *is* with the language of competent speakers; and my Wittgensteinian "reminders"— in responding to the opening paragraphs of Hawthorne's *Knowledge and Lotteries*, in responding on behalf of Austin to "relevant-alternatives" contextualist accounts of "know," and elsewhere in my work (see Baz 2012a and 2012b)—have all been meant to get the reader to look at, and see, *that* differently, and to see that, looked at and seen differently, the language we (competent adults) use does not sponsor many of the (sorts of) questions and difficulties that have exercised analytic philosophers.

But the idea that *what* we acquire, when we become competent speakers of our first language, is essentially separate from *how* it is acquired seems to me deeply mistaken.[1] As we have seen in the case of Jackson, and as we will see shortly in the case of Bartsch and Wellman's account of the acquisition of "know," a particular way of looking at, and seeing, competent adult language tends to go together with a particular way of looking at, and seeing, its acquisition. Conversely, if I could get the reader to look at and see differently the acquisition of philosophically troublesome words such as "know," that should also encourage her or him to look at and see differently the adult, competent use of those words.[2]

6.1 The Current Empirical Evidence

Empirical evidence for the "Augustinian," representational-referential and atomistic-compositional conception of language could only have come from studies that recognize a viable alternative to that conception and are designed to test one conception *as against the other*. I am aware of no study of that sort that has generated evidence favoring the representationalist conception of language over its Wittgensteinian-Merleau-Pontian alternative. Most extant studies of language acquisition suffer from two serious shortcomings in this respect. First, they *presuppose* the empiricist ("Augustinian") picture of language and therefore are not designed to *test* it. Paul Bloom, whose book on the acquisition of first language is considered by many to provide the definitive statement of our current empirical knowledge of the subject, says this, for example: "Within psychology, grasp of the conditions underlying category membership is usually described as a concept, and the concept that is associated with a word is usually described as the word's meaning" (Bloom 2000: 145).[3]

---

[1] As Wittgenstein suggests as early as PI: 6.

[2] Moreover, it has often been argued, sometimes directly against Wittgenstein's critique of the tradition of Western philosophy, that unless our words had meanings separable from use—the sort of meanings envisioned by proponents of the representational conception—we would not be able to explain their acquisition and our ability to use and understand them in combinations we have never encountered before (see, for example, Soames 2003: 128–9, 147). The alternative model I will propose in section 6.2 disarms that argument. The model shows how we can take the use of "know," rather than anything you might think of as its "representational content," as primary, and not just when the word is acquired.

[3] The same combination of ideas is expressed by Elbourne, who contends that "concepts are mental representations that allow us to classify things we come across and access

Bloom is here expressing *not a conclusion* reached on the basis of the studies he discusses, but rather a *presupposition* that guides and informs those studies, as well as Bloom's interpretation of their findings. The other, related shortcoming of most empirical studies of first language acquisition is that they focus almost exclusively, as Geurts has noted in his review of Bloom 2000, on "words denoting middle-sized observable objects" (Geurts 2000).[4] Bloom himself acknowledges, in response to charges such as Geurts's, that "this is where the data is" (Bloom 2001: 1127). Consequently, the (representational) theory of language acquisition defended by Bloom, however plausible it may seem to be when it comes to *those* words, has no obvious extension to words such as "know"; and the empirical findings he cites therefore have no clear bearing on the central issue of this book. Not unless one *presupposes* that all words function in more or less the same way and are acquired in more or less the same way, which is precisely what I've been questioning.

One extensive study that does focus on the acquisition of some of the philosophically troublesome words—the ones Wittgenstein proposes may not aptly be understood on the model of "object and designation" (PI: 293)—is presented in Bartsch and Wellman 1995 (hereafter B&W).[5]

---

memorized information about them" (Elbourne 2011: 26), and then also contends that "we do not need to profess allegiance to any particular theory of concepts in order to hold the view that word meanings are concepts" (Elbourne 2011: 29).

[4] The only significant exception in Bloom's book is the chapter on number words, in which he actually moves away from the broadly Augustinian picture that informs the rest of his discussion. Tomasello also notes that studies of first language acquisition tend to focus almost exclusively on common nouns, and to ignore altogether performative and expressive expressions (Tomasello 2003: 24, 47, 87). A similar complaint is put forward by Nelson (Nelson 2009: 282–3).

[5] There have also been quite a lot of studies of children's grasp of the difference between "factive" mental state verbs such as "know" and "non-factive" mental state verbs such as "believe" or "think" (see Dudley et al. 2015, and references therein). Those studies, interesting as they may be in other respects, have no clear bearing on the main concern of this chapter. They mostly focus on children's understanding of "third-personal" utterances of the form "N knows/thinks/believes that such and such" and in particular on the extent to which, or the point at which, children know that utterers of sentences of the form "N knows that such and such" normally take it for granted that such and such, whereas utterers of sentences of the form "N thinks/believes that such and such" normally do not. The reason why these studies are neither here nor there when it comes to the main concern of this chapter is that they are not designed to test a representationalist, "truth-conditional" understanding of the difference between "factive" and "non-factive" mental state verbs, *as against* a broadly pragmatist understanding of that difference—the sort of understanding I suggested, on behalf of Austin, in section 4.2 of Chapter Four.

The study focuses on words such as "know," "believe," "think," and "want" that according to the authors "refer" to the "mental states" of knowing, believing, thinking, and wanting (see B&W: 62). Bartsch and Wellman proceed on the basis of a Cartesian conception on which our own "mental states" are epistemically available to us unproblematically, whereas the mental states of others are "of course . . . internal and unobservable" and must be posited or inferred or assumed by us on the basis of, and as a way of explaining and predicting, their ("external") behavior (B&W: 4–6). From the perspective of both Wittgenstein and Merleau-Ponty, this Cartesian conception is deeply problematic; but this issue must here be set aside, since it would distract us from the central concern of this book.

For the purposes of this book, the question is whether the findings cited by Bartsch and Wellman support the conception of language that underwrites the philosophical method of cases in its traditional form. Do their findings support the assumption that "know" and its cognates, for example, are first and foremost instruments for categorizing worldly "items"—here, I suppose, people and their mental states or epistemic relations to propositions, or facts—even apart from any context of significant use of these words, and that competent speakers may therefore reasonably be expected to understand the theorist's question of whether the protagonist of some described case knows this or that, and to answer that question (mostly) "correctly," just on the basis of their mastery of the words and their familiarity with the case in question? The answer to this question seems to me to clearly be negative.

Focusing for the sake of brevity and simplicity just on "know" and its cognates, I note first that when Bartsch and Wellman attempt to specify the (type of) mental state these words refer to they end up with a rather elaborate and complex disjunction that initially includes "a belief that is felt to be justified, assumed to be true, or that enjoys markedly higher conviction than one described by *think*" (B&W: 40) and is later expanded to allow that "know" is also used "to describe success and successful actions, when, for example, we say we know how to do something, or know an answer meaning we can correctly state it" (B&W: 59). This minimally suggests that there is no *one* "pattern" that children need to come to be able to recognize and use "know" and cognates for, but rather a family of patterns that relate to each other in a variety of ways.

But the real issue goes deeper. The real issue is that it is not at all clear that the best way to explain empirically the acquisition and use of a philosophically troublesome word such as "know" is to posit some worldly-cum-mental pattern, or even a family of patterns, to which the word refers and *thereby* becomes fit for its various uses. Bartsch and Wellman *presuppose* from the outset that the words whose acquisition they study refer to such patterns, and hold on to that presupposition *despite*, rather than *because of,* the empirical findings they discuss. On the alternative conception of language presented in Chapter Five, the use of a word should be taken as *primary*, and consideration of the use of a word on some occasion (or set of occasions) is the best way of telling what, if anything, it is used by the speaker to refer to on that occasion.[6] It seems to me that Bartsch and Wellman's data actually speak in favor of this alternative understanding—an alternative that does not so much as come into view in their discussion.

Bartsch and Wellman note early on that many of our common uses of words such as "know," "think," and "remember" involve no "genuine psychological reference" (B&W: 32), but rather fulfill "pragmatic conversational functions" (B&W: 20–1). Even by their count, which I will shortly question, genuine psychological reference was found in only 40 percent of all of the uses of "mental terms" by young children (B&W: 43). This minimally suggests that Jackson's and Bloom's Augustinian story—on which the child *first* learns what item, or category of items, the word refers to, and then comes to use the word *for it*—is misguided, at least when it comes to *those* words. It also suggests that words *need not* refer to (name, denote) particular (types of) worldly items in order to be fit for the uses we put them to.

Now, for Bartsch and Wellman's purposes it does matter that at least *some* of the utterances analyzed in their study may aptly count as involving "genuine reference" to a "mental state"; for those are the utterances that are supposed to reveal children's developing "theory of mind" (B&W: vii). In many cases, however, this theoretical purpose, or

---

[6] Compare Chomsky, who urges that we "drop the empirical assumption that words pick out things, apart from particular usages" (Chomsky 1995: 23). Chomsky's focus has been on words such as "house," or "London," and he offers compelling reasons for thinking that what some such word picks out, on an occasion of its use, is a function of the "interests and concerns" that inform that particular usage (Chomsky 1995: 22). I am proposing, and have argued at some length in Baz (2012a), that when it comes to philosophically troublesome words such as "know," or "cause," we should drop the assumption that they are always, or even primarily, in the business of picking out things.

framework, leads Bartsch and Wellman to force a representational-referential interpretation on their data.

For example, very many of the uses of "know" that they count as genuinely referring to a mental state are in the "I don't know" construction. To fit this fact into the representational story they wish to tell, they propose that the reference here is to "the mental state of ignorance" (B&W: 42), or that those uses of "know" feature in "discussions about ignorance" (B&W: 58), whereas it would be far more natural, and less misleading, to describe at least most of those uses as *expressions* of—rather than *descriptions* of, let alone *discussions about*—ignorance, or, more precisely, as expressions of the inability to do something or to answer some question. As Tomasello notes (Tomasello 2003: 106), the expression children learn to use and respond to is typically not "I don't know" but rather "I dunno," and children acquire it not as a combination of separate words that by virtue of their meanings and the way they are put together attribute to their utterer the property of not knowing, or being ignorant of, this or that. Rather, they acquire it as what Tomasello calls "an utterance-level construction" (Tomasello 2003: 114). For the child learning to speak, as for most speakers of English, "I dunno" is "a fixed expression with a single coherent meaning equivalent to a shrug of the shoulders" (Tomasello 2003: 106). "I dunno," as commonly used, is no more representational in its function, no more refers to or describes the speaker's independently existing mental state, than a shrug of the shoulders. "I dunno" is, and is acquired as, an intersubjectively shared instrument that enables speakers—not to report on their own "inner" mental state, but rather—to make certain kinds of intersubjectively significant moves in contexts of shared activity.[7]

Or consider Bartsch and Wellman's disjunctive characterization, mentioned above, of the mental state to which "know" presumably refers. The first two disjuncts—"a belief that is felt to be justified, [or] assumed to be true"—seem to be taken on the authority of the tradition, rather than on the basis of close analyses of actual use; and they bring with them a host of difficulties for the representational view of language, and for philosophical theorizing about knowledge that proceeds on the basis of answers to the

---

[7] For this way of looking at language and at the acquisition of language see Canfield (1993), and Turnbull and Carpendale (2009).

theorist's questions. One difficulty, which I discussed in Chapter Four,[8] is that in contexts in which the conversants have accepted some justification—some basis for the claim that such and such—as good enough for all intents and purposes, the (theorist's) question of whether they *know* that such and such normally drops out as irrelevant: the participants can, and normally do, competently go on with words or deeds without having to attend to that question, let alone answer it. Another difficulty, also mentioned in section 4.2 of Chapter Four, is that in situations in which the participants assume or take for granted the obtaining of some fact—and so, if you will, the truth of some belief— "know" would normally be used in the sense of "(already) being familiar with" that fact, and so not in the philosopher's sense of having an epistemically super-strong or even infallible relation to that fact.[9] (Bartsch and Wellman briefly consider the idea that "knowing that such and such" may sometimes mean something analogous to being in "(physical) contact with part of the world," but dismiss it out of hand, and without any argument, as a "misconstrual" (B&W: 54–5).)

Bartsch and Wellman's third disjunct—"[a belief] that enjoys markedly higher conviction than one described by *think*"—is meant to accommodate, I suppose, the common use of "I know" to *express*, not describe or report, conviction. As Wittgenstein notes, when used in *that* sense, "I know" may be replaced without loss by "I'm sure" (Wittgenstein 1969: 8). And it matters for our purposes that "know" may only thus be used (i.e., to *express* conviction) *in the first person*—a fact that is problematic from the perspective of the representational-referential view of language, but is wholly unproblematic from the Wittgensteinian-Merleau-Pontian perspective that takes use, rather than reference or representational content, to be primary. For while it is conceptually, or grammatically (in the Wittgensteinian sense of that word), possible for me to *describe* or *report* any state of the other that I am able to describe or report when it is mine, there is of course no reason to assume that it should similarly be possible for me to *express* states or positions of the other just because it is possible for me to express them when they are mine.

---

[8] And in greater detail in Baz 2012a and 2012b.
[9] I elaborate on this (sort of) use of "know" and its cognates, and give examples, in Baz 2012a.

More generally, Bartsch and Wellman note that of the 40 percent of the utterances that on their count involved genuine psychological reference, 79 percent(!) were in the first person (B&W: 62). Since Bartsch and Wellman are committed to the idea that in all of those utterances the words were used to "describe" (B&W: 40, 59) or "comment on" (B&W: 39) a person's mental state—be it one's own or someone else's—they have a hard time explaining the predominance among them of utterances in the first person. Their two hypotheses are, first, that children "simply prefer to talk about themselves" and, second, that children "at first conceive of only their own [mental states]" (B&W: 62). The second, Cartesian proposal, which strikes me as quite incredible, is immediately undermined by the fact that first person uses of "mental terms" continue to predominate even after the child has started to use those words in the second and third person (B&W: 63). The first proposal seems merely ad hoc. Rather than supposing that children simply prefer to talk about their own mental states, it seems to me far more plausible that, just like the adults from whom they learn the language, they use combinations of words featuring "know" (for example) to make *intersubjectively significant moves* in the course of intersubjectively significant interactions with other people; and, unlike representational or descriptive moves, very many of those moves have no second or third person variants.[10]

Ultimately, however, the question is not whether one could find a referent—if only in the form of an indefinitely long and complex disjunction—for every word in our language, or find some referent for a word for every occasion on which it is used. For of course one could *always* insist that "know" refers to *knowing* (or to *knowledge*), just as one could insist that "true" refers to *truth*, "five" refers to *the number five*, and "and" refers to *conjunction*. Such an insistence, as Wittgenstein notes (PI: 13), would be not so much false as empty. The real question is whether it offers, or at least points in the direction of, genuine understanding of the acquisition and use of our words, or only creates the illusion of such an understanding.

---

[10] This Wittgensteinian reading of the empirical data has been argued for by Tomasello. On the basis of studies showing the overwhelming predominance of the first-person singular in young children's use of "think," for example, he draws the natural conclusion that "for many young children *I think* is a relatively fixed phrase meaning something like *maybe*" (Tomasello 2009: 80).

Rather than continuing to discuss in detail all of the findings cited by Bartsch and Wellman and showing that they are not only not incompatible with, but actually support the Wittgensteinian-Merleau-Pontian understanding of language as against the representationalist understanding, I will now move to propose an alternative model, inspired by that understanding, of the acquisition of words such as "know." The model, which is also inspired by Tomasello's (Wittgensteinian) "usage-based" or "social-pragmatic" theory of language acquisition (Tomasello 2003, 2008, and 2009; see also Nelson 1996, 2009; and Turnbull and Carpendale 1999), is fundamentally different from the one Jackson assumes in his defense of the method of cases; and it is safe to say that it is better supported by the empirical evidence than Jackson's "Augustinian" account of the acquisition of "knowledge."

6.2 The Alternative Model

I begin by noting that I've shifted the discussion from the acquisition of "knowledge" to the acquisition of "know" (and its cognates). As far as ordinary, non-philosophical discourse is concerned, the verb is far more prevalent; and it most certainly comes first in the order of acquisition. Replace the theorist's "Does the protagonist know that such and such?" with, say, "Does the protagonist's true belief that such and such rise to the level of knowledge?" (Bach 2005: 62–3), or "Is the evidence that has led the protagonist to form the true belief that such and such good enough for knowledge that such and such?" (see Fantl and McGrath 2002: 67), and all plausibility would leak out of Williamson's, Cappelen's, and Jackson's claim of continuity. Even the seemingly more innocent "Does the protagonist possess the knowledge that such and such?" would be unnatural, and biased in favor of the representationalist conception of language. Jackson, as we saw, *presupposes* that conception, so his choice to discuss the singular substantive "knowledge" rather than the verb "know" is *motivated*: given the general story he wants to tell about language, he needs an item (or set of items) that competent speakers may come to recognize; and he needs a word that names or refers to it. Our use of the *verb* "know," Jackson and other proponents of the representationalist conception assume, depends upon an ability to detect *knowledge*—the (type of) item to which "know" presumably refers.

But the assumption, I now intend to show, is unwarranted, and not at all compulsory. My aim in what follows is not to tell an alternative story that is accurate in every detail about how English-speaking children actually come to be competent employers of "know" and its cognates. No one can tell *that* story. Nor is there good reason to suppose that there is a detailed story to tell that is true of all English-speaking children. What I present is better seen as a *model* of how English-speaking children come to master these words; and the model may be thought of as a Wittgensteinian "object of comparison" that is meant to invite the reader to look differently at how children come to master words such as "know" (see PI: 130 and 144). The model, which is fundamentally different from the one Jackson assumes, is inspired by Merleau-Ponty and Wittgenstein, as well as by Michael Tomasello's (Wittgenstein inspired) "social-pragmatic" theory of first-language acquisition. Moreover, the model receives support from the sort of empirical findings cited in section 6.1—the kind of support that cannot be claimed for the representationalist model.[11]

On the alternative model, it is not *instances of knowledge* that the child must learn to discern in order to become a competent employer of "know" (and its cognates), but rather different types of humanly signifi-cant *situations* in which constructions featuring "know" may be called for and do significant work of one type or another. The pattern the child needs to learn to pick out and follow is not some general pattern in which *knowledge* presumably consists and to which "knowledge" presumably refers—*that* pattern need not exist; the only reason to assume its exist-ence being prior commitment to the representationalist conception of language—but rather a pattern, and in fact several different and variously related patterns, of *usage* of constructions featuring "know" (or one of its cognates).[12] As Tomasello has summarized recent empirical findings about how children learn their native language:

Word learning does not consist in the child engaging in a reflective cognitive task in an attempt to make correct mappings of word to world, but rather it emerges

---

[11] It should be noted that almost everybody agrees that something like the model I am about to propose is correct when it comes to "function words" such as logical connectives and prepositions such as "of" or "by"; very few would propose that the only way to explain the acquisition and use of *those* words is to posit (types of) worldly items to which they refer (though I suppose many would still maintain that their meaning should be understood primarily in terms of their contribution to the representational content of utterances). My aim in what follows is to show that such positing may also be misguided in the case of words such as "know."

[12] See Tomasello 2003: 29–31 and 100.

naturally from situations in which children are engaged in social interactions in which they are attempting to understand and interpret adult communicative intentions as expressed in utterances.   (Tomasello 2003: 89)

"The *speaking* of a language," Wittgenstein notes, "is part of an activity" (PI: 23). Normally, the child first hears and begins to use "know," and most of her other early acquired words, in the context of shared, significant activities into which utterances are woven: changing a diaper, preparing and eating a meal, going to the store or for a walk, taking a bath, playing, and so on. These shared activities often take the form of what Bruner calls "formats"—"patterned situations that enable adult and child to cooperate in the 'passing on' of a language" (Bruner 1983: 10), or "routinized and repeated interaction[s] in which an adult and a child *do* things to and with each other" (Bruner 1983: 132). The primary use of words in these activities, as Katherine Nelson observes, is "pragmatic, not symbolic": "Language uses in these shared activities help to mark them, to move them forward, but language is not initially used to *represent* them as such in the child's cognitive or communicative productions" (Nelson 1998: 91).

Thus, for example, relatively early on, English-speaking children normally come to use the construction "I don't know"—or, more realistically, "I dunno." As I've already proposed, following Tomasello, they acquire this expression not as a combination of separate words that by virtue of their meanings and the way they are put together attribute to their utterer the property of not knowing this or that, but rather as "an utterance-level construction" (Tomasello 2003: 114)—as "a fixed expression with a single coherent meaning equivalent to a shrug of the shoulders" (Tomasello 2003: 106).

The complexity, including what may aptly be thought of as *compositional* complexity, of non-linguistic, "merely" bodily gestures such as a shrug of the shoulders often goes unnoticed, and mostly goes underappreciated.[13] This makes it hard to see the natural continuity between such gestures and linguistic utterances, and to think of the latter on the

---

[13] Camp, citing Grice with apparent approval, says that while bodily gestures do stand in systematic relation with other significant acts—verbal and non-verbal—they lack "any discernible internal structure" and have no "parts in the way that sentential utterances do" (Camp 2016: 119). I do not mean to deny or downplay the differences, but I find the idea that bodily gestures have no internal structure and complexity to be mistaken.

model of the former. It is therefore worth reminding ourselves that non-linguistic, bodily gestures have both what may be thought of as syntax and what Wittgenstein has called "grammar." Fogel et al. 2000, for example, have identified four different "types" of smiles in babies as young as six months old who were engaged in play with their mothers; and they have found that the "same" smile, geometrically speaking, means different things—expresses different "emotions," as they put it— depending on its gestural accompaniments and on its intersubjective context. Smiles with a particular distinct form, when combined with a gaze directed at the mother and appearing at a certain particular stage of a game, for instance, have a different meaning from that of smiles of the "same" form that are combined with a gaze turned away from the mother or appear at a different stage of the game.

Shrugs too have syntax and Wittgensteinian grammar. Just like an utterance of "I dunno," a shrug of the shoulders is sometimes *called for* by the situation. When not discoverable as called for in any way or as appropriate to the situation, a shrug—if it could even be called that— would be incomprehensible: the shrugger would, and could, mean nothing by it. When in place, a shrug may carry various kinds and degrees of commitment for the shrugger, depending both on the situation and on its gestural-expressive accompaniments. And it can be found "justified" or "unjustified"—perfectly acceptable, or somehow problematic or otherwise challengeable. Correlatively, responses to a shrug also need to be called for and appropriate: for example, a shrug may only compe-tently be challenged or rebuked in certain ways but not others, depend-ing on its form (manner, style) and context. Competent shruggers will know these sorts of things; and competent employers of "I dunno" will know them as well. They will know them, not in the sense of articulating them to themselves explicitly or even being able to articulate them (fully), but rather in the sense of exhibiting sensitivity and adhering to them in their bodily or linguistic shrugs, and in their responses to other people's use of these gestures. If knowing *these* sorts of things—in *this* sense of "knowing"[14]—means (partially) possessing the concept of knowledge and knowing what knowledge is, then competent shruggers (partially)

---

[14] Compare Davidson 2006: 256, on the mostly tacit, non-propositional knowledge that is manifested in linguistic competence.

possess the concept of knowledge and know what knowledge is. And yet, surely, one could be a competent employer of shrugs—whether bodily or verbal—without being able to detect some worldly pattern that is specifiable and detectible apart from any context of significant shrugging, and to which shrugs refer.

But we are only at the beginning. The child who has started to use "I dunno" more or less as we do is still far from being a master of "know" and full possessor of our concept of knowledge. She still has quite a way to go. So let us continue to follow her. In addition to "I dunno," she will also hear early on, and ultimately come to use, the exclaimed "I know" that has the force of a signal meaning something like "I have an idea," "I can answer this question," "I can go on," "I can do it (myself)"; and the "I know" of sympathy ("I know you're tired"); and the "I know" of sharing an affective response (—"Mommy, Daddy is being silly."— "I know!"). Later on, I suppose, she will learn the "I know" that functions as a "proposition modifier" that is used to expresses confidence and has the force of "I am sure" ("I know you'll forget!"),[15] and the "I know" that has the force of, roughly, "I already have the information," or "You don't need to tell me." Probably later, and I suspect *much* later, she may hear and ultimately come to use "I know" in the sense Austin focuses on, in which it has roughly the force of "(You should) take my word for it."[16] She will also hear and ultimately come to use competently the question "How do you know?"—the question on which Austin focuses in "Other Minds" and which is normally used for inviting the other to tell us her basis for asserting something; and she will learn what sorts of responses to this question are acceptable, and which ones are unhelpful, silly, outrageous, unreasonable, or otherwise incompetent. And so on and so forth. I lay absolutely no claim to have given an exhaustive list, not even

[15] See Tomasello 2003: 252. And compare Wittgenstein: "The difference between the concept of 'knowing' and the concept of 'being certain' isn't of any great importance at all, except where 'I know' is meant to mean: I *can't* be wrong. In a law-court, for example, 'I am certain' could replace 'I know' in every piece of testimony. We might even imagine its being forbidden to say 'I know' there" (Wittgenstein 1969: remark 8).

[16] The last "I know" is the one that Austin has famously, some would surely say infamously, compared to "I promise," with the aim of showing that "I know" is not "a descriptive phrase" (Austin 1979: 98–103). Though I think Austin's comparison is insightful when it comes to *this* particular use of "I know," and useful for Austin's overall purposes in "Other Minds," he ill-advisedly ignores other uses of the phrase, not to mention other uses of "know" and cognates.

of just the general types of usages of the "I know" construction. The list, though at any given moment finite, is potentially inexhaustible.[17]

Being able to use competently these and other more or less closely related constructions featuring "know," and to respond competently to other people's use of them, is, as Williamson notes (Williamson 2005: 11–12; see also PP: 216), our ordinary and normal criterion for grasping the meaning of "know," and hence for possessing the concept of knowledge. So, by this criterion, the child will ultimately come to grasp the meaning of "know" and possess the concept of knowledge. But at no point in the process will she need to be able to discern some single pattern in which knowledge consists, which is detectable in the world apart from any context of significant employment of "know" or one of its cognates, and to which these words always refer, regardless of how (if at all) they are used.

I do not deny that the uses of "know" and cognates mentioned above, and other uses of these words, are more or less closely and more or less straightforwardly related to each other. What the child acquires is a historical product that is the result of *natural* evolution—by which I do not mean Darwinian, causally driven evolution, but rather evolution propelled by what speakers find natural (compare Tomasello 2003: 13). And this means that the various uses and senses of "know" should be expected to have, precisely, a *natural* unity. What I have questioned is the assumption that underlying this unity, and ensuring it, is a worldly pattern in which knowledge consists and to which "know" and its cognates (and "knowledge") refer—a pattern whose instances may be detected even apart from any context of significant use of these words.

The above idea of natural unity harks back to Wittgenstein's notion of "family resemblance" (PI: 67), except that Wittgenstein applies the notion to the different objects named by the same word, whereas I am expanding the notion to refer to different usages of the same word. And it also matters that the identification of family resemblance is often ad hoc: we often come to see the resemblance between a parent and their child, for example, only after we know of their relation. It is quite easy to think of examples of languages that have evolved differently from each other, in such a way that the work normally done by means of some word

---

[17] If this sounds hyperbolic, consider Cavell's discussion of the "projection" into new contexts/uses of "feed," and of "put" (Cavell 1979: 180ff).

in one of those languages is divided among several different words in another language; and it is also possible that some of that work is not done by any particular word in the other language.[18] Some of the similarities suggested to us by our language may thus remain unpronounced, and unperceived, for those at home in some other language, and vice versa.

To be sure, in order to become a competent employer of "know" and its cognates the child will need to use and understand these words as parts of combinations of words she has never encountered before, and in new contexts. Merleau-Ponty says that this ability to "transcend" and thereby "transform" what is given to us defines us not just as speakers, but in every aspect of our experience.[19] Essentially the same ability for what Cavell calls "projection" (Cavell 1979: 180ff) is manifested by the child who, having experienced his mother hiding her face with her hands and then revealing it as she exclaims "peek-a-boo," comes one day to hide *his* face with *his* hands and to reveal *it* as he exclaims "peek-a-boo"—not merely in imitation of his mother, but assuming the role of the agent initiating the game—and later on comes to hide his whole body, or a doll, behind the sofa, and then reveal *it* as he exclaims "peek-a-boo."[20]

Similarly, having only heard and responded to *others* saying "I dunno," *our child* will at some point come to say "I dunno" in an appropriate context, and to competently follow upon other people's responses to her "I dunno." Having, at any given point, only heard the expression used in response to finitely many questions, she will need to understand it when it is used, and to use it herself, in response to some other question. Having only heard the "I know" of sympathy used in the context of, say, someone's being in pain, she will understand and respond appropriately to

---

[18] It is well known that different languages divide differently the work done by prepositions, which is why use of prepositions is so challenging for non-native speakers. Another example would be languages such as German, French, or Hebrew, in which a different word is used for "knowing" in the sense of "being acquainted with someone or something." Another example is Japanese, in which, according to Stephen Stich (personal communication), neither of the two words that most closely translate the English "know" is "factive."

[19] Indeed, he argues that our perception itself is characterized by this creative power—the power for "human elaboration" (Merleau-Ponty 1964: 59).

[20] For a description of such non-primarily-linguistic creative projections, see Bruner 1983: 54. Tal Baz (personal communication) tells me that children on the autistic spectrum who have a hard time with the projection of words into new contexts, also have a hard time with such non-linguistic projections, and that the latter difficulty is an excellent predictor for the former.

"I know you're tired"; and one day she may stroke her doll and spontaneously say "I know you're hungry," without ever having used or even heard *that* particular combination of words before. Having used "I know" in the sense of "You don't need to tell me," she may naturally and spontaneously come to use "she knows" in the sense of "you don't need to tell her" (though it is far more likely that she will have heard the third-person construction used in this sense before she herself uses it). Having only heard and participated in finitely many exchanges in which the "How do you know?" construction is used and responded to, she will come to be able to respond competently (reasonably, acceptably, helpfully . . .) to the question, and to be able to assess and challenge competently other people's responses to that question, in indefinitely many new (types of) contexts. And so on and so forth. At no point in the process, will the child need to be able to detect some worldly pattern—identifiable apart from any context of significant employment of "know" or one of its cognates—in which knowledge consists and to which "knowledge" refers.[21] Projecting "know" into new contexts no more requires that we come to identify an item or type of item to which it always refers than projecting a particular, geometrically identified form of smile from one (sort of) context to another, in which it may have a quite different meaning, requires that we be able to identify an item to which this particular, geometrically identified form of smile always refers.[22] As Tomasello puts it, summarizing the results of numerous studies of first language acquisition:

[C]hildren do not have to create each of their utterances from the ground up, using meaningful words . . . , but rather they integrate together in various ways many different kinds of already constructed constructions, each with an associated communicative function.   (Tomasello 2003: 305; see also 307)

---

[21] Compare Kukla: "We cannot simply presuppose the idea that there is *a thing*—knowledge—that our lay language and intuitions grope at and which is the *same thing* that epistemologists are trying to theorize and precisify. It may well be that what we really have on our hands is a loose cluster of epistemic phenomena with no common core or essence" (Kukla 2015: 207).

[22] Compare Fodor's saying that "concept learning is essentially inductive extrapolation" (Fodor 1975: 42). Fodor's use of "induction" betrays an over-intellectualization of the process, by my lights. He and I also have very different ideas of what the learner extrapolates *from*, and *to*. Fodor understands both in representational terms. Part of my aim in presenting the alternative model is to break through the apparent obviousness of Fodor's assertion, or to contest the way Fodor and others have tended to understand it.

The child does not begin with words and morphemes and glue them together . . . ; rather, she starts with already constructed pieces of language of various shapes, sizes, and degrees of abstraction (and whose internal complexities she may control to varying degrees), and then "cuts and pastes" these together in a way appropriate to the current communicative situation.   (Tomasello 2003: 310)

The combinatorial complexity and expandability of language has often been cited as a decisive consideration in favor of the representational view of language, on which the meaning of a word is primarily a matter of what item, or set or type of items, it refers to.[23] Following Wittgenstein, Merleau-Ponty, and Tomasello, I am suggesting that it is not. The undeniable fact that we can use and understand combinations of words we have never encountered before does not mean that the words must come with the sort of meanings or "representational contents" envisioned by the Augustinian. *Pace* Jackson and many others, what gets combined, when words are competently combined, need not be "representational contents" altogether separable from function. Rather, what get combined may precisely be *functions*, which may or may not aptly be described as "representational." Furthermore, *which* functions are combined in some particular utterance may not be determined, or determinable, apart from a determination of the function, or sense, of the utterance as a whole. This, if you think about it, is really just Frege's famous "context principle" (Frege 1999: x), but now applied to language no longer seen through a representationalist prism.

"In human linguistic communication," Tomasello proposes following Wittgenstein, "the most basic unit of intentional action is the utterance as a relatively complete and coherent expression of a communicative intention, and so the most fundamental unit of language learning is stored exemplars of utterances" (Tomasello 2003: 296; see also Tomasello 2009: 72); and for this reason, "identifying the functional roles of components of utterances is possible only if the child has some (perhaps imperfect) understanding of the adult's overall communicative intention—because

---

[23] Thus, for example, Schoubye and Stokke move seamlessly and without argument from observing that "the meaning of the constituents of a sentence S and the order in which these are combined intuitively constrain what S can be used to say (relative to a context)"—which, but for their puzzling use of "intuitively," is a perfectly innocuous truism—to the far from innocuous idea that there is therefore a "minimal proposition" that is expressed by S (Schoubye and Stokke 2016: 774).

understanding the functional role of X means understanding how X contributes to some larger communicative structure" (Tomasello 2003: 297; see also Tomasello 2009: 73). In Chapter Five, I put what is essentially the same point by saying that you cannot tell what contribution a word makes to the overall sense of an utterance before you see that overall sense.

In order to become a competent employer of "know" and its cognates, the child will need to get the hang of the use of different types of constructions featuring these words. She will need to learn their occasions and their different sorts of significance: what (sorts of) positions in the interpersonal world one assumes in using certain (types of) expressions in certain (types of) ways in certain (types of) contexts; what the conditions are for taking some particular position or another by means of these words; and what commitments (liabilities, risks) one takes upon oneself when using the words in one way or another, and in responding in one way or another to other people's use of them.[24] At no point in this process of learning will the child need to map "know" and its cognates onto the world—not if the mapping is supposed to hold independently of any context of significant use of the words, and to connect individual words to individual, independently existing *items* or *types of items* that are identifiable apart from how those words are used.[25] Though becoming fully competent with "know" and its cognates requires varying degrees and kinds of what may be called abstraction, at no point in the process of acquisition does the speaker need to arrive at some *final* level of abstraction that supposedly underlies, governs, and unifies *all* uses of these words. Not until she starts philosophizing within the framework of the representationalist conception of language, at any rate; and when she comes to do *that*, if she does, she may in fact be chasing, not worldly items or patterns to which our words have come to refer, but rather, as Price suggests, shadows cast by the ways we talk (Price 2011: 319).

---

[24] This sort of learning, as Merleau-Ponty argues (see Phenomenology: 142ff), is bodily and perceptual, but not merely mechanical: the acquisition is a matter of how we come to perceive and (mostly) unreflectively respond to given situations—manifesting in our behavior an *understanding* of those situations, but an understanding that is not encoded in rules or concepts.

[25] For a forceful and sustained argument against the "mapping" picture of language, see Price 2011.

6.3 Objections and Responses

I have argued that the representational-referential and atomistic-compositional conception of language rests on no *empirical* evidence—no evidence that supports it as against the alternative, Wittgensteinian-Merleau-Pontian conception I have presented. This does not mean that there are no considerations that may seem to speak in its favor, and against the alternative conception I have proposed. In this section, I discuss three general considerations that may be invoked—and which have actually been invoked, often in response to the works of Wittgenstein and Austin, and those inspired by them—in support of the representational-referential and atomistic-compositional conception.

The first objection is based on Williamson's setup for his argument against the epistemic conception of analyticity, and goes something like this: *Following Wittgenstein, Merleau-Ponty, and Tomasello, you say, for example, that uttering "I dunno," when done in a suitable context, is an act, a gesture, that, normally, has roughly the same meaning as that of a shrug of the shoulders. And you say (following Merleau-Ponty) that the meaning of the utterance, just like the meaning of the non-linguistic gesture, is inseparable from it, and not aptly thought of in terms of reference to some worldly item (or pattern), or type of item, in which knowledge (or its absence, for that matter) consists. However, you are thinking about linguistic reference altogether incorrectly. What the child's, or anyone else's, "know" refers to is not a matter, or direct function, of how she uses it on some occasion or set of occasions. As Williamson has proposed, "each individual uses words as words of a public language; their meanings are constitutively determined not individually, but socially, through the spectrum of linguistic activity across the community as a whole" (PP: 98). When speakers use a word as a word of a public language, they thereby "[allow] its reference in their mouths to be fixed by its use over the whole community," and "reference can supervene on underlying facts in ways far from transparent to native speakers" (PP: 124). The referential properties of expressions of the language may "supervene on lower-level facts," for example on "causal connections between uses of those expressions and objects in the environment" (Williamson 2011: 503). The child in your story is on her way to becoming a member of the community of English speakers. Whatever she does with her "I dunno" and however she means it, what her truncated "know" refers to is what "know" refers to in that community—namely,* (the factive mental state of) knowledge.

This objection begs the question against the alternative conception of language that I have been proposing, and against the alternative model presented in section 6.2. It *presupposes* without evidence or argument the existence of the "objects" to which our philosophically troublesome words are supposed to refer; and then it proposes a (rather sketchy) story about how the relation of reference between our words and those "objects" gets established.[26] However, at least when it comes to philosophically troublesome words such as "know," "understand," "mean," "free," and so on, the "objects" to which these words supposedly refer are, *at best*, theoretical posits—objects whose existence we must *assume*, in order for there to be the sort of referents for our words required by the representationalist conception.[27] Less happily, these "objects" may just be philosophically constructed chimeras. On the alternative conception of language that I have proposed, following Wittgenstein and Merleau-Ponty, we need not presuppose those objects—they drop out of consideration without any loss, theoretical or other.

I fully agree with Williamson that speakers of a language are not individually masters or determiners of what they mean or may reasonably be taken to mean with their words, and hence are not masters or determiners of their words' meanings. As I've said, following Wittgenstein and Merleau-Ponty, the meaning of a word, and hence what uses it is fit for, or may be found fit for, is a function of the history of its use, as we've inherited it. The question, however, is whether that meaning is best understood in terms of reference to independently existing, and context *in*sensitively identifiable, worldly items. So far, we have been given no reason for thinking that it is, and therefore no reason for believing in Williamson's referents.

The next consideration is significantly older than the first and has widely been taken to decisively support the representationalist conception of language. It originates from Peter Geach (1960, 1965) and John Searle (1999) and may be put as follows: *Following Wittgenstein, Merleau-Ponty, and Tomasello, you say, for example, that uttering "I dunno," when done in a suitable context, is an act, a gesture, that, normally, has roughly the*

---

[26] As I've already noted that Williamson's story is sketchy is something he himself acknowledges (Williamson 2011: 503).

[27] And objects of study for Williamson's and Cappelen's "metaphysician" (see PP: 18–19; PWI: 30, fn. 2; and Cappelen and Lepore 2005: 155–75).

same meaning as that of a shrug of the shoulders. And you say (following Merleau-Ponty) that the meaning of the utterance, just like the meaning of the non-linguistic gesture, is inseparable from it, and not aptly thought of in terms of reference to some worldly pattern, or type of pattern, in which knowledge (or its absence, for that matter) consists. This, however, ignores the ways in which one utterance may, and often actually does, logically connect with others. For example, someone's "I dunno" may be responded to by someone else's "How can you not know?! Of course you do!" or simply "You (do) know." If this imagined conversation is genuine and the second person actually succeeds in challenging and even contradicting the first, then, surely, the first person's (truncated) "know" must mean the same thing that the second person's "know" means. In other words, even though they are clearly doing different things with their words—making different gestures with them, if you will—both speakers are talking about the same thing: namely, the first person's knowledge (or lack thereof) of some proposition. If they didn't talk about the same thing, they'd be talking past each other. So, pace Merleau-Ponty, there must be a semantic, or purely referential, meaning to the words that is prior to and separable from whatever gestural-pragmatic meaning each individual utterance has. Otherwise, true communication, and logical relations between different utterances, would be impossible, or merely illusory.

This line of objection to my alternative conception and model trades on three features. The first is a conflation of *the meaning of "x"* and *what someone, on occasion, means by "x,"* or *what "x," as used by someone on a particular occasion, means.*[28] The second is the fact that *in English* we can

---

[28] This sort of conflation is pervasive, and I think symptomatic, in Davidson, who talks about what someone is using her words to mean on some occasion (Davidson 2006: 253), or about what someone "means by his words" (Davidson 2006: 260), but also says that the answer to *that* may be given by a dictionary definition (Davidson 2006: 253). This is because he thinks of linguistic understanding in terms of translation or disquotation. But, as I've already noted, I may be unsure what you mean, here and now, by "x," even though I have no doubt that the meaning of "x"—as a dictionary would give (or indicate) it—is the same for you and for me. For Davidson, understanding a word on some particular occasion of use is essentially a matter seeing what concept it expresses or what word in my idiolect expresses the concept that word expresses (Davidson 2006: 259). The kind of context-sensitivity that most clearly and directly gives trouble to the minimal assumption, however, is a matter of the indefinitely many ways that a word, having the meaning it has in our language—the sort of thing that could be gleaned by consulting a dictionary—could be used, or meant. If you and I are competent speakers of English, and I'm not sure what you mean *here* by "cause," in asking "Did A cause B?"—because the context of our conversation leaves what you *could*

say of two people that they mean, or do not mean, the same *thing* by some word, and can also say of two words that belong to two different languages and have more or less the same function in their respective languages that they mean the same *thing*. The third feature is the all-too-typical highly abstract nature of the "examples" of conversations that are used to support this line of objection.

It might help to begin with a few Wittgensteinian reminders. Contemporary mainstream analytic philosophers tend to dismiss such "ordinary language" reminders, on the ground that they cannot by themselves settle weighty theoretical issues. I agree. It should be noted, however, that the following reminders are not *meant* to settle weighty theoretical issues. On something like the contrary, they are meant to ensure that no weighty theoretical issue is taken to have been settled on the basis of nothing more than contingent facts about linguistic usage—here, usage of the English word "mean."

So, first, "What So and So means by 'x'" (or "How So and So means 'x'") is normally used in reference to some *particular* utterance or set of utterances made by So and So *in some particular context*, not in reference to *all* of So and So's uses of "x." There is normally no correct answer to the question of what So and So means by "x" *in general*.

Second, and relatedly, we normally ask "What does So and So mean by 'x'?" when there is some particular lack of clarity—some difficulty in understanding So and So's use of "x" *on some particular occasion* (or set of occasions). Apart from some such lack of clarity, it would normally make no sense to ask what So and So means by "x." Apart from some actual or envisioned particular lack of clarity, a correct (appropriate) response to "What does So and So mean by 'x'?" would be "What do *you* mean? What do you find unclear?"[29]

Third, in order to say what So and So meant by "x" on some occasion, or how she meant her "x," we normally give a *paraphrase* of her word(s)—that is, we give *more words*; and we often paraphrase her

---

mean by that word (too) indefinite—it would do me no good to be told that by "cause" you mean cause, or "cause" (Davidson, as I've noted, is inconsistent in his use of quotation marks for the "translating" word, and precisely because he conflates what someone means by "x," here and now, with the meaning of "x" in her idiolect).

[29] Compare Wittgenstein: "The question 'What do I mean by that?' is one of the most misleading ways of talking (*Redeweisen*). In most cases one might answer: 'Nothing at all— I *say*...'" (Wittgenstein 1981: remark 4, I have slightly amended Anscombe's translation).

utterance as a whole, even when the question was about some particular word. A good paraphrase conveys to the audience how So and So's "x"— or really how *she*, the speaker—is to be understood *here*, in *this* context. It most certainly does not give the audience some *thing*, or *type of thing*, to which "x," or So and So's "x," *always* refers.

Fourth, it is true that we can sometimes say in English of two or more people that they do or do not mean the same *thing* by a word—again, normally in reference to the way they have *actually used* the word on some occasion (or set of occasions); but that does not mean that there is literally and metaphysically some one *thing* (or set, or type, of things) that they have both somehow meant with their word.

And fifth, while it is also true that we can say in English of two *words*— typically words that belong to two different languages—that they mean the same thing, this is normally best understood as meaning that the two words have more or less the same function, or set of functions, in their respective languages.[30] It does not mean that there is some one *thing* that they both somehow mean. (What might it mean for a *word* to *mean* a *thing*?)

Now go back to the "example" of linguistic exchange that is supposed to support the above objection to my alternative model of "know(ledge)" acquisition: one person says "I dunno" and the other responds with, for example, "What do you mean you don't know? Of course you do!" or maybe simply with "You do know." What do the two imaginary conversants mean by "know" (or what remains of it in the first person's "I dunno" and in the second person's "of course you do")? Geach, Searle, and other proponents of the representational-referential and atomistic-compositional conception have supposed that this question makes clear sense as it stands, and that we could answer it correctly without knowing anything about the context of the exchange (as long as we know that the conversants are speaking "seriously and literally"). The question, they have supposed, could aptly be answered by saying "By 'know' the two conversants mean *knowledge*, or *the knowledge state (or relation)*."[31]

---

[30] Davidson puts it right when he says that when we take it that Mrs. Malaprop says "epitaph" because she confuses it with "epithet," we take it that her "epitaph" has *"all the powers* ['epithet'] has for many other people" (Davidson 2006: 262, my emphasis; in the square brackets I have corrected what I take to be a typographical error).

[31] Recall Cappelen's saying that "think," in any (serious and literal) utterance of "I think (this or that)," "denotes the psychological state people are in when they think" (PWI: 38).

That, however, only gives an illusion of sense. Italicizing one's words does not ensure that there is anything clear one means by them.

My own answer to the question what the two conversants imagined above mean by "know" is that we cannot sensibly answer it until we know more about the circumstances of the exchange.[32] The first person's "I dunno" could have come in response to the second person asking her what she wants for dessert, for example. If so, it may mean something like "several things appeal to me and it is hard for me to choose between them" or maybe something like "Nothing really appeals to me"; and the second person's words may mean something like "Come on! There must be something you prefer. (You always say you don't know, but then always end up choosing the tiramisu)." Or the first person's "I dunno" could have come in the course of working on a jigsaw puzzle and in response to the second person's question "Where is the piece that goes here?" In that case, the "I dunno" may mean something like "I haven't found it yet" or "I think it may have gotten lost" and the second person's words may mean something like "Come on! Stop pulling my leg. I know you have it." Or maybe the utterer of "I dunno" is just learning to do jigsaw puzzles, and she does not trust herself to be able to find the right piece, in which case the second person's words may mean something like "Trust yourself. You can do it." Or the "I dunno" may come in response to the second person asking when she will finally get a dog, in which case it may mean something like "I am not willing to make a commitment about this at this point," and the second person's "What do you mean you don't know?!" may mean something like "The decision is all in your hands, and there is no good reason for you to decline to give me a definite answer, one way or another." And so on and so forth.

In each of the above exchanges and indefinitely many others we could imagine, if there is no misunderstanding, no breakdown in communication, the two parties *could* intelligibly be said, given an appropriate context, to be talking about the same thing; but note that what they could be said to be *talking about* would normally *not* be what they could be said to *mean by*

---

[32] One important complication I ignore for simplicity's sake is that the answer to this question is normally context-dependent. The correct answer normally depends on what particular difficulty in understanding the speaker, or what potential misunderstanding on the part of the person asking the question, it may reasonably be expected to seek to alleviate, given *its* context.

"know": in most cases, if we were asked what they were talking about we would have to say something about, or paraphrase, the exchange as a whole, or *its* topic; to answer that they were both talking about (the first person's) *knowledge* (or lack thereof) would be incompetent.

The two conversants *might* also be said—though I find it hard to imagine a context in which saying it would be natural—to *mean the same thing* by "know" (or what remains of it in "I dunno" and in "Of course you do"). But here too, what they could intelligibly be said to mean by "know" is a matter of what—given their circumstances and the history of the word—they would most reasonably be taken to have committed themselves to in uttering it, and what we think would best help our audience to understand their exchange as a whole. Whatever the context of the envisioned exchange and the context of our reflecting on it, we've so far been given no reason to suppose there is some one (type of) *thing*—identifiable apart from those contexts—that both conversants are talking about, or mean.

I said that normally the answer to the question, "What does So and So mean by 'x'?" takes the form of a paraphrase. I have argued that there is no reason to suppose that there is *one* paraphrase that could serve as the correct answer to the question of what is meant by "know" in all of its possible uses. (If there were, philosophers could be said to have the "analysis of knowledge" that most of them have by now given up on finding.) Moreover, insofar as there's a paraphrase that may seem apt in a wide range of possible uses, it can be expected to be just as problematic or indeterminate in what *it* means as the original constructions featuring "know." For example, "(being) able to answer correctly some salient question" may seem like a good paraphrase of "know" in many common types of contexts—though not in all contexts and, importantly, not in the skeptical contexts on which philosophers have tended to focus! A quick reflection reveals, however, that in different contexts "being able to answer correctly some salient question" would need to be meant in different ways, in order to successfully paraphrase "know" (where it can successfully paraphrase it). Though not nearly as multifunctional as "know," "being able to answer correctly some salient question" is also indeterminate in what it may mean and therefore tricky to capture when taken apart from any context of significant use.

As for logical relations between utterances, I have nowhere denied that one utterance featuring "know" may bear on others in ways that may be called "logical." On the contrary, I have proposed that the sense of an utterance may best be thought of in terms of the difference it may reasonably be found to make in the conversation, and more broadly in the situation, where that centrally includes the commitments its producer may reasonably be found to have created, both for herself and for others, in producing it.[33] So the sense of an utterance, as I am thinking of it, *is* in large measure a matter of what (intelligible) responses on the part of others, as well as what (intelligible) continuations on the part of its producer, it makes possible or calls for, and how it affects the significance of various possible responses and continuations. This, however, does not mean that the senses of utterances, and what may be thought of as logical relations between utterances, are a function of determinate things that each of their constituents taken in isolation means, or of determinate commitments that each of those constituents taken in isolation carries regardless of context and independently from human judgment and sensibility.

By ordinary everyday criteria, to know the meaning of "know" (and possess the concept of knowledge) is to know how to use it competently in a wide enough range of contexts, and how to respond competently to other people's use of it. The above line of objection to my alternative model has given us no reason to suppose that *that* requires an ability to detect—apart from any context of significant employment of the word—some item, or some general type of items, in which knowledge consists and to which "know" refers. The "examples" of conversations that have been used by Geach, Searle, and their followers as evidence for the representationalist conception of language would only seem to support that conception to someone who was *already* presupposing it. Only someone already committed to that conception would take it that the meaning of a word may unproblematically be referred to as "the (type of) thing (or item) the word—as such, and hence on every occasion—means."[34]

The third consideration has also widely been taken to speak for the representational-referential and atomistic-compositional conception of

---

[33] This, in broad outline, is how Robert Brandom (1994, 2008) has proposed that we think of linguistic meaning. See also Williams 2004.

[34] In Baz 2012a, I discuss in detail Geach's example (in Geach 1965) of an inference featuring "know," and I argue that it does not show what Geach takes it to show—namely, that "know" has a representational meaning that determines, by itself and regardless of how the word is used, the contribution it makes to the sense of utterances in which it features.

language, and so by implication against the alternative model of the acquisition of "know(ledge)" that I have proposed. It received its most influential articulation from Paul Grice (in Grice 1989), and may be put as follows: *You speak about finding words* called for *in a situation, or in place. This, however, obscures the distinction between semantics and pragmatics. Thus, for example, one may find "I dunno" called for—in the sense of finding it very* tempting to say *"I dunno" (perhaps in order to be let off some hook), or of thinking that it would do the other person some good* to think one did not know—*and yet for all that* know *(the proposition in question). The opposite case is also possible: one may have no reason whatsoever to say "I dunno" in some situation—actually saying it in that situation would be, qua human act, incomprehensible because altogether pointless—and yet say something* true *in uttering "I dunno," because (by hypothesis) she would not know (the proposition in question). These sorts of cases show that there must be a purely representational meaning to the words, which is separable from, and logically prior to, the significance or point of some utterance of them. When given all of the relevant facts, competent employers of "know" should therefore, in principle, be able to tell whether someone* knows *this or that, even apart from any reason for saying that she knows or does not know it. This is why they should be able to answer the theorist's question, and answer it mostly correctly.*

Just like the previous lines of objection to my alternative model, this one too *presupposes* the representational-referential and atomistic-compositional conception of language. If, as I have proposed, there are indefinitely many different ways expressions featuring "know" could be meant—indefinitely many different possible (kinds of) answers to the question "What did So and So mean (in uttering any one of those expressions)?" or "What did So and So mean by 'know'?"—depending on the context of So and So's utterance and on the context in which the question is asked, then why suppose that the imagined maker of the above Gricean objection has succeeded in saying something clear or determinate by means of *her* "know"? The objection *assumes* that we are saying something clear in saying, for example, "someone's utterance of 'I dunno' may be justified in some sense or even appropriate and yet false because *she knows,* or may be altogether pointless and yet true because *she does not know.*" It *assumes* that "know(s)" means something clear and determinate *here.* But if, *pace* the representationalist conception, the meaning of a word is better seen not as what *it*, by itself, means or says, but as its potentiality for being used by speakers (or thinkers) for saying (or thinking) different things in different contexts, then the assumption is mistaken.

We may well *have the sense* of saying something clear in uttering sentences featuring "know" apart from any particular context of significant use; but that, as Wittgenstein suggests, may be due to the fact that we could easily enough imagine contexts in which the words *would be* used for saying something clear (Wittgenstein 1969: remark 10); or we could tacitly be relying on a picture of "knowledge"—as a super-strong connection between a mind and a fact, for example—or on an abstraction that captures one general sort of way of meaning "know," but not others.

The objection also misunderstands the notion of "the point of an utterance" as I have used it in this book. What I mean by "the point of an utterance" is what Merleau-Ponty means by "the meaning (sense, *sens* in French) of an utterance." Merleau-Ponty, as we saw, says that he is proposing "a new meaning of the word 'meaning'" (Phenomenology: 146), precisely in that meaning, as he here understands it, is something *inseparable from the human act of expression that has it*; the meaning is embodied in the act and cannot be perceived, grasped, or articulated apart from it. That's how I mean "the point of an utterance." The above objection, by contrast, takes "the point of an utterance" to mean something like "the reason for making the utterance," and takes it that the utterance can have a clear and determinate (truth-evaluable) "content" independently of whatever reason one may or may not have for making it. Where "reason for making an utterance" is meant *in this way*, it simply does not mean what I mean by "the point of an utterance."

To be sure, there may be, at any given moment, truths expressible by means of constructions featuring "know," which one has no good reason to actually express, and perhaps good reasons to keep to oneself. *Pace* Grice, however, this truism does not imply that those constructions may express those truths even apart from being meant in one way or another in a context suitable for *thus* meaning them.[35]

---

[35] Travis presses this point very clearly and compellingly in response to Grice's critique of philosophers such as Wittgenstein and Austin. "The issue," Travis argues on behalf of the philosophical works Grice has meant to undermine, "is one of *making sense*; not one of what we wouldn't say" (Travis 1991: 241).

Conclusion

On Going (and Getting) Nowhere with Our Words

And now finally consider, in light of the alternative way of looking at language that I have offered in Chapters Five and Six, the peculiar context in which the theorist's question is raised and answered. By design, both the question and the answer are not supposed to have any particular point: there is no particular intention—solicited by or responsive to some particular perceived situation—that the words expressing the question are "following up," as Merleau-Ponty puts it, and to which the respondent is called upon to respond. There is therefore an important sense in which neither the words expressing the theorist's question nor the words expressing answers to it are being *used*; no significant position in an interpersonal world is taken by means of those words, either by the one uttering the question or by the one attempting to answer it (often, one and the same person). In other words, there is no *actual speaker* in that artificial context—a person who finds herself in some significant situation and commits herself by means of the words to some non-merely-theoretical stand. There are only the case and the familiar words, and they are assumed by both armchair and experimental philosophers to suffice. What the theorist's question asks, what some particular answer to it means, and whether the answer is correct—all that is taken to be determined just by the words themselves and by the case.

The method of cases as commonly practiced by either armchair or experimental philosophers should therefore be distinguished from the practice of those who, following Wittgenstein and Austin, proceed philosophically by way of asking themselves "what we should say when, *and so why and what we should mean by it*" (Austin 1979: 181, emphases altered).

The latter form of practice invites us to project ourselves imaginatively into situations of speech—situations in which we could, and normally would, be *using* our words; and its aim is to bring out and elucidate the possible—that is, intelligible—uses of the philosophically troublesome word(s), and the worldly conditions of those uses, and thereby to show that the philosopher responded to has failed to say anything clear with his words, or failed to say what he evidently wanted and needed to say given his theoretical commitments and ambition. The former form of practice, by contrast, invites us to "apply" our words to cases from a metaphysically detached position, in an artificial context in which, by design, nothing hangs on what we say or think—nothing, that is, but some theory. The theorist is inviting us to *do nothing in particular* with our words, and so it may appear as though he is inviting us to do *less* with them than we normally and ordinarily do. Following Wittgenstein, we may say that in the theorist's context all friction has been removed, and so it would seem that the conditions are ideal (PI: 107). And then we find ourselves getting entangled in intractable difficulties, unable to make any real progress. Our words are instruments for taking steps—making intersubjectively significant moves; but in order to enable us to take those steps, they require the friction of everyday situations and real (or else imagined) stakes.

This does not mean that we are altogether in the dark when we attempt to understand and answer the theorist's question, or that our answers are wholly arbitrary and revelatory of nothing potentially interesting. What it does mean, however, is that what guides us in giving our answers is at best an abstraction, and at worst a picture—of knowledge as a super-strong connection between a mind and a fact, for example—that we have formed for ourselves and come to associate with that abstraction.

Being guided by an abstraction or by a picture *could* be harmless. It might be theoretically harmless, if what speakers normally and ordinarily mean by the expression in question *is* a matter of what worldly item, or constellation, they mean to refer to and if the nature of the item or constellation varies little across different contexts of speech. This *might* be the case with expressions such as "contains milk" or "weighs 79 kilos," though contemporary contextualists such as Charles Travis have argued that not even such philosophically innocent expressions are fit for application to cases apart from some particular context.[1] At any rate,

---

[1] See Travis 1989 and 1997.

when the theorist invites us to "apply" words whose normal and ordinary
functioning in discourse is not merely or purely or even primarily that of
conveying information about the world, or communicating Fregean
thoughts (see PI: 304), and whose history points in no single direction—
words whose ordinary and normal use is guided by what Austin describes
as "models" that are "overlapping, conflicting, or more generally simply
disparate" (Austin 1979: 203)[2]—then it should only be expected that the
answers we find ourselves inclined to give to the theorist's questions will
tend to be "unsystematic,"[3] and to conflict with the answers others find
themselves inclined to give.[4] And it is also no wonder that we find it

---

[2] Compare Nichols and Ulatowski, who propose that responders to Knobe's "intentional
action" experiments were each guided by one of two different "interpretations" of "intentionally" (Nichols and Ulatowski 2007: 356). And compare also Fischer, Engelhardt, and
Herbelot, who, partly inspired by Austin, note that the theorist's context is "insufficiently
rich", which allows the theorist to develop arguments—Fischer et al. focus on the "Argument
from Illusion"–that trade on the indeterminate sense of key words in those arguments.
(Fischer et al. 2015: 281). This, they propose, allows the philosopher to lead us (and himself)
astray: realizing that the philosopher is (must be) using "looks,", "seems," or "appears" in a
rather uncommon, "purely phenomenal" sense, we grant him that a round coin viewed
sideways (for example) looks elliptical to us; but another, more "dominant," "doxastic" sense
of the word, is then relied upon to draw the conclusion that we are mistaken–are under
"illusion"–about the shape of the object in front of us, which in turn is taken to mean that we
are not really seeing it, but rather some sort of an intermediary (see Fischer et al. 2015: 271-4).
The *general form* of this diagnosis may be applicable to some cases of philosophical difficulty;
but I'm not entirely sure about its specifics. I'm not sure there is an ordinary, "purely
phenomenal" use of "looks," "seems," or "appears," on which the coin viewed sideways
looks, seems, or appears elliptical (under normal conditions)–not even if we (try to) suspend
what we know, or think we know, about its actual shape. My own sense is that when the
philosopher invites us to realize that "a round coin seems elliptical when viewed sideways"
(Fischer et al. 2015: 272), and from there leads us to the conclusion that we do not see the coin
itself, but only some sort of an intermediary, he is relying, from beginning to end, not on any
of the more or less ordinary uses of "looks," "seems," or "appears," but on a compelling *picture*
of perception. It is the picture that gives rise to and sustains the illusion of sense (and truth)
here, not any of the ordinary and normal uses of the words the philosopher employs. And it is,
as Cavell has argued (in Cavell 1979), the inherent plasticity of language—the creativity it
affords—that prevents us from ruling out *in advance* that the philosopher has succeeded in
putting his words to intelligible use. The failure to make (clear enough) sense must here, as
elsewhere, be *made out, shown*.

[3] See Gendler and Hawthorne 2005.

[4] Paul Horwich puts the essential point well when he writes:

> Our intuitive judgments—our basic a priori convictions—are intractably
> messy. Not only do we discover this to be so, but it should be unsurprising
> that we do. For the linguo-conceptual practices that are explicitly articulated
> in such judgments evolved under a variety of shifting and often conflicting

natural to describe ourselves as *intuiting* our answers to the theorist's question, whereas we would normally not be inclined to describe ourselves as intuiting our answers to everyday questions. *Pace* Cappelen, the talk of philosophical "intuition" is neither a mere "tick" or "virus" (PWI: 22), nor merely a dispensable hedge (PWI: 47 and 83). It aptly and successfully registers the sense of lacking sufficient orientation in the theorist's peculiar context—of standing nowhere in particular and having nowhere in particular to go to with one's words.

How could this sort of philosophical idleness be avoided? I do not think there is only one way to avoid it, let alone a recipe for how to avoid it. In the Appendix, I will compare and contrast two different ways—Wittgenstein's and Merleau-Ponty's—of proceeding philosophically *and* meaningfully. But the upshot of this book is that the *first* step in avoiding philosophical idleness is to acknowledge that the sense of our words—including the words of our philosophizing—is not ensured by anything that they bring with them from one occasion of use to another, but rather is a matter of what *we* may most reasonably be found to mean by them, or how *we* may most reasonably be found to mean them, given the history of their employment, the circumstances of their utterance, and the irreducible power speakers have of making, perceiving, and responding to more or less creative sense (as well as nonsense).

constraints (—including our practical and intellectual needs, our limited cognitive powers, and our physical and social environments). So we are almost always left with concepts that are too complex, and/or too vague, and/or too open ended, and/or too family-resemblance-like, and/or too paradox-prone, to be captured by simple definitions, or rules, or guiding theories. (Horwich 2016: 134–5)

Phenomenology and the Limitations of the Wittgensteinian Grammatical Investigation

In Chapter Five, and in other moments in this book, I present Merleau-Ponty and Wittgenstein as allies. The alternative conception of language that I present in that chapter and then go on to support empirically in Chapter Six—the conception on which the minimal assumption is false and the philosophical method of cases is therefore fundamentally misguided—draws equally from each of those two philosophers. This striking alliance between Wittgenstein and one of the most important voices of "Continental" philosophy only goes so far, however. There are deep and important differences between these two philosophers—differences in philosophical method and, relatedly, in what, for each one of them, constitutes what may be described as the basic and general form of philosophical difficulty. My aim in this appendix is to say where I see Wittgenstein and Merleau-Ponty as parting ways, and to explain why, where they do part ways, I choose (for now) to continue with Merleau-Ponty.

A.1 Merleau-Ponty and Wittgenstein: Affinity and Distance

A good place to take initial measure of both the affinity and the distance between Merleau-Ponty and Wittgenstein is the preface to the *Phenomenology of Perception*, which may be read as a response to the at-the-time widespread notion that the still relatively young phenomenological movement in philosophy is plagued by confusion about its own nature and aims. The confusion is (allegedly) evidenced by the fact that the Husserlian search for a priori phenomenological essences is contradicted, so to speak, both in spirit and in practice, by Heidegger's phenomenological existentialism that takes as hopelessly misguided any attempt to understand the human subject apart from her "being-in-the-world"—that is, apart from her finding herself always already *situated* and *responding* to her situation prior to any reflection, unable to ever extricate herself, not even in thought, so not even when she philosophizes, from her ties to the world. This widespread notion of a fundamental rift within the phenomenological movement, Merleau-Ponty proposes, rests on a misunderstanding of the nature and aim of the Husserlian phenomenological investigation and search for essences. "[W]e cannot subject our perception of the world to philosophical scrutiny," he writes, "without ceasing to be identified with that act of positing the world, with that interest in it which delimits us, without drawing back from our commitment which is itself thus made to appear as a spectacle, without passing from the *fact* of our existence to its *nature*, from the Dasein to the Wesen" (Phenomenology: xiv). This, however, does not mean that the Husserlian search for Wesen aims at releasing us, philosophically, from our Dasein, Merleau-Ponty continues. Rather, it is meant to enable us to "become acquainted with and to prevail over [Dasein's] facticity" (Phenomenology: xv).

A little later, Merleau-Ponty says this: "It is the office of language to cause essences to exist in a state of separation which is in fact merely apparent, since through language they still rest upon the ante-predicative life of consciousness" (Phenomenology: xv). This passage expresses two ideas that suggest deep affinity between Merleau-Ponty and the later Wittgenstein. The first is the idea that it is of the very nature of language to create or give rise to the idea of essences that are separable from their particular instances or manifestations, and separable too from the particular uses we make of the words that "express" them.[1] The second is the idea that this separability is merely apparent, since it is precisely through language that those essences are in fact tied to the ante-predicative life of consciousness—that is, to our pre-reflective being-in-the-world. The later Wittgenstein would agree, I think, that the essential repeatability of a word, "x," may naturally give rise, especially when we seek to *explain* theoretically our acquisition and use of words, to the idea that there *must* be something—call it the meaning (or concept) of "x," or the essence of Xhood—which is common to all of the things we (correctly) call "x," makes them all cases of X, and is separable, in principle, from our particular uses of "x." Wittgenstein would also agree that the separable meanings or essences thus envisioned are illusory, because, as his remarks on rule following make clear, the meaning of "x" is not separable from the use(s) ordinarily and normally made of "x," by particular people under particular circumstances.

Moreover, given what he says in the above passage, and given what we saw in Chapter Five (cf. Phenomenology: 391), it would seem that Merleau-Ponty should have no objection to the fundamental Wittgensteinian insight that many traditional philosophical difficulties arise when we assume, or imagine, that our words have meanings separable from their concrete uses by particular human beings in particular humanly significant situations, and that those

---

[1] I remind the reader that I use quotation marks, here and elsewhere, to register that the word is a technical, or quasi-technical term which is part of a philosophical jargon—which means that I am, in effect, quoting, even though I'm not quoting anyone in particular—and to signal that the word, thus used, may only give us the illusion of sense, while covering up real difficulties.

meanings, by themselves, may ensure the sense of what we say by means of those words—regardless of whether, or how, *we* (may reasonably be found to) actually use or mean those words. Nor, it would seem, should Merleau-Ponty have any objection to the Wittgensteinian idea that an important step in dissolving philosophical difficulties *thus* generated is to remind ourselves of the ordinary and normal uses of the philosophically troublesome words, and thereby to "lead those words back from their metaphysical to their everyday use" (PI: 116).

So far, we seem to have found a striking affinity between Wittgenstein and Merleau-Ponty. That's the affinity that I have worked out in some detail in Chapter Five. But I have been quoting Merleau-Ponty selectively. Interspersed among the passages I have quoted are other passages that seem to suggest a deep *dis*agreement between him and Wittgenstein. In those passages, Merleau-Ponty writes critically not directly about Wittgenstein, certainly not about the *later* Wittgenstein—who was, at the time the *Phenomenology* was written, still in the process of coming into his own, and unknown to Merleau-Ponty—but about the Vienna Circle. It does not matter for my purposes what or how much Merleau-Ponty actually knew about the Vienna Circle and the evolving thinking of its members, nor whether he is doing justice in these passages to that thinking. What matters for my purposes is that some of what he says in those passages appears to put him in direct opposition to the later Wittgenstein, and to undermine the above appearance of far-reaching agreement between the two of them.

The Vienna Circle's "logical positivism," Merleau-Ponty writes, "is the antithesis of Husserl's thought," because "[whatever] the subtle changes of meaning which have ultimately brought us, as a linguistic acquisition, the word and concept of consciousness, *we enjoy direct access to what it designates*" (Phenomenology: xv, my emphasis). "Seeking the essence of consciousness," he says a few lines later, "will therefore not consist in developing the *Wortbedeutung* of consciousness and escaping from existence into the universe of things said; it will consist in rediscovering my actual presence to myself, the fact of my consciousness which is in the last resort what the word and the concept of consciousness mean" (Phenomenology: xv).

Now, it is true that the later Wittgenstein does not think of the meanings of words in the way that members of the Vienna Circle such as Schlick and Carnap did. But still, Merleau-Ponty here contends, in effect, that the essence of consciousness (perception, experience, seeing, touching, moving . . .) is not going to be found by way of investigating or clarifying the meaning of the word(s)—not even, I suppose, if we think of those meanings as best revealed in our ordinary and normal *use* of the word(s). And the idea that we could investigate consciousness (perception, experience . . .) *directly*, so to speak—that is, not by way of investigating our use of the word(s)—and *thereby* become clearer about what the word(s) or concept(s) in the last resort mean(s), appears to rely on the sort of representational-referential ("Augustinian") picture of language that the *Investigations* presents as lying at the root of any number of traditional philosophical difficulties.

This seemingly stark disagreement between Merleau-Ponty and Wittgenstein is then reinforced, of course, by the fact that Merleau-Ponty's phenomenological investigation as presented in the *Phenomenology of Perception*, while arguably no less descriptive and therapeutic, takes a very different form from Wittgenstein's grammatical investigations as presented in the *Investigations*. There are many more appeals in the *Phenomenology* to empirical findings concerning both normal and abnormal behavior and perception than reminders about "the kind of statements that we make about phenomena" (PI: 90); and while Wittgenstein too suggests that a commitment to objectivist thinking as epitomized by science lies at the roots of many of our philosophical difficulties (cf. PI: 308), Merleau-Ponty's confrontation of that form of thinking—his attempt to show that it is fundamentally incapable of answering *its own* questions when it comes to human perception and behavior (Phenomenology: 72)—is far more direct and systematic. Indeed, whereas it is important to Wittgenstein to emphasize that his own teaching is not that of a *theory* (PI: 109), Merleau-Ponty has no problem presenting himself as offering a *theory* of perception (cf. Phenomenology: 203).

In sections A.2 and A.3, I will offer an understanding of this seemingly fundamental disagreement between Merleau-Ponty and Wittgenstein. I will propose that what we have here is not so much a fundamental disagreement, as a fundamental difference in *the sort of philosophical difficulty* to which each of these two philosophers is primarily responding. The difficulties to which Wittgenstein primarily responds arise when "language goes on holiday" (PI: 38)—they stem, as I have said, from the idea that our words have meanings separable from their uses, and that those meanings may *by themselves* ensure the sense of what we say by means of those words when we do philosophy, and sustain *substantive* philosophical difficulties. In the face of difficulties *thus* generated, the best response may well be therapy by way of the deliberate assembling of grammatical reminders that aim to reveal the difficulties as artificially created and self-imposed—resting on nothing but non-compulsory and poorly supported theoretical commitments.

In Merleau-Ponty's case, on the other hand, the fundamental difficulty is that of uncovering and clarifying our pre-reflective experience—that is, our experience before we reflect on it with the attempt to understand it theoretically, or explain it empirically—and the world *as perceived* prior to being *thought*, or thought (or talked!) *about*. And the difficulty is hard to overcome because these experiences and world tend to disappear, or get distorted, under reflection, and in particular under the sort of reflection that takes its bearing from what we take ourselves to *know* objectively about the world and about ourselves.

Wittgensteinian grammatical reminders *could* aid us in overcoming this difficulty, by bringing out the *expressive* dimension of our use of words, especially in
those moments when we seek to give voice to our experiences, and by distinguishing those uses of language from those uses that primarily aim at "conveying
information about the external world" (see Wittgenstein 1980a: 899). But those
reminders, I am about to propose, will only take us so far in bringing out and
elucidating our pre-reflective experience; and they *might* actually lead us astray.
Here the *basic* method, or methods, will need to be different. And this, I will
finally propose, is what Wittgenstein himself was coming to realize when, in his
final years, he tried to become clearer about what he called "aspect perception."

A.2 Wittgensteinian Grammar and Phenomenology

Merleau-Ponty and Wittgenstein, I have proposed, may be seen as walking a
considerable distance together, philosophically: both would agree that language
is, at once, the source of certain types of philosophical difficulties and the means
by which those difficulties may be overcome—that at the same time that language
encourages us to look for separable essences, it can redirect us to our existence in
the world in which we first and foremost find ourselves and others, and in which
meaning originally appears.

So far so good. But suppose we want to understand—and moreover understand in their interrelatedness—phenomena such as the following: the way in
which our bodies are perceived by us, or present to us, when geared toward some
particular task, or when we gesture or dance creatively, or when we are at rest; the
way, or ways, in which our past, and the past of our culture, are present in our
present—the way in which we are related to, and draw upon, the history of a
word in putting it to use, for example, or the way in which a childhood trauma, or
some collective trauma, may still be affecting how we look at and respond to
things without our being aware of that; the way in which *others* are present in
our world—the way in which as soon as our gaze falls upon the body of another
"the objects surrounding it immediately take on a fresh layer of significance"
(Phenomenology: 353), for example, or the way in which, in encountering another,
we are already communicating our response to the encounter *to her*, and cannot
avoid communicating to her *some* such response; the way or ways in which
people may deceive themselves—know and at the same time not know that they
have lost a limb (as in cases of a phantom limb), for example, or a friend (see
Phenomenology: 80ff); our ability to create reflective distance between ourselves
and some given situation—which is itself dependent upon our ability to relegate
much of our engagement with the world to habitual responses (cf. Phenomenology: 87)—and our inability to avoid placing ourselves, thereby, in yet another
(related) situation whose meaning is never fully within our grasp, or control

(cf. Phenomenology: 357ff); the way in which the meaning, not only of an utterance, but of anything we might do next, is shaped and constrained by our situation and history, as well as by our language and culture, but at the same time is left indeterminate by them (cf. Phenomenology: 450 and 453); the way in which our death lies altogether outside of our life, and yet affects the significance of every one of its moments (cf. Phenomenology: 364) . . . These are some of the phenomena that the *Phenomenology of Perception* seeks to elucidate. I've given this fairly long list, because I am about to suggest that a Wittgensteinian gram- matical investigation can only take us so far when it comes to elucidating such phenomena; and I wanted to make clear why, if I'm right about this, we may want to go further than it can take us.

Since what we wish to understand are, ultimately, phenomena of *meaning*— or, more precisely, *meaningful phenomena in their meaningfulness*—and the way, or ways, in which those phenomena relate to each other in our experience, I take it to be clear that the understanding we are looking for may not be arrived at from the objectivist, third-personal perspective of empirical science. The phenomena we wish to understand may only be understood and elucidated from the per- spective of someone who has the capacity to perceive and respond to meaning, and by her exercising of that very capacity.

This, I have argued elsewhere (Baz 2012a and Baz 2016a), is also true of Wittgenstein's grammatical investigations and the practice of ordinary language philosophy: the question what utterance makes (what) sense, and under what conditions, is not a question that empirical science could answer for us. The Wittgensteinian or ordinary language philosopher's invitation to consider "what we should say when," or "[how the philosophically troublesome word] is actually used in the language in which it has its original home" (PI: 116, translation amended), I have proposed in the Conclusion to this book, is an invitation to project ourselves imaginatively, in our capacity as competent speakers, into situations of speech—situations in which the philosophically troublesome words would actually be *used*—and thereby to find what makes (what) sense *to us*, and under what conditions.

So far, still so good. The *limitations* of the Wittgensteinian grammatical investigation stem from what Merleau-Ponty, following Husserl, refers to as our "natural attitude." The natural attitude, according to Husserl, is that of being "immersed naively in the world" and "accept[ing] the experien*ced* as such" (Husserl 1998: 14, my emphasis)— focusing on "objects, values, goals," rather than "on the experien*cing* of [one's] life" (Husserl 1998: 15, my emphasis; see also Husserl 1970: 119 and 144). Husserl's "bracketing," or *epoché*, is meant to counteract our tendency to focus on objects (broadly understood) and overlook our experiencing of them—to overlook, that is, how those objects actually present themselves to us, and how we relate to them, before we begin to reflect on and theorize about perception from the perspective of the natural sciences.

Merleau-Ponty invokes the Husserlian notion of "the natural attitude" in the passage from the preface mentioned above, in which he talks about how "our existence is too tightly held in the world to be able to know itself as such at the moment of its involvement" (Phenomenology: xv). He comes back to that idea early in the first chapter of the *Phenomenology*, when he says that "we are caught up in the world and . . . do not succeed in extricating ourselves from it" (Phenomenology: 5). This natural involvement with the world, which Merleau-Ponty later refers to as our "obsession with being" (Phenomenology: 70), culminates in the constitution of an objective world, which (failing to heed Kant's warnings!) we tend to think of as "a world in itself" (Phenomenology: 41)—fully and finally determinate, and wholly independent from our experience of it (cf. Phenomenology: 47).

"The natural attitude . . . " Merleau-Ponty writes, "[throws] me into the world of things, [and thereby] gives me the assurance of apprehending a 'real' beyond appearance, the 'true' beyond illusion" (Phenomenology: 39). "Real" and "true" are in quotation marks in this last passage, precisely in order to alert us to the tendency to understand these terms in their objectivist sense. From the phenomenological perspective, the phenomenal world, the world "I live through" (Phenomenology: xvii), is more real than the objective world, the world I "think," since we construct, posit, the latter on the basis of the former;[2] and the truth of objective judgments presupposes "the experience of truth" (Phenomenology: xvi)—that is, the experience of coming to *see* something aright (see Phenomenology: 302ff).

The main obstacle to understanding perception, and hence behavior, Merleau-Ponty argues, is the tendency to take the objective world—that is, the world as objectively construed—as the starting point of our theorizing about perception. In trying to reconstruct perception on the basis of what we take ourselves to already know objectively, we commit what Merleau-Ponty, following Köhler, calls "the experience error": "we make perception out of things perceived . . . And since perceived things themselves are obviously accessible only through perception, we end up understanding neither" (Phenomenology: 5). "Our perception," he similarly says later on, "ends in objects, and the object once constituted, appears as the reason for all the experience of it which we have had or could have" (Phenomenology: 67). The task of the *Phenomenology* would accordingly be

to rediscover phenomena, the layer of living experience through which other people and things are first given to us, the system of "self-others-things" as it comes into being; to reawaken perception and foil its trick of allowing us to forget it as a fact and as perception in the interest of the object which it presents to us and of the rational tradition to which it gives rise. (Phenomenology: 57)

---

[2] See (Husserl 1970: 127).

Now, if it is of the essence of normal perception to overlook itself in the interest of the object which it presents us, then it is only to be expected that our ordinary and normal use of words would participate in, and reflect, that overlooking of our pre-reflective experience. Consider the extent to which our ordinary and normal talk focuses on objects and their objective constellations—who said or did what to whom, and when; who saw what (object or fact); what has been decided; what's the plan for the evening; at what time the meeting takes place; how much money we've got left; who won the game . . . —rather than on how we experience them *before* we think, or talk, *about* them. And consider also the extent to which, in our *deliberate* initiation of our children into language we teach them what things are called and how to describe their objective constellations. As I've emphasized in Chapter Six, there is *much else* that we do with words, with and around our children, including even when we teach them what things are called; but the *focus* is on things and how they stand, not on how we relate to them experientially, or perceptually.

The tendency to focus on objects and overlook our experiencing of them, I'm proposing, manifests itself in our use of words, including the words that might be thought to refer to the sorts of phenomena Merleau-Ponty is interested in. Thus, for example, "meeting (or encountering) another" is not ordinarily or normally used in the context of describing the *experience* of meeting (or encountering) another; "losing a friend" is not ordinarily or normally used in the context of describing the *experience* of losing, or having lost, a friend; "home," or "being at home," is not ordinarily or normally used in the context of describing the *experience* of being at home, or of coming home; and so on. For this reason, elucidating the grammar of "meeting another," "losing a friend," "(being at) home," and so on—as that grammar reveals itself in our ordinary and normal use of those words, or in our sense of when they would make (what) sense and under what conditions—is not likely to do much to bring those experiences more clearly into view. On something like the contrary, focusing on the Wittgensteinian grammar of such expressions *might* encourage us, as I will propose in section A.3, to take the objectivist perspective as primary and commit the "experience error."

To be sure, if Merleau-Ponty is right, then to project oneself imaginatively into situations of significant speech is to project oneself imaginatively into the phenomenal world—the world in which words may be elicited from us or found called for, and against the background of which they acquire their particular sense(s). Leading words back from their metaphysical to their everyday use (PI: 116) thus partakes of the work of phenomenology.[3] I do not deny this. Nor, again, am I saying that all, or even most of our ordinary and normal discourse is in the business of representing objects and facts. On the contrary, in Chapter Five and Six I have proposed—following Wittgenstein and Merleau-Ponty and going

---

[3] "Linguistic phenomenology," Austin suggests at some point (Austin 1979: 182); but he does not think about it in quite the way that I'm thinking about it here.

against the grain of how language is commonly thought about in contemporary analytic philosophy—that our words are instruments for doing many different kinds of things, only some of which may aptly be thought of as "representing" or "describing" the world. My point is just that we do not primarily, or commonly, use language in order to describe, or express, the perceptual phenomena that Merleau-Ponty seeks to elucidate, and which according to him constitute "the core of primary meaning round which the acts of naming and expression take shape" (Phenomenology: xv). And this means that reminding ourselves of the kinds of statements we make about *those* phenomena will not take us far in uncovering pre-reflective experience, and that they are bound to remain, precisely, *in the background* of the Wittgensteinian grammatical investigation. The difficulty is to make them come to the fore, without distorting them. This is the difficulty of phenomenology, as Merleau-Ponty understands and practices it.

The *Phenomenology of Perception* employs several methods that aim at enabling us to overcome that difficulty. Chief among those methods is the careful description of perceptual and behavioral phenomena, normal and abnormal, and the attempt to show that those phenomena defy objectivist-scientific understanding, as well as different forms of rationalist understanding. They become comprehensible only when we look at them from the phenomenological perspective.

On the phenomenological understanding, the "phenomenal world"—that is, the world *as perceived* and *responded to* prior to being *thought about*—is to be distinguished from the objective world (which we construct on the basis of the phenomenal world); and the human subject may be identified with the phenomenal human body—the *lived*, or *living* body, as Husserl calls it (cf. Husserl 1970: 107)—which is again to be distinguished from the human body as paradigmatically thought about and understood by science. The phenomenal body, be it our own or another person's, is a power of engagement and communication with the phenomenal world: it is geared toward that world, takes hold of it in various ways—with the gaze, with the hand, with words, and in other ways—and responds to its solicitations. The phenomenal body and the phenomenal world are *internally related* to each other, in the sense that neither can be understood apart from its relation to the other: the latter is perceived as a field of actual and potential engagement by the former; the former is perceived as a power of actual and potential engagement with the latter (cf. Phenomenology: 132 and 441).

As I have already noted, the phenomenological understanding of perception and behavior is an understanding from *within*: "I cannot gain a removed knowledge" of the internal relation between the phenomenal body and the phenomenal world, Merleau-Ponty writes (Phenomenology: 75); I can only understand the living body by "enacting it myself, and insofar as I am a body which rises toward the world" (Phenomenology: 75).

As can be seen in this last quotation, in attempting to get us to recognize the phenomenological perspective, and recognize its truth, Merleau-Ponty is not relying on the ordinary and normal use, hence sense(s), of words such as "see," "hear," "body," "world," and so on. On something like the contrary, he relies heavily on figurative, creative language, as when he talks here of the body as "rising toward the world," or talks elsewhere of the hand when used for touching something as "shoot[ing] through like a rocket to reveal the external object . . . " (Phenomenology: 92), or of our phenomenal body, when we lean with our hands against a desk, as trailing behind our hands "like the tail of a comet" (Phenomenology: 100). And when he does employ terms such as "body," "physical world," "causalities," and so on, that may naturally be understood in their ordinary and normal—that is, objectivist—sense, he typically, or at least initially, puts them in quotation marks, in order to signal that he is inviting us to understand each one of them in a new, phenomenological sense (cf. Phenomenology: 83 and 115). So he is using those words, and invites us to understand them, in what Wittgenstein would call a "secondary meaning" (PI, Part II (hereafter "PPF"): remark 216). And this means that he is leading them, *not* back to, but rather, in a sense, away from, the language in which they have their original home.

A.3 The Limitations of the Wittgensteinian Grammatical Investigation: The Case of Aspect Perception

One type of experience that brings out in a rather dramatic way the difference between the objective world and the world as pre-reflectively perceived, and brings out the role *we* play in bringing about the unity and sense of the latter, is the dawning, or lighting up, of what Wittgenstein calls "aspects." (That we play a role in bringing about the unity and sense of the *former* is arguably Kant's most important insight.) Merleau-Ponty invokes that type of experience several times in the *Phenomenology*. Early on, he gives the example of the Necker cube in support of his claim that "ordinary experience draws a clear distinction between sense experience and judgment" (Phenomenology: 34). In the case of the Necker cube, he says, "even if I *know* that it can be seen in two ways, the figure in fact refuses to change its structure and my knowledge must await its intuitive realization" (Phenomenology: 34); and this, he says, shows that "judgment is not perception" (Phenomenology: 34). The Gestalt psychologists appealed to phenomena of aspect-switch as a way of challenging the tendency to seek to understand perception on the basis of the world we know, or think we know, objectively, and more specifically in order to refute the "constancy hypothesis"— the hypothesis, namely, that there is a one-to-one correlation between the objects we perceive, as known and understood objectively, and our perceptual experience of them (cf. Köhler 1947: 55 and 70).

In what became section xi of part II of the *Investigations* ("PPF"), Wittgenstein introduces the topic of aspect perception by distinguishing between two uses, hence senses, of the word "see" (PPF: 111). So he identifies the subject matter of his investigation *grammatically*; and in many of his remarks on aspects he seeks to further elucidate grammatically "the *concept* [of noticing an aspect] and its place among the concepts of experience" (PPF: 115). As I have argued elsewhere (Baz 2009), in order to attain clarity about the grammar of "seeing" a Wittgensteinian aspect—or for that matter any other concept of experience— we need to do more than just remind ourselves of particular isolated forms of words that may be used to describe or otherwise give voice to our experience. We need also to remind ourselves of "the occasion and purpose" of those phrases (PPF: 311). "It is necessary to get down to the application (*Anwendung*)" (PPF: 165), to ask oneself "What does anyone tell me by saying 'Now I see it as . . . '? What consequences has this piece of communication? What can I do with it?" (PPF: 176, translation amended; see also Wittgenstein 1980a: 339). A striking feature of virtually all of the readings of Wittgenstein's remarks on aspects with which I am familiar, is that they fail to heed *this* Wittgensteinian call altogether.[4] The use of the relevant terms—where that importantly includes the *philosopher's* use of them—tends to be neglected in favor of theoretical commitments and ambitions.[5]

By his own testimony, however, Wittgenstein continued to find the phenomena of aspect perception extremely perplexing until the very end of his life.[6] I want to suggest that Wittgenstein's difficulties with aspects stem, at least in part, from the inherent limitations of his grammatical inquiry: it is suitable for elucidating the concept of "aspect (dawning)" and its place among our concepts of experience, but less suitable for elucidating the *experience* of aspect dawning and its relation to other features and dimensions of our perceptual experience.

In fact, an important tenet of Wittgenstein's grammatical investigation is that it is meant, among other things, to turn our attention *away* from our experiences. This can be seen in the remarks on aspects, where Wittgenstein again and again

---

[4] In Baz 2009, I discuss in considerable detail Wittgenstein's grammatical elucidation of "(noticing an) aspect."

[5] As a result, "aspect" as used by philosophers who present themselves as interpreting Wittgenstein has come to mean, literally, just about everything and anything one might be said to perceive. Thus, for example, Severin Schroeder writes: "[W]henever something is seen (and not only looked at inanely or absent-mindedly) *some* aspect of it must be noticed, be it only certain shapes or colors" (Schroeder 2010: 366). But how exactly, or in what sense, is the color of an object or its shape an *aspect*? Not, I believe, in Wittgenstein's sense. As I note in the text, Wittgenstein explicitly distinguishes between an aspect and 'a property of the object' (PPF: 247).

[6] Ray Monk reports that not long before death, and after many years of thinking about the topic, Wittgenstein said to his friend Maurice Drury: "Now try and say what is involved in seeing something as something; it is not easy. These thoughts I am now having are as hard as granite" (Monk 1991: 537).

calls upon his reader (or himself) to "*forget*, forget that you have these experiences yourself" (Wittgenstein 1980b: 531), not to try to "analyze your own inner experience" (PPF: 188), and to think about aspect perception from a third-person perspective (PPF: 241 and 204). This, I have argued elsewhere (Baz 2011), is an effective and well-motivated approach when it comes to the sort of philosophically troublesome concepts that are the focus of the first part of the *Investigations*: "learning," "understanding," "meaning," "naming," "thinking," "reading," "intending," and so on. When it comes to concepts such as *those*, the attempt to elucidate them by way of reflection on "what happens in us" when we learn, understand, think, intend, and so on, is bound to lead us astray.[7] Here, what is needed is what Cavell has insightfully called Wittgenstein's "undoing of the psychologizing of psychology" (Cavell 1969: 91). The problem with "aspect-dawning" (and therefore with "aspect" as Wittgenstein uses it), however, is that, unlike "learning," "understanding," "naming," and so on, it *does* refer to a *particular sort of experience*—an experience, moreover, that is internally related to, and therefore revelatory of, the rest of our perceptual experience. And however far we may go in elucidating the language-game(s) in which we give voice to that experience, and in this way elucidate the *concept* of "noticing an aspect," here the experience *is* in the last resort what the word and concept of "(noticing an) aspect" mean (Phenomenology: xv). No amount of Wittgensteinian grammar would be much help to someone unfamiliar with the experience, or incapable of having it.

   To be clear, it is open to Wittgenstein, just as it is open to Merleau-Ponty and to everyone else, to try to *describe the experience* of the dawning, or lighting up, of an aspect, or, for that matter, any other sort of experience. And this is something that Wittgenstein actually does in some of his remarks, including early on in section xi of PPF when he characterizes the experience of aspect-dawning by means of the example of being struck by the likeness of one face to another, and writes "I *see* that [the face] has not changed; and yet I see it differently" (PPF: 113). My point has just been that when he does *that*, Wittgenstein is no longer engaged in the grammatical investigation of philosophically troublesome words or concepts by way of the perspicuous representation of language-games, but rather is moving, as Cavell puts it, "to regions of a word's use which cannot be assured or explained by an appeal to its ordinary language games" (Cavell 1979: 189). And my two further proposals are, first, that in attempting to elucidate the experience of aspect-dawning in its relation to other experiences and dimensions

---

[7] I do not say, and do not think, that reflection from the first-person perspective on *experiences* of learning, understanding, naming, and so on, is necessarily misleading, or that it has no value. All I say, following Wittgenstein, is that it is not the way to go when our goal is to disentangle *conceptual* entanglements.

of our experience Wittgenstein is not as helpful, or as effective, as Merleau-Ponty, whose methods of inquiry are more suitable for *that* task; and, second, that he sometimes betrays a tendency to be misled by grammar into taking the objectivist perspective on perception as primary. Let me end by saying a little more about this.

At least on first approximation, in the first use of "see" Wittgenstein describes, we may see what is, and *cannot* see what is not, anyway there to be seen—objectively, third personally, independently from whether we see it or not. Examples of objects of sight of this first category would be "a red circle over there" (PPF: 121), a knife and a fork (PPF: 122), and a conventional picture of a lion (PPF: 203). In its second use, "see" is used to refer to, or express, the seeing of "aspects"—the seeing of a resemblance between a face you are looking at and another, for example, where seeing the resemblance is not a matter of seeing (judging) *that* there is an objectively establishable resemblance between the two faces, but rather is a matter of undergoing a particular kind of experience in which you all of a sudden come to see the other face *in* the face you are looking at, so that the latter *comes to look different.*

"What I perceive in the dawning of an aspect," Wittgenstein writes, "is not a property of the object, but an internal relation between it and other objects" (PPF: 247). The notion of "internal relation" (*interne Relation*) is drawn from Gestalt psychology and is, importantly, a *perceptual* notion, not an objective, third-personal notion.[8] Two (or more) perceived things (objects, elements) stand in an internal relation to each other when their perceived qualities are not independent of the perceived relation between them. Here is a passage from Kurt Koffka that illustrates what is meant by the notion: "Two colors adjacent to each other are not perceived as two independent things, but as having an inner connection which is at the same time a factor determining the special qualities A and B themselves" (Koffka 1999: 221). According to Gestalt psychology, what we perceive, at the most basic level, is not atomic sensations that we must then somehow synthesize into significant wholes, but rather unified, significant wholes, where the perceived qualities of the elements of a perceived whole, and so the specific contributions those elements make to the overall perceived significance of that whole, are not perceptually independent from that perceived overall significance.

The duck-rabbit provides a simple illustration of this. When you see it as a rabbit, say, you see the two "appendages" as ears; but your seeing them as ears is

---

[8] Schroeder muddles the issue by speaking of the similarity that strikes us as at once "an internal relation" (Schroeder 2010: 359) and "an objective feature of the object, namely a relation of likeness between it and some other object" (Schroeder 2010: 360). But a similarity thought of as an objective feature is not—cannot conceptually be—an *internal* relation.

not independent of your seeing the whole thing as a rabbit. Perceptually, the ears are (seen as) ears only when the whole thing is (seen as) a rabbit. One important thing this means is that your seeing the duck-rabbit as a rabbit cannot be *explained* as the outcome of your seeing this portion of the drawing as ears, that portion as mouth, another portion as the back of the head, and so on. The rabbit aspect is not synthesized from elements that have their "rabbit-part" significance independently of being elements of that overall aspect. On the other hand, if you took the basic elements of our perception of the duck-rabbit to only have objectively establishable, geometrical properties, and so to be devoid of any rabbit (and equally duck) significance, then you would never be able to explain, on *that* basis, why those elements got synthesized into the rabbit aspect, say, rather than the duck aspect. This shows that the perception of significant wholes should be taken as primary.

Another case of Gestalt perception, which is at the heart of Wittgenstein's understanding of philosophical difficulty, is that of linguistic meaning, or sense. As we saw in Chapter Five, on Wittgenstein's (and Merleau-Ponty's) view, which may be seen as a development of Frege's "context principle," the basic unit of linguistic sense is neither the isolated word, nor the isolated string of words, but an utterance—a human *act* performed against the background of the history of the language, the culture, and of the individual participants. Phenomenologically— which means, from the perspective we all occupy as speakers engaged in discourse, as opposed to theoreticians reflecting on it academically—analysis presupposes synthesis: the contribution made by each word to the overall sense of an utterance is not independent from, and therefore cannot *explain*, that overall sense.

It is important to note that internal relations hold not just among the perceived elements of perceived things but also, and equally fundamentally, between perceived objects and the background against which they are perceived. This is likely to be missed by those who mostly focus, in their reflection on aspect perception, on the examples of schematic drawings and deliberately ambiguous figures, which are typically encountered in the artificial context of a psychology lab or philosophy classroom. Even here, the perceived objects stand in internal relations to other objects, as Wittgenstein notes; but the way in which foreground and background are internally related in normal perception, and therefore change together, does not come out clearly in their case. It comes out far more clearly in the more natural cases of aspect dawning.[9]

(That the analysis of perceptual experience presupposes its synthesis and therefore cannot explain it is one of Kant's fundamental insights, and his most basic objection to empiricist-mechanical accounts of how unity arises in our

---

[9] I discuss the internal relation between figure and background, and give real-life examples, in Baz, forthcoming.

experience. Kant saw that we must play an active role in bringing about— "constituting," as the phenomenologists later came to say—the unity of our experience. What Kant missed, the phenomenologists have argued, is the possibility, and reality, of a perceived unity that, while in some clear sense intelligible and intersubjectively shareable, is not objectively establishable, or conceptually capturable.[10] As I've said, the dawning of Wittgensteinian aspects brings out especially clearly the distinction between what we *perceive* and what we objectively *think* (or know), and the reality of intersubjectively shareable, nonconceptual, perceptual synthesis, or unity.)

Now go back to the experience Wittgenstein describes of being struck by the similarity between two faces. A similarity understood as an objective property of the faces is an *external* relation between them: each face has its objective properties, which one may come to know without knowing anything about the other face, and those properties determine whether, and if so to what extent, the two may count (context-dependently) as bearing some objective similarity to each other. And so you may look at a face and see (first sense), or have someone point out or demonstrate to you, that there is some visible similarity between it and another, where seeing *that* need not involve, or bring about, *any* change in how you visually experience the face you're looking at: its perceived Gestalt (physiognomy, expression) need not change at all.

By contrast, in the experience Wittgenstein describes, the perceived Gestalt of the face you're looking at changes; and what dawns on you here is an *internal* relation between the one face and the other, precisely because the perceived relation—of similarity—is inseparable from the perceived change in the overall physiognomy or expression of the face. The perceived qualities of each of the two faces that make them bear a similarity to each other are not independent, perceptually, from our perception of the similarity.[11] (Again, they *could be*: we could recognize an objectively establishable similarity between the faces—a similarity that may simply be *known* to be there, and which does not depend on anyone's visual experience of the face. But that would not be the seeing of a Wittgensteinian aspect—the *seeing* of one thing *as* another. As Wittgenstein notes, even the person he calls "aspect-blind" and defines as someone "lacking in the capacity to see something *as something*" should be able to recognize

---

[10] In the preface to the *Phenomenology*, Merleau-Ponty says that Kant made an important move toward recognizing, and recognizing the fundamental importance of, nonconceptual-and-yet-intersubjectively-sharable-perceived synthesis in his account of beauty in the *Critique of Judgment* (Phenomenology: xvii).

[11] Compare Lakoff and Johnson who argue that the "cross-domain" similarities expressed by metaphors are not objective similarities that are there anyway but rather are similarities that we "project"—that is, we *see* one domain *as* (similar to) another (cf. Lakoff and Johnson 2003: 244–5).

objective similarity and "execute such orders as 'Bring me something that looks like *this*'" (PPF: 257).)

Now let's go back to Wittgenstein's two uses of "see." There is no denying that the first use is in some clear sense *primary*, and the second use is in some clear sense *secondary*: not only do we learn the first use before we learn the second, and not only is the first far more common than the second, but it also seems clear that the second use is parasitic on the first—that we could not have learned the second use if we were not already familiar with the first. This, however, is just what we should expect if our being-in-the-world, and hence our everyday use of words, reflects the natural attitude; and it would therefore be a mistake to take this *grammatical* primacy as evidence for the relative *phenomenological* primacy of seeing in the first sense.

This mistake is made by Charles Travis in his otherwise careful and compelling account of what he calls "perception" (Travis 2013). Travis's account is premised on two Fregean dichotomies. The first is that between things in the objective "environment" (cf. Travis 2013: 60) and metaphysically private, individually owned "*Vorstellungen*" (cf. Travis 2013: 62ff and 82ff). Appealing throughout to the grammar of "see" in Wittgenstein's first use of the word, in which "what someone saw is bounded by what there was, anyway, to be seen" (Travis 2013: 411)—"something which can form images on retinas" (Travis 2013: 100)—Travis insists that only the former are proper objects of perception, and that failure to acknowledge this would lead us straightaway to positing objects of the second kind as objects of perception, which he takes—correctly in my view— to be hopeless. The problem for Travis is that Wittgensteinian aspects are objects of perception that fall on neither side of his dichotomy: their presence is not objectively establishable (you'd be neither wrong nor literally blind if you couldn't see a particular aspect); they *are* partly dependent on us ("are subject to the will" (PPF: 256)); *and yet* it makes perfect sense to call upon others to share (the seeing of) an aspect with you, whereas—by definition, as it were—it would make no sense to call upon another to share a Fregean *Vorstellung* with you.

The second dichotomy Travis insists on is that between what *perception* presents us with, and *our response* to what it presents us with—a response that for Travis must be an act of *thought* that cannot affect *what we perceive* (cf. Travis 2013: 411; and Travis 2015: 49). But, as I've already noted, the seeing of Wittgensteinian aspects reveals our power to affect *what we perceive*, rather than, and separably from, what we think, or judge.

Aware of the difficulty, and attempting to "do away with any . . . impression of a threat" to his general account (Travis 2013: 13), Travis insists again and again that the set of related phenomena Wittgenstein is investigating under the title of "aspect perception" is "unusual" (Travis 2013: 102 and 180), "*recherché*" (Travis 2013: 411), or "special" (Travis 2015: 45); and he goes as far as to claim that "see" in Wittgenstein's "second use" is not even used for talking about or expressing *seeing* (Travis 2013: 102 and 411). And here, I'm proposing, his faithful adherence to Wittgensteinian grammar has led him astray.

To be clear: the *dawning* of a Wittgensteinian aspect *is* a rather esoteric, or anyway unusual, phenomenon; and insofar as it is essential to Wittgensteinian aspects that they *dawn*—they cannot, I have argued elsewhere (Baz 2000), be perceived *continuously* while remaining (what Wittgenstein calls) *aspects*—the seeing of Wittgensteinian aspects is esoteric, or anyway unusual. However, insofar as the second use of "see" refers us to a level of experience in which we play an active role in bringing about the unity and sense—the overall expression or physiognomy, the pre-reflective significance—of what we perceive and respond to prior to any objective judgment or thought about what we perceive, it may nonetheless refer us to what comes first *in the order of perception*.

It is this *phenomenological* primacy that Koffka speaks about when he says that "phenomena such as 'friendliness' and 'unfriendliness' are extremely primitive—even more so, perhaps, than that of a blue spot" (Koffka 1999: 134), or that "an object looks attractive or repulsive before it looks black or blue, circular or square" (Koffka 1999: 230). Merleau-Ponty expresses similar ideas, but goes even further, when he argues that, before they are identified objectively, even shapes and colors are perceived physiognomically (cf. Phenomenology: 61), within the context of a temporally extended perceptual field of actual and potential bodily engagement—a field whose elements form a system in which they are all internally related to each other (cf. Phenomenology: 46–7, 52ff, 209ff, and 313), so that colors have *affective* and *motor* significance (Phenomenology: 210), and the blue of a carpet, for example, "would never be the same blue were it not a woolly blue" (Phenomenology: 313). But we are likely to miss much of this, and to fail to appreciate how radically we would need to break from the objectivist perspective in order to truly understand our perceptual experience, if we mostly focus, as Wittgenstein did, on the ambiguous figures, schematic drawings, and other objects that are encountered in the artificial context of doing philosophy, or psychology. Those are useful for the elucidation of the grammar of "aspect-dawning," but problematic if taken as paradigmatic of the experience of aspect dawning.

"Cases of ambiguous perception in which we can at will choose our anchorage," Merleau-Ponty writes, referring precisely to the sorts of examples Wittgenstein primarily considers, "are those in which our perception is artificially cut off from its context and its past, in which we do not perceive with our whole being, in which we play a game with our body and with that generality which enables it at any time to break with any historical commitment and to function on its own account" (Phenomenology: 279–80). Normally, how we see things is tied to the whole of our perceptual field, with its horizons of language and culture and our personal and impersonal history, and therefore is not subject to the will in the way that seeing the duck-rabbit as a duck, or a rabbit, is subject to the will. Normally, we *find ourselves* seeing things one way or another. And yet we do play a role in how we see things, as is evidenced by the dawning of aspects in the natural course of everyday experience, by the fact that it makes sense to *call upon* or *invite* others, as well as to *try*, to see things one way or another, and by the all-too-familiar fact that others often *perceive* things—not just *think* about them—very differently from us. But we are likely to miss the active role we play in how the world presents itself to us perceptually, or to unduly dismiss it, as Travis has done, if we take "seeing" in its first use, and the objectivist perspective more generally, as primary.

In many of Wittgenstein's remarks on aspects, he engages with the ideas of Gestalt psychologists; and in a number of those remarks, he betrays a tendency to take seeing in the first sense, and therefore the objectivist perspective, as primary (cf. Wittgenstein 1980a: 1035; and Wittgenstein 1980b: 474).[12] This comes out most clearly when he responds to Köhler's idea that when figure and background switch for us as we look at figures such as the "double-cross," lines that we previously saw as "belonging together" are no longer seen as "belonging together," and vice versa (Köhler 1947: 100–1, and 108).[13] Wittgenstein protests that Köhler's account is misleading, because "the radii that belonged together before belong together now as well; only one time they bound an 'arm,' another time an intervening space" (Wittgenstein 1980a: 1117). But, as Merleau-Ponty notes early on in the *Phenomenology of Perception* (Phenomenology: 4) and as empirical studies have shown (see Köhler 1947: 108; Baylis and Driver 1993; and Block 2010), we *actually do perceive* the outline of the figure we focus on as *belonging to the figure*, and *not* to its background (or intervening space), whose shape is *perceptually indeterminate* (cf. Phenomenology: 13; and Köhler 1947: 107); and this, despite the fact—of which Köhler was well aware!—that when we consider the matter *objectively*, the outline of the figure is equally the outline of its background. Köhler was not forgetting or ignoring the objective, or objectivist, perspective. He was *challenging* the tendency, to which Wittgenstein has here succumbed, to take it as the starting point when attempting to describe and understand the world *as pre-reflectively perceived* (cf. Köhler 1947: 55). Moreover, being fully aware of the way in which our ordinary and normal use of words encourages the objectivist understanding of perception, Köhler proposed that in order to do

---

[12] Eilan has recently proposed, and has on good evidence taken Wittgenstein to propose, that seeing in the first sense comes first in the order of perception as well—that the Wittgensteinian aspect merely "overlays the physical object, as seen, and its apparent shape and colours" (Eilan 2013: 9).

[13] My aim in what follows is not to defend Köhler—I might be reading him *too* charitably (by my lights)—but to underscore the limitations of Wittgenstein's grammatical investigation.

justice to our perception we would need *new concepts*, such as the *phenomenal* concepts of "belonging together" and "organization" (cf. Köhler 1947: 80).[14] As I have noted, Merleau-Ponty would have included "color" and "shape"—and equally "movement," "location," "size," and other words that are primarily used to refer to objective properties—among the words that would need to be understood phenomenologically if we are to understand our perception of color, shape, movement, and so on.

Nor, finally, did Köhler thereby commit himself to positing *inner* or metaphysically *private* objects—what Travis would call "*Vorstellungen*"—as our objects of sight. In proposing that the (phenomenal) "organization" of what we see is no less basic than colors and shapes—or, going in the other direction, that colors and shapes too are pre-reflectively perceived and responded to within the context of a unified field and are subject to contextual and attitudinal effects[15]—he did not proceed, as Wittgenstein suggests he did, from "the idea of the visual impression as an inner object" which is "a chimera; a queerly shifting construction" (PPF: 134).[16] The dichotomy between what's "external" and what's "internal" is itself an objectivist dichotomy. The phenomenal world—the world in which the outline of a figure "belongs" to it, faces have expressions, cities have tempers (Phenomenology: 24), and words are meaningful—being prior in the order of perception to the objectivist world, and perspective, is neither aptly thought of as "external" nor aptly thought of as "internal"; and it is not to be found, or explored, by anything we may aptly think of as "introspection" (see Phenomenology: 57). To ask where it is, objectively, is to ask a bad question. But it *is* where we first and foremost find ourselves, and others.

---

[14] The subtitle of Köhler's book *Gestalt Psychology* is "An Introduction to New Concepts in Modern Psychology." It is true that in the particular passage Wittgenstein seems to be citing (Wittgenstein gives no exact reference) Köhler is not careful to put "belong together" and "organization" in quotation marks or scare quotes, as he does elsewhere (cf. Köhler 1947: 80), as a way of signaling that the words are not to be taken in their common, objectivist, sense; but that may well be because, by that point, he is already counting on his reader to know that he means these terms to refer to "*visual* facts" (Köhler 1947: 108, my emphasis), as contrasted with physical facts.

[15] As was made evident by the case of the white-gold/blue-black dress that befuddled internet surfers a little while ago (see https://en.wikipedia.org/wiki/The_dress_(viral_phenomenon)).

[16] Eilan too accuses Köhler of positing "*internal* phenomenal objects" (Eilan 2013: 15, my emphasis).

References

Armstrong, S. L., Gleitman, L. R., and Gleitman, H. (1999). 'What Some Concepts Might Not Be'. In Margolis and Laurence (1999): 225–59.

Austin, J. L. (1964). *Sense and Sensibilia*. New York: Oxford University Press.

Austin, J. L. (1979). *Philosophical Papers*. New York: Oxford University Press.

Austin, J. L. (1999). *How to Do Things with Words*. Cambridge, MA: Harvard University Press.

Bartsch, K. and Wellman, H. (1995). *Children Talk about the Mind*. New York: Oxford University Press.

Baylis, G. C. and Driver, J. (1995). 'Visual Attention and Objects: Evidence for Hierarchical Coding of Location'. *Journal of Experimental Psychology: Human Perception and Performance* 19: 451–70.

Baz, A. (2000). 'What's the Point of Seeing Aspects?' *Philosophical Investigations* 23: 97–121.

Baz, A. (2009). 'On Learning from Wittgenstein; or What Does it Take to *See* the Grammar of Seeing Aspects?' In *Seeing Wittgenstein Anew*. W. Day and V. Krebs (eds.). New York: Cambridge University Press, pp. 227–48.

Baz, A. (2011). 'Seeing Aspects and Philosophical Difficulty'. In *The Oxford Handbook of Wittgenstein*. Marie McGinn and Oskari Kuusela (eds.). New York: Oxford University Press, pp. 697–713.

Baz, A. (2012a). *When Words Are Called For*. Cambridge, MA: Harvard University Press.

Baz, A. (2012b). 'Must Philosophers Rely on Intuitions?' *Journal of Philosophy* 109: 316–37.

Baz, A. (2014). 'Whose Dream Is It Anyway?' *International Journal for the Study of Skepticism* 4: 263–87.

Baz, A. (2016a). 'Ordinary Language Philosophy'. In *The Oxford Handbook of Philosophical Methodology*. Herman Cappelen, Tamar Gendler, and John Hawthorne (eds.). New York: Oxford University Press, pp. 112–29.

Baz, A. (2016b). 'The Sound of Bedrock: Lines of Grammar between Kant, Wittgenstein, and Cavell'. *European Journal of Philosophy* 24: 607–28.

Baz, A. (forthcoming). 'Motivational Indeterminacy'. *European Journal of Philosophy* DOI: 10.1111/ejop.12163.

Bealer, G. (1998). 'Intuition and the Autonomy of Philosophy'. In *Rethinking Intuition: The Psychology of Intuition and Its Role in Philosophical Inquiry*. M. DePaul and W. Ramsey (eds.). Oxford: Rowman and Littlefield, pp. 201–40.

Bealer, G. (2000). 'A Theory of the A Priori'. *Pacific Philosophical Quarterly* 81: 1–30.

Block, N. (2010). 'Attention and Mental Paint'. *Philosophical Issues* 20: 23–63.

Bloom, P. (2000). *How Children Learn the Meanings of Words*. Cambridge, MA: MIT Press.

Bloom, P. (2001). 'Precis of *How Children Learn the Meanings of Words*'. *Behavioral and Brain Sciences* 24: 1095–134.

Brandom, R. (1994). *Making It Explicit*. Cambridge, MA: Harvard University Press.

Brandom, R. (2008). *Between Saying and Doing*. New York: Oxford University Press.

Bruner, J. (1983). *Child's Talk: Learning to Use Language*. New York: W. W. Norton & Company.

Bruner, J. (1990). *Acts of Meaning*. Cambridge, MA: Harvard University Press.

Buckwalter, W. (2010). 'Knowledge Isn't Closed on Saturdays'. *Review of Philosophy and Psychology* 1: 395–406.

Camp, E. (2016). 'Conventions' Revenge: Davidson, Derangement, and Dormativity'. *Inquiry* 59: 113–38.

Canfield, J. (1993). 'The Living Language: Wittgenstein and the Empirical Study of Communication'. *Language Sciences* 15: 165–93.

Cappelen, H. (2012). *Philosophy without Intuitions*. New York: Oxford University Press.

Cappelen, H. (2013). 'Nonesense and Illusions of Thought'. *Philosophical Perspectives, Philosophy of Language* 27: 22–50.

Cappelen, H. and Lepore, E. (2005). *Insensitive Semantics*. Malden, MA: Blackwell Publishing.

Carpendale, J., Hammond, S., and Lewis, C. (2010). 'The Social Origin and Moral Nature of Human Thinking'. *Behavioral and Brain Sciences* 33: 334.

Carston, R. (2002). *Thoughts and Utterances*. Malden, MA: Blackwell.

Cavell, S. (1969). *Must We Mean What We Say?* New York: Cambridge University Press.

Cavell, S. (1979). *The Claim of Reason*. New York: Oxford University Press.

Chomsky, N. (1995). 'Language and Nature'. *Mind* 104: 1–61.

Clarke, T. (1972). 'The Legacy of Skepticism'. *Journal of Philosophy* 69: 754–69.

Cohen, S. (1998). 'Contextualist Solutions to Epistemological Problems: Scepticism, Gettier, and the Lottery'. *Australasian Journal of Philosophy* 76: 289–306.

Cohen, S. (1999). 'Contextualism, Skepticism, and the Structure of Reasons'. *Philosophical Perspectives* 13: 57–89.

Conant, J. (1998). 'Wittgenstein on Meaning and Use'. *Philosophical Investigations* 21: 222–50.

Cova, F., Dupoux, E., and Jacob, P. (2010). 'Moral Evaluation Shapes Linguistic Reports of Others' Mental States, Not Theory of Mind'. *Behavioral and Brain Sciences* 33: 334–5.

Cullen, S. (2010). 'Survey-Driven Romanticism'. *Review of Philosophy and Psychology* 1: 275–96.

Cummins, R. (1998). 'Reflections on Reflective Equilibrium'. In *Rethinking Intuitions: The Psychology of Intuition and Its Role in Philosophical Inquiry*. M. DePaul and W. Ramsey (eds.). Oxford: Rowman and Littlefield, pp. 113–28.

Davidson, D. (2001). *Inquiries into Truth and Interpretation*. New York: Oxford University Press.

Davidson, D. (2006). 'A Nice Derangement of Epitaphs'. In *The Essential Davidson*. E. Lepore and K. Ludwig (eds.). New York: Oxford University Press.

DeRose, K. (1992). 'Contextualism and Knowledge Attributions'. *Philosophy and Phenomenological Research* 52: 913–29.

DeRose, K. (1995). 'Solving the Skeptical Problem'. *Philosophical Review* 104: 1–52.

DeRose, K. (2002). 'Assertion, Knowledge, and Context'. *Philosophical Review* 111: 167–203.

DeRose, K. (2005). 'The Ordinary Language Basis for Contextualism, and the New Invariantism'. *Philosophical Quarterly* 55: 172–98.

DeRose, K. (2011). 'Contextualism, Contrastivism, and X-Phi Surveys'. *Philosophical Studies* 156: 81–110.

Deutsch, M. (2015). *The Myth of the Intuitive*. Cambridge, MA: MIT Press.

Devitt, M. (2011). 'Experimental Semantics'. *Philosophy and Phenomenological Research* 82: 418–35.

Dudley, R., Orita, N., Hacquard, V., and Lidz, J. (2015). 'Three-year-olds' Understanding of *Know* and *Think*'. In *Experimental Perspectives on Presuppositions*. F. Schwarz (ed.). New York: Springer, pp. 241–53.

Eilan, N. (2013). 'On the Paradox of Gestalt Switches: Wittgenstein's Response to Kohler'. *Journal for the History of Analytic Philosophy* 2: 1–19.

Elbourne, P. (2011). *Meaning—A Slim Guide to Semantics*. New York: Oxford University Press.

Fantl, J. and McGrath, M. (2002). 'Evidence, Pragmatics, and Justification'. *Philosophical Review* 111: 67–94.

Feldman, R. (2007). 'Critical Study: John Hawthorne, *Knowledge and Lotteries*'. *Philosophy and Phenomenological Research* 75: 211–26.

Fischer, E. and Collins, J. (2015). *Experimental Philosophy, Rationalism, and Naturalism*. New York: Routledge.

Fischer, E., Engelhardt, P., and Herbelot, A. (2015). 'Intuitions and Illusions'. In Fischer and Collins (2015): 259–92.

Frege, G. (1979). 'Notes for Ludwig Darmstaedter'. In *Posthumous Writings*. H. Hermes, F. Kambartel, and F. Kaulbach (eds.). Chicago: University of Chicago Press, pp. 253–7.

Frege, G. (1999). *The Foundations of Arithmetic*. Austin, J. L. (tr.). Evanston, IL: Northwestern University Press.

Fodor, J. (1975). *The Language of Thought*. Cambridge, MA: Harvard University Press.

Fodor, J. (1987). *Psychosemantics*. Cambridge, MA: MIT Press.

Fodor, J. (1999). 'Information and Representation'. In Margolis and Laurence (1999): 513–24.

Fogel, A., Nelson-Goens, G. C., Hsu, H. C., and Shapiro, A. F. (2000). 'Do Different Infant Smiles Reflect Different Positive Emotions?' *Social Development* 9: 497–520.

Geach, P. (1960). 'Ascriptivism'. *Philosophical Review* 69: 221–5.

Geach, P. (1965). 'Assertion'. *Philosophical Review* 74: 449–65.

Gendler, T. and Hawthorne, J. (2005). 'The Real Guide to Fake Barns: A Catalogue of Gifts for Your Epistemic Enemies'. *Philosophical Studies* 124: 331–52.

Gettier, E. (1963). 'Is True Justified Belief Knowledge?' *Analysis* 23: 121–3.

Geurts, B. (2000). 'Review of Bloom 2000: How Children Learn the Meanings of Words'. *Linguist List* posting 11.1151. http://linguistlist.org/issues/11/11-1151.html.

Giora, R. (2003). *On Our Mind*. New York: Oxford University Press.

Gleitman, L. and Papafragou, A. (2005). 'Language and Thought'. In *The Cambridge Handbook of Thinking and Reasoning*. K. Holyoak and B. Morrison (eds.). New York: Cambridge University Press, pp. 633–62.

Goldman, A. (2007). 'Philosophical Intuitions: Their Target, Their Source, and Their Epistemic Status'. *Grazer Philosophische Studien* 4: 1–26.

Goldman, A. and Pust, J. (1998). 'Philosophical Theory and Intuitional Evidence'. In *Rethinking Intuitions: The Psychology of Intuition and Its Role in Philosophical Inquiry*. M. DePaul and W. Ramsey (eds.). Oxford: Rowman and Littlefield, pp. 179–97.

Goldstein, K. (1948). *Language and Language Disturbances*. New York: Grune and Stratton.

Grice, P. (1989). *Studies in the Way of Words*. Cambridge, MA: Harvard University Press.

Gustafsson, M. (forthcoming). 'Wittgenstein on Using Language and Playing Chess: The Breakdown of an Analogy, and Its Consequences'. In *Finding One's Way through Wittgenstein's Philosophical Investigations—New Essays on §§1–88*. E. Bermon and J.-P. Narboux (eds.). New York: Springer.

Hales, S. D. (2006). *Relativism and the Foundation of Philosophy*. Cambridge, MA: MIT Press.

Hansen, N. (2013). 'A Slugfest of Intuitions: Contextualism and Experimental Design'. *Synthese* 90: 1771–92.

Hansen, N. and Chemla, E. (2013). 'Experimenting on Contextualism'. *Mind and Language* 28: 286–321.

Hart, H. L. A. and Honoré, T. (1985). *Causation and the Law*. 2nd edition. New York: Oxford University Press.

Hawthorne, J. (2004). *Knowledge and Lotteries*. New York: Oxford University Press.

Horowitz, A. (2015). 'Experimental Philosophical Semantics and the Real Reference of "Gödel"'. In Fischer and Collins (2015): 204–58.

Horwich, P. (2012). *Wittgenstein's Metaphilosophy*. Oxford: Clarendon Press.

Horwich, P. (2016). 'Wittgenstein's Global Deflationism'. In *The Oxford Handbook of Philosophical Methodology*. H. Cappelen, T. Gendler, and J. Hawthorne (eds.). New York: Oxford University Press, pp. 130–46.

Hume, D. (1993). *An Enquiry Concerning Human Understanding*. Indianapolis, IN: Hackett.

Husserl, E. (1970). *The Crisis of the European Sciences and Transcendental Phenomenology*. Carr, D. (trans.). Evanston, IL: Northwestern University Press.

Husserl, E. (1998). *The Paris Lectures*. Koestenbaum, P. (trans.). Norwell, MA: Kluwer Academic Publishers.

Ichikawa, J. (2012). 'Experimentalist Pressure gainst Traditional Methodology'. *Philosophical Psychology* 25: 743–65.

Ichikawa, J. (2013). 'Review of *Philosophy without Intuitions*'. *International Journal of Philosophical Studies* 21: 111–31.

Jackendoff, R. (1999). 'What Is a Concept, That a Person May Grasp It?' In Margolis and Laurence (1999): 225–59.

Jackson, F. (1998). *From Metaphysics to Ethics*. New York: Oxford University Press.

Jackson, F. (2009). 'Thought Experiments and Possibilities'. *Analysis* 69: 100–9.

Jackson, F. (2011). 'On Gettier Holdouts'. *Mind and Language* 26: 468–81.

Kant, I. (1998). *Critique of Pure Reason*. P. Guyer and A. Wood (eds. and trans.). New York: Cambridge University Press.

Kant, I. (2000). *Critique of the Power of Judgment*. P. Guyer (ed.), Guyer, P. and Mathews, E. (trans.). New York: Cambridge University Press.

Kaplan, D. (1989). 'Demonstratives'. In *Themes from Kaplan*. J. Almog, J. Perry, Wettsteinand H. (eds.). New York: Oxford University Press, pp. 481–563.

Knobe, J. (2003). 'Intentional Action in Folk Psychology: An Experimental Investigation'. *Philosophical Psychology* 16: 309–24.

Knobe, J. (2004). 'Intentional Action and Side Effects in Ordinary Language'. *Analysis* 63: 190–4.

Knobe, J. (2007). 'Experimental Philosophy and Philosophical Significance'. *Philosophical Explorations* 10: 119–22.

Knobe, J. (2010). 'Person as Scientist, Person as Moralist'. *Behavioral and Brain Sciences* 33: 315–65.

Knobe, J., Buckwalter, W., Nichols, S., Robbins, P., Sarkissian, H., and Sommers, T. (2012). 'Experimental Philosophy'. *Annual Review of Psychology* 63: 81–99.

Knobe, J. and Nichols, S. (2008). 'An Experimental Philosophy Manifesto'. In *Experimental Philosophy*. New York: Oxford University Press, pp. 3–14.

Koffka, K. (1999). *The Growth of the Mind: An Introduction to Child-Psychology.* Ogden, R. M. (trans.). New York: Routledge.

Köhler, W. (1947). *Gestalt Psychology: An Introduction to New Concepts in Modern Psychology.* New York: Liveright.

Kornblith, H. (2002). *Knowledge and Its Place in Nature.* New York: Oxford University Press.

Kornblith, H. (2015). 'Naturalistic Defenses of Intuition'. In Fischer and Collins (2015): 151–68.

Kukla, R. (2015). 'Delimiting the Proper Scope of Epistemology'. *Philosophical Perspectives* 29: 202–16.

Lakoff, G. and Johnson, M. (2003). *Metaphors We Live By.* 2nd edition. Chicago, IL: University of Chicago Press.

Lance, M. and Kukla, R. (2009). *Yo! and Lo!* Cambridge, MA: Harvard University Press.

Lewis, D. (1980). 'Index, Context, and Content'. In *Philosophy and Grammar.* S. Kanger and S. Öhman (eds.). Dordrecht: Reidel, pp. 79–100.

Lewis, D. (1983). *Philosophical Papers*, Vol. 1. New York: Oxford University Press.

Lewis, D. (1984). 'Putnam's Paradox'. *Australasian Journal of Philosophy* 62: 221–36.

Lewis, D. (1996). 'Elusive Knowledge'. *Australasian Journal of Philosophy* 74: 549–67.

Locke, J. (1975). *An Essay Concerning Human Understanding.* P. Nidditch (ed.). New York: Oxford University Press.

Ludlow, P. (2014). *Living Words.* New York: Oxford University Press.

Ludwig, K. (2007). 'The Epistemology of Thought Experiments: First Person versus Third Person Approaches'. *Midwest Studies in Philosophy* 31: 128–59.

Machery, E. (2011). 'Thought Experiments and Philosophical Knowledge'. *Metaphilosophy* 42: 191–214.

Machery, E. (2015). 'The Illusion of Expertise'. In Fischer and Collins (2015): 188–203.

Machery, E., Mallon, R., Nichols, S., and Stich, S. (2004). 'Semantics, Cross-Cultural Style'. *Cognition* 92: B1–B12.

Malmgren, A. (2011). 'Rationalism and the Content of Intuitive Judgments'. *Mind* 121: 263–327.

Margolis, E. and Laurence, S. (eds.) (1999). *Concepts: Core Readings.* Cambridge, MA: MIT University Press.

McDowell, J. (1994). *Mind and World.* Cambridge, MA: Harvard University Press.

Merleau-Ponty, M. (1964). *Signs.* McCleary, R. (trans.). Evanston, IL: Northwestern University Press.

Merleau-Ponty, M. (1996). *Phenomenology of Perception*. Smith, C. (trans.). New York: Routledge.

Millikan, R. G. (1999). 'A Common Structure for Concepts of Individuals, Stuffs, and Real Kinds: More Mama, More Milk, and More Mouse'. In Margolis and Laurence (1999), pp. 525–48.

Monk, R. (1991). *The Duty of Genius*. New York: Penguin Books.

Nado, J. (2015). 'Intuition, Philosophical Theorizing, and the Threat of Skepticism'. In Fischer and Collins (2015): 204–21.

Nagel, J. (2012). 'Intuitions and Experiments: A Defense of the Case Method in Epistemology'. *Philosophy and Phenomenological Research* 85: 495–527.

Nanay, B. (2015). 'Experimental Philosophy and Naturalism'. In Fischer and Collins (2015): 222–39.

Nelson, K. (1998). *Cognitive Development: Emergence of the Mediated Mind*. New York: Cambridge University Press.

Nelson, K. (2009). 'Wittgenstein and Contemporary Theories of Word Learning'. *New Ideas in Psychology* 27: 275–87.

Nichols, S. and Ulatowski, J. (2007). 'Intuitions and Individual Differences: The Knobe Effect Revisited'. *Mind and Language* 22: 346–65.

Price, H. (1996). *Time's Arrow and Archimedes' Point: New Directions for the Physics of Time*. New York: Oxford University Press.

Price, H. (2001). 'Causation in the Special Sciences: The Case for Pragmatism'. In *Stochastic Causality*. D. Constantini, M. C. Galavotti, and P. Suppes (eds.). Stanford: CSLI Publications, pp. 103–20.

Price, H. (2011). *Naturalism without Mirrors*. New York: Oxford University Press.

Price, H. (2013). *Expressivism, Pragmatism, and Representationalism*. New York: Cambridge University Press.

Quine, W. V. O. (1976). 'Truth by Convention'. In *Ways of Paradox*. Cambridge, MA: Harvard University Press, pp. 77–106. Originally published in *Philosophical Essays for A. N. Whitehead*. O. H. Lee (ed.). New York: Longmans (1935).

Quine, W. V. O. (1991). 'Two Dogmas in Retrospect'. *Canadian Journal of Philosophy* 21: 265–74.

Recanati, F. (2004). *Literal Meaning*. Cambridge: Cambridge University Press.

Recanati, F. (2010). *Truth-Conditional Pragmatics*. New York: Oxford University Press.

Rosch, E. and Mervis, C. (1975). 'Family Resemblances: Studies in the Internal Structure of Categories'. *Cognitive Psychology* 7: 573–605.

Ryle, G. (2000). *The Concept of Mind*. Chicago, IL: Chicago University Press.

Schaffer, J. (2004). 'From Contextualism to Contrastivism'. *Philosophical Studies* 119: 73–103.

Schaffer, J. (2005). 'What Shifts? Thresholds, Standards, or Alternatives?' In *Contextualism in Philosophy*. G. Preyer and G. Peter (eds.). Oxford: Oxford University Press, pp. 115–30.

Schaffer, J. (2006). 'The Irrelevance of the Subject: Against Subject Sensitive Invariantism'. *Philosophical Studies* 127: 87–107.

Schoubye, A. and Stokke, A. (2016). 'What Is Said?'. *Noûs* 50: 759–93.

Schroeder, S. (2010). 'A Tale of Two Problems: Wittgenstein's Discussion of Aspect Perception'. In *Mind, Method, and Morality: Essays in Honour of Anthony Kenny*. J. Cottingham and P. M. S. Hacker (eds.). New York: Oxford University Press, pp. 352–71.

Searle, J. (1978). 'Literal Meaning'. *Erkenntnis* 13: 207–24.

Searle, J. (1999). *Speech Acts*. New York: Cambridge University Press.

Sgaravatti, D. (2015). 'Thought Experiments, Concepts, and Conceptions'. In Fischer and Collins (2015): 132–50.

Simchen, O. (forthcoming). 'Metasemantics and Singular Reference'. *Noûs* 10.1111/nous.12136: 1–21.

Soames, S. (2003). *Philosophical Analysis in the Twentieth Century, Volume 2: The Age of Meaning*. Princeton, NJ: Princeton University Press.

Sosa, E. (1998). 'Minimal Intuition'. In *Rethinking Intuitions: The Psychology of Intuition and Its Role in Philosophical Inquiry*. M. DePaul and W. Ramsey (eds.). Oxford: Rowman and Littlefield, pp. 257–70.

Sosa, E. (2007a). 'Intuitions: Their Nature and Epistemic Efficacy'. *Grazer Philosophische Studien* 74: 51–67.

Sosa, E. (2007b). *A Virtue Epistemology: Apt Belief and Reflective Knowledge*. New York: Oxford University Press.

Sosa, E. (2009). 'A Defense of the Use of Intuitions in Philosophy'. In *Stich and His Critics*. D. Murphy and M. Bishop (eds.). Malden, MA: Blackwell, pp. 101–12.

Sosa, E. (2011). 'Can There Be a Discipline of Philosophy and Can It Be Founded on Intuitions?' *Mind and Language* 26: 453–67.

Sperber, D. and Wilson, D. (1986/1995). *Relevance: Communication and Cognition*. Oxford: Blackwell.

Stanley, J. (2000). 'Context and Logical Form'. *Linguistics and Philosophy* 23: 391–434.

Stanley, J. (2005). *Knowledge and Practical Interests*. New York: Oxford University Press.

Stanley, J. (2008). 'Philosophy of Language in the Twentieth Century'. In *The Routledge Companion to Twentieth Century Philosophy*. M. Dermont (ed.). New York: Routledge, pp. 382–437.

Stich, S. (1988). 'Reflective Equilibrium, Analytic Epistemology, and the Problem of Cognitive Diversity'. *Synthese* 74: 391–413.

Swain, S., Alexander, J., and Weinberg, J. (2008). 'The Instability of Philosophical Intuitions: Running Hot and Cold on Truetemp'. *Philosophy and Phenomenological Research* 76: 138–55.

Tobia, K., Buckwalter, W., and Stich, S. (2012). 'Moral Intuitions: Are Philosophers Experts?' *Philosophical Psychology* 26: 629–38.

Tomasello, M. (2003). *Constructing a Language*. Cambridge, MA: Harvard University Press.

Tomasello, M. (2008). *Origins of Human Communication*. Cambridge, MA: MIT Press.

Tomasello, M. (2009). 'The Usage-based Theory of Language Acquisition'. In *The Cambridge Handbook of Child Language*. E. Bavin (ed.). New York: Cambridge University Press, pp. 69–88.

Travis, C. (1989). *The Uses of Sense*. New York: Oxford University Press.

Travis, C. (1991). 'Annals of Analysis'. *Mind* 100(398): 237–64.

Travis, C. (1997). 'Pragmatics'. In *A Companion to the Philosophy of Language*. B. Hale and C. Wright (eds.). Oxford: Blackwell, pp. 87–107.

Travis, C. (2013). *Perception*. New York: Oxford University Press.

Travis, C. (2015). 'Suffering Intentionally?' In *Wittgenstein and Perception*. M. Campbell and M. O'Sullivan (eds.). New York: Routledge, pp. 45–62.

Turnbull, W. and Carpendale, J. (1999). 'A Social Pragmatic Model of Talk: Implications for Research on the Development of Children's Social Understanding'. *Human Development* 42: 328–55.

Turnbull, W. and Carpendale, J. (2009). 'Talk and Children's Understanding of Mind'. *Journal of Consciousness Studies* 16: 140–66.

Weatherson, B. (2014). 'Centrality and Marginalization' (Symposium on Cappelen 2012). *Philosophical Studies* 171: 517–33.

Weinberg, J. (2007). 'How to Challenge Intuitions Empirically without Risking Skepticism'. *Midwest Studies in Philosophy* 31: 318–43.

Weinberg, J. (2015). 'Humans as Instruments'. In Fischer and Collins (2015): 171–87.

Weinberg, J., Gonnerman, C., Buckner, C., and Alexander, J. (2010). 'Are Philosophers Expert Intuiters?. *Philosophical Psychology* 23: 331–55.

Weinberg, J., Nichols, S., and Stich, S. (2001). 'Normativity and Epistemic Intuitions'. *Philosophical Topics* 29: 429–60.

Williams, M. (2004). 'Context, Meaning, and Truth'. *Philosophical Studies* 117: 107–29.

Williamson, T. (2000). *Knowledge and Its Limits*. New York: Oxford University Press.

Williamson, T. (2004). 'Philosophical "Intuitions" and Skepticism about Judgment'. *Dialectica* 58: 109–53.

Williamson, T. (2005). 'Armchair Philosophy, Metaphysical Modality, and Counterfactual Thinking'. *Proceedings of the Aristotelian Society* 105: 1–23.

Williamson, T. (2007). *Philosophy of Philosophy*. New York: Oxford University Press.

Williamson, T. (2009). 'Replies to Kornblith, Jackson and Moore'. *Analysis* 69: 125–35.

Williamson, T. (2011). 'Reply to Boghossian'. *Philosophy and Phenomenological Research* 82: 498–506.

Wittgenstein, L. (1958). *The Blue and Brown Books*. Oxford: Blackwell.

Wittgenstein, L. (1969). *On Certainty*. G. E. M. Anscombe and G. H. von Wright (eds.). Anscombe, G. E. M. (trans.). New York: Harper and Row.

Wittgenstein, L. (1978). *Philosophical Grammar*. Kenny, A. and Rhees, R. (trans.). Berkeley, CA: University of California Press.

Wittgenstein, L. (1980a). *Remarks of the Philosophy of Psychology*, Vol. I. G. E. M. Anscombe and G. H. von Wright (eds.). Anscombe, G. E. M. (trans.). Oxford: Blackwell.

Wittgenstein, L. (1980b). *Remarks of the Philosophy of Psychology*, Vol. II. G. E. M. Anscombe and G. H. von Wright (eds.). Luckhardt, C. G. and Aue, M. A. E. (trans.). Oxford: Basil Blackwell.

Wittgenstein, L. (1980c). *Culture and Value*, G. H. von Wright (ed.). Winch, P. (trans.). Chicago, IL: University of Chicago Press.

Wittgenstein, L. (1981). *Zettel*. G. E. M. Anscombe and G. H. von Wright (eds.). Anscombe, G. E. M. (trans.). Oxford: Blackwell.

Wittgenstein, L. (2009). *Philosophical Investigations*. Anscombe, G. E. M., Hacker, P. M. S., and Schulte, J. (trans.). Malden, MA: Wiley-Blackwell.

Index